Summer Exhibition Illustrated 2016

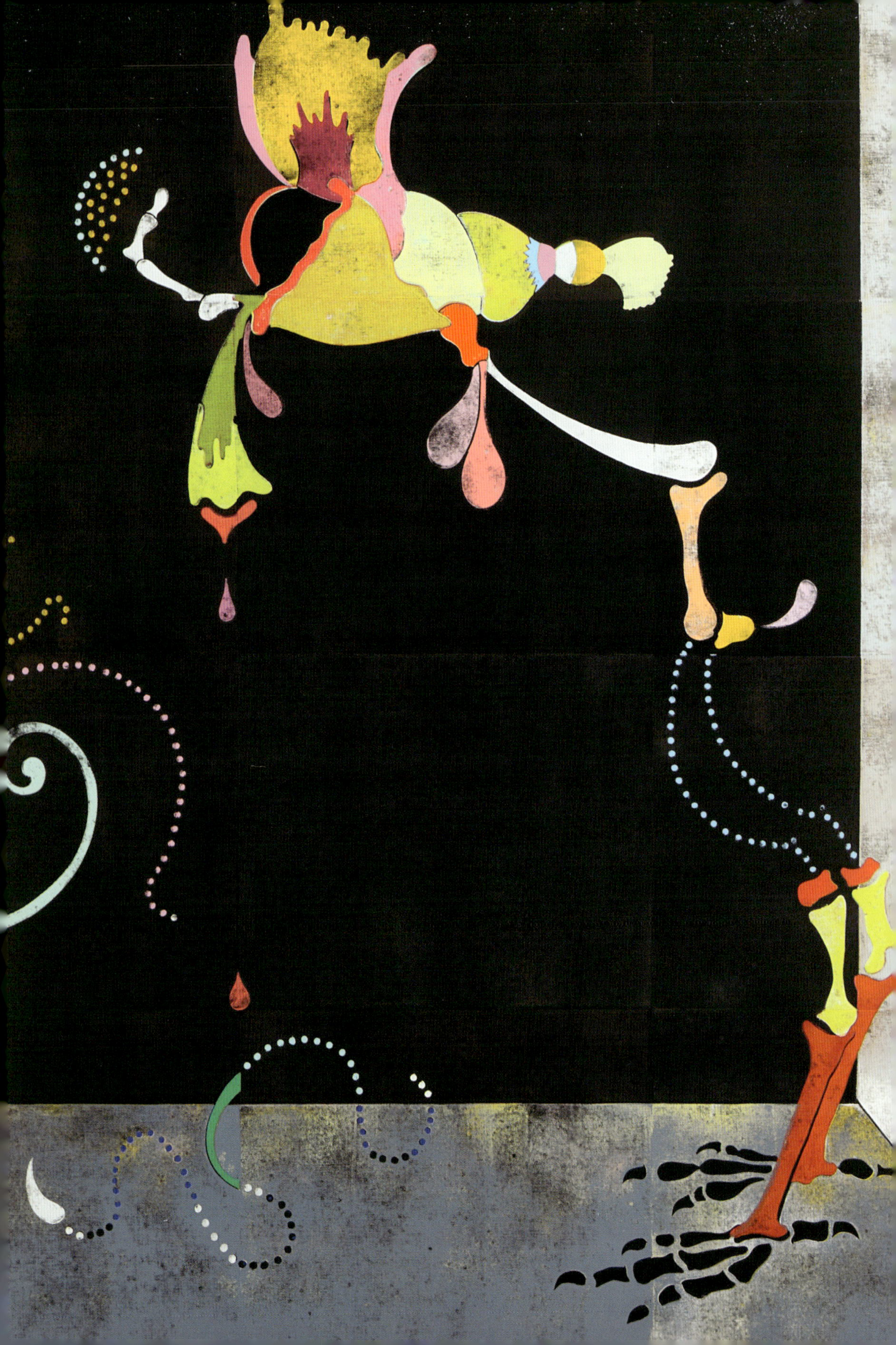

A Selection from the 248th Summer Exhibition
Edited by Richard Wilson RA

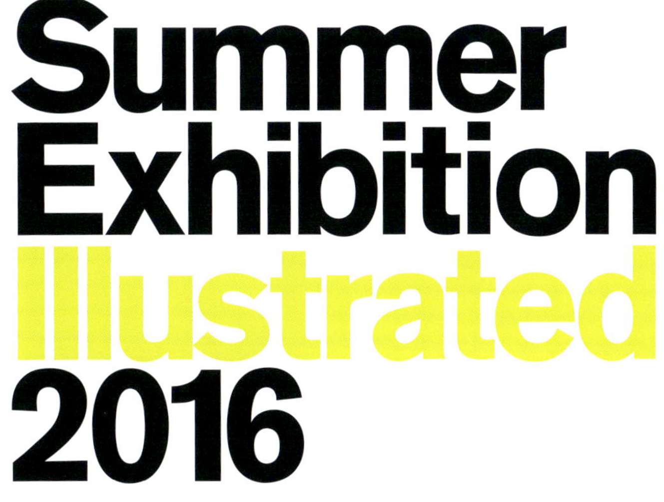

Sponsored by

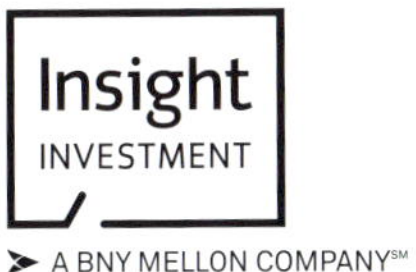

Royal Academy of Arts

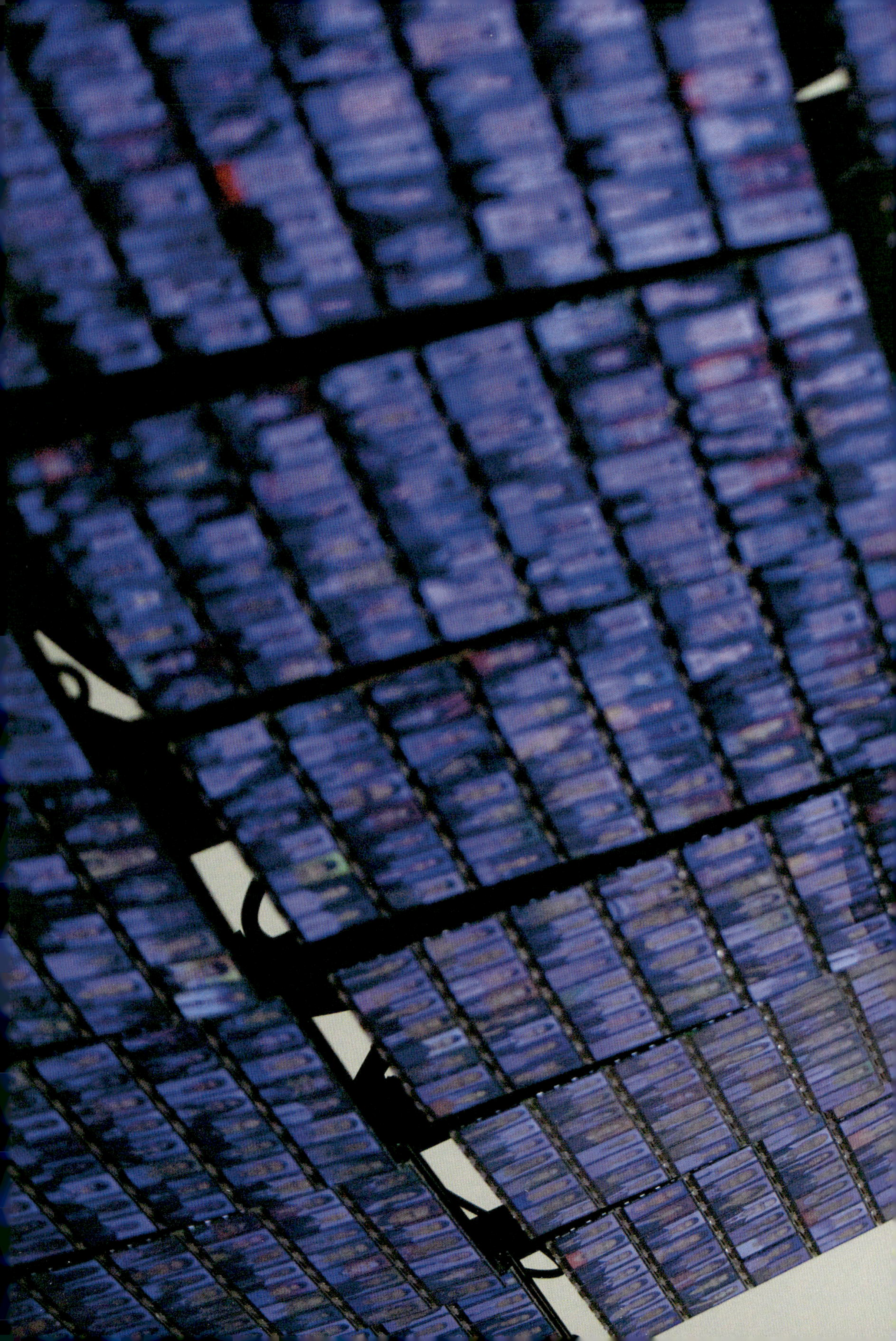

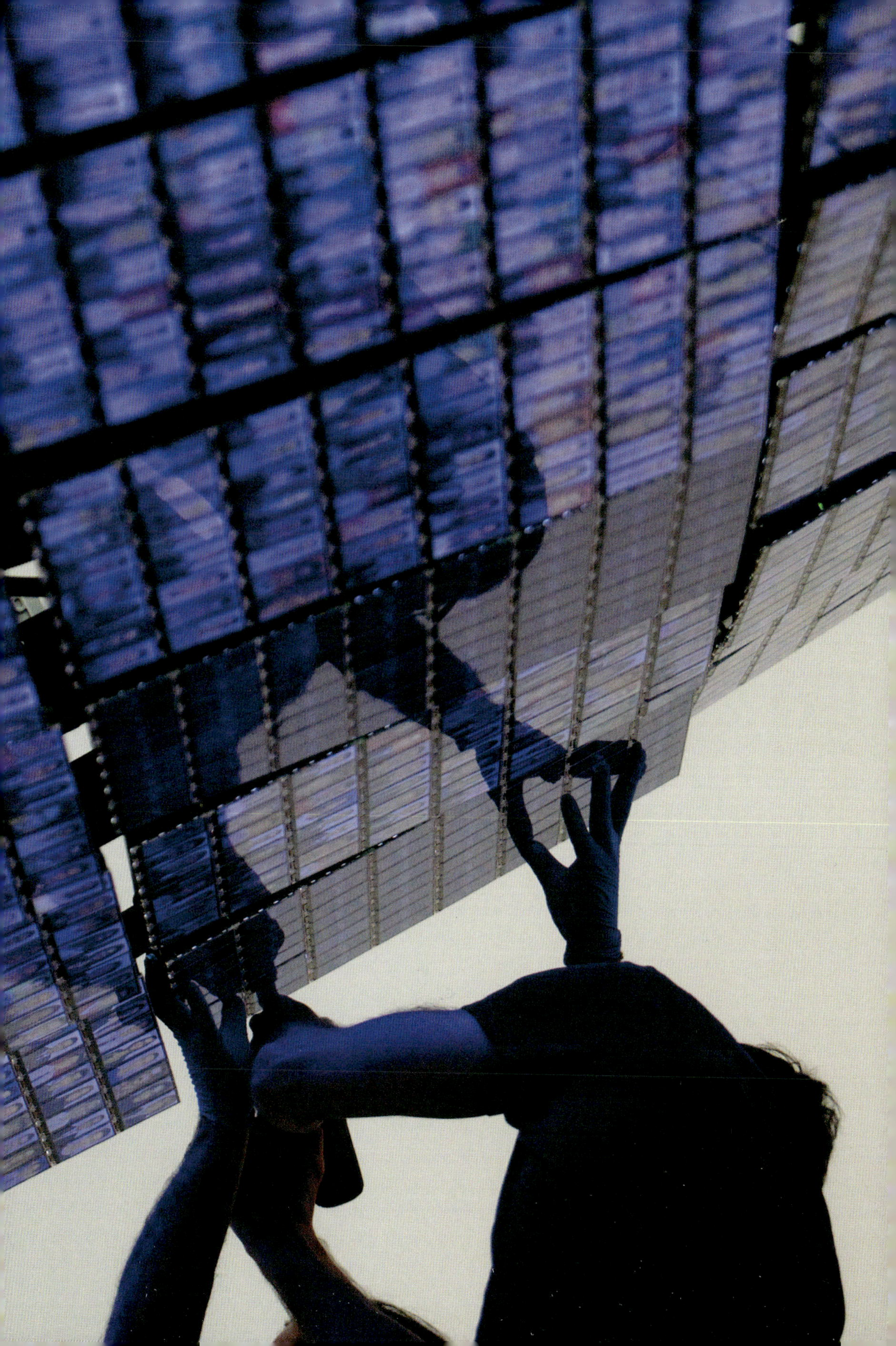

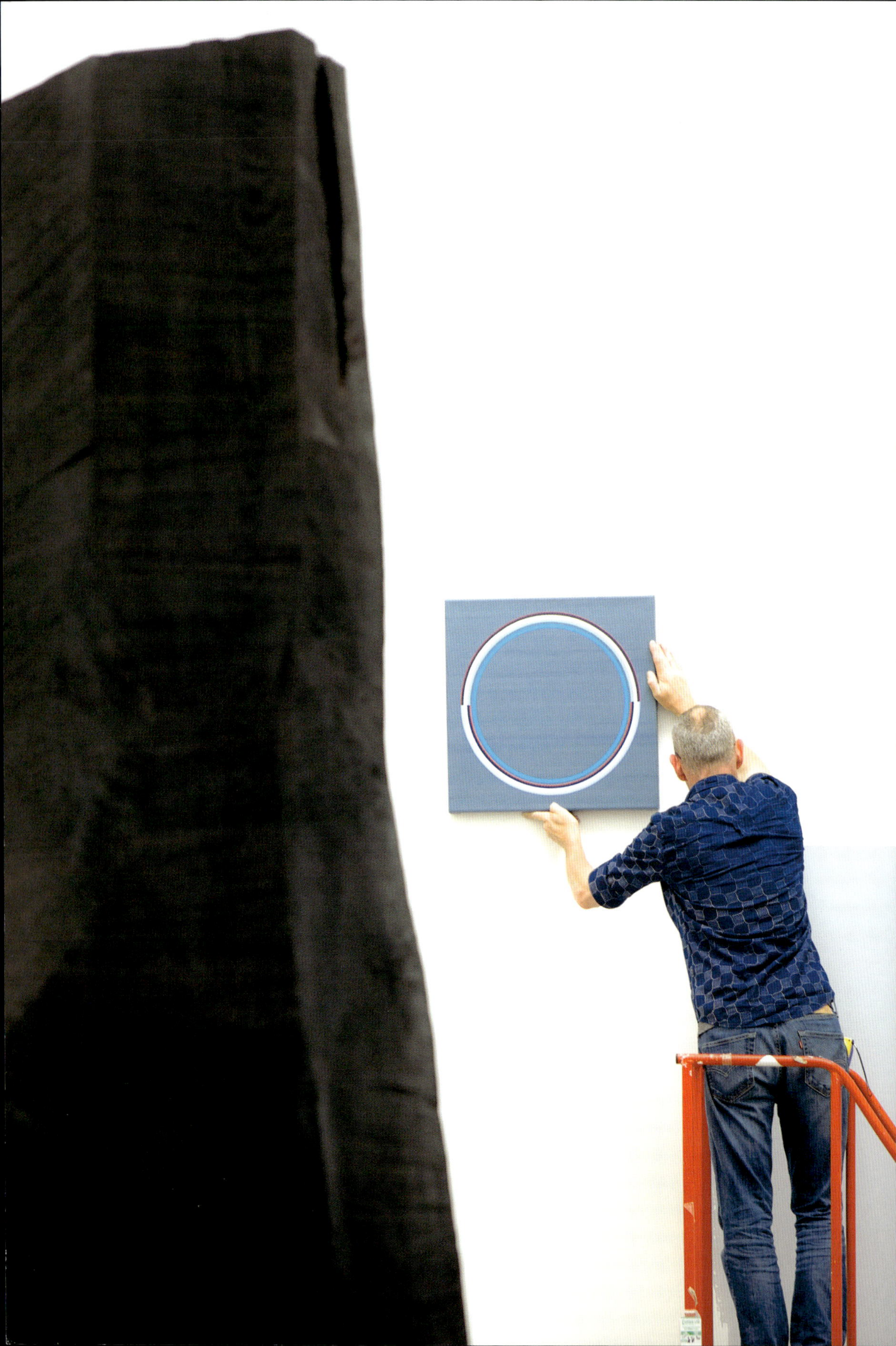

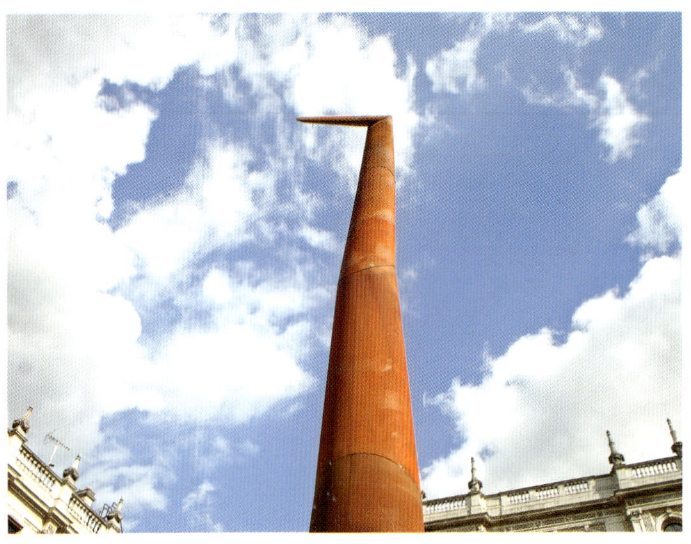

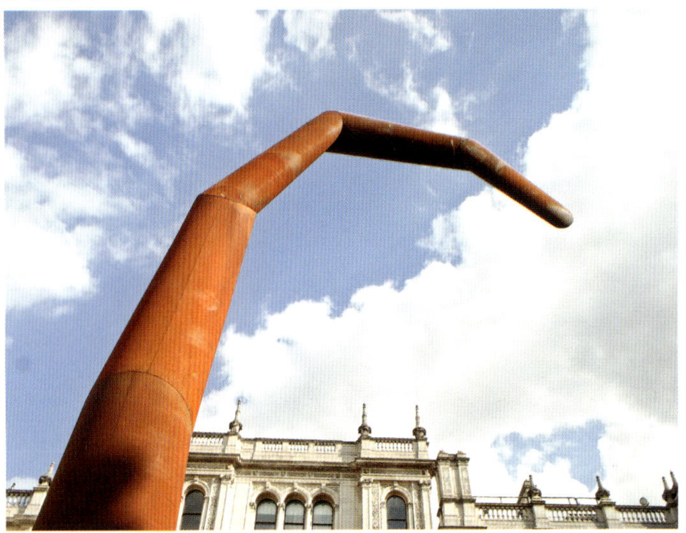

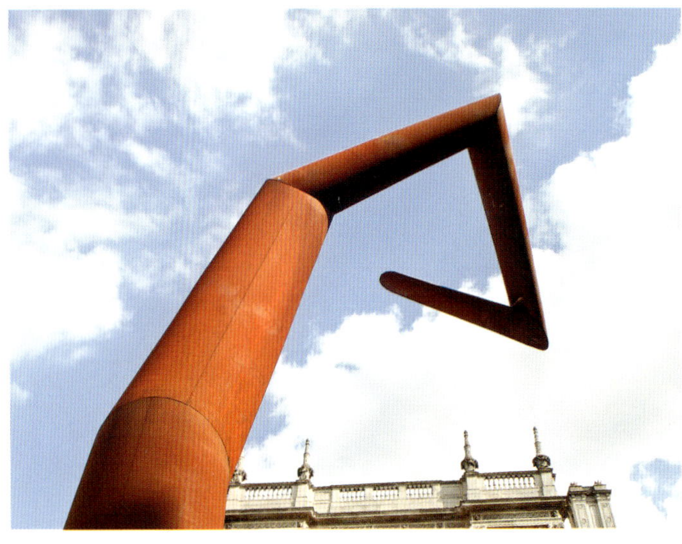

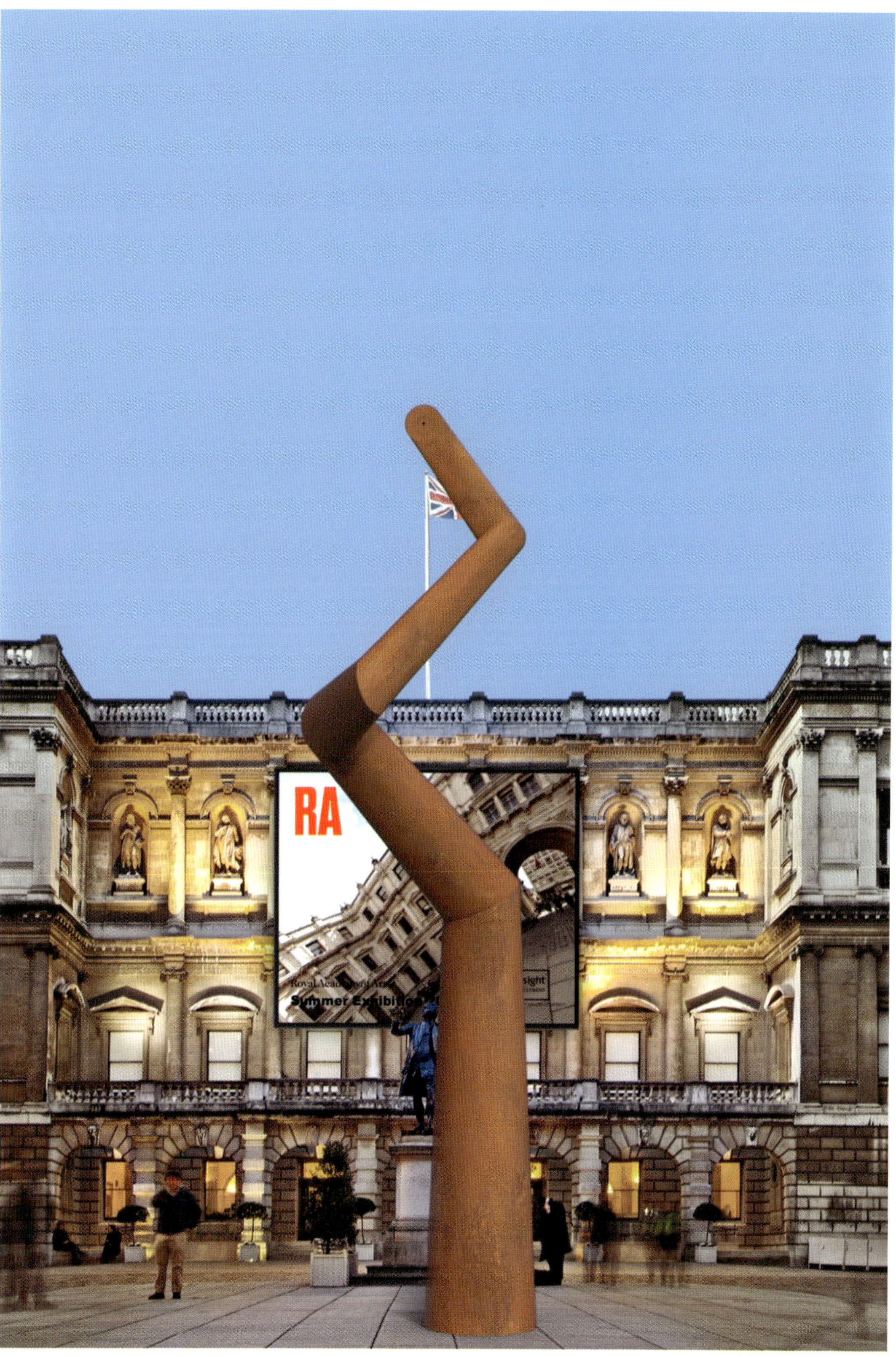
RA

Sponsor's Foreword

For nearly a quarter of a millennium the Royal Academy Summer Exhibition, the world's largest open-submission exhibition, has set the stage for both established and emerging artists, consistently providing a unique and enlightening perspective on contemporary art.

Insight Investment, a proud sponsor of the Summer Exhibition for more than a decade, embraces true challenge and innovation, qualities that the curatorial stewardship of leading British sculptor and Royal Academician, Richard Wilson, brings to life.

This year promises to be yet another spectacular showcase. Provocative works from Gilbert & George sit alongside an atmospheric photographic installation from Jane and Louise Wilson's seminal series Chernobyl, before leading to a crescendo of vision in Kutluğ Ataman's *The Portrait of Sakıp Sabancı*. Many of this year's works unite a diverse group of celebrated, international artistic duos and the curator's unique vision transcends throughout.

In this, its 248th year, the illustrious creative history of the Summer Exhibition continues to inspire. As we enter the second decade of our partnership, we hope you will share our delight at the triumph of this cornerstone of British culture as it offers artists a pre-eminent platform to showcase their work to an international audience.

Abdallah Nauphal
Chief Executive Officer

Insight
INVESTMENT
A BNY MELLON COMPANY℠

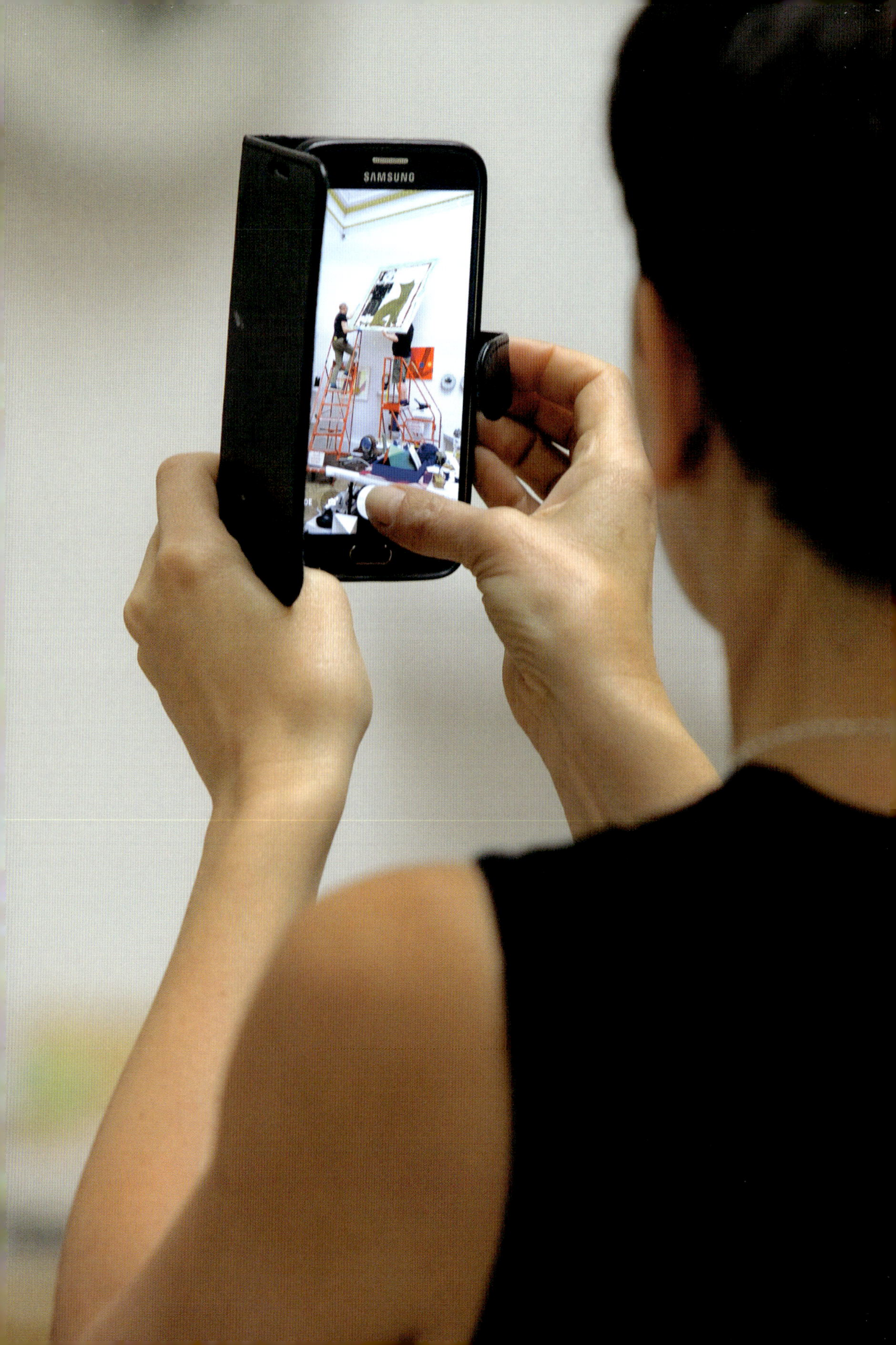
SAMSUNG

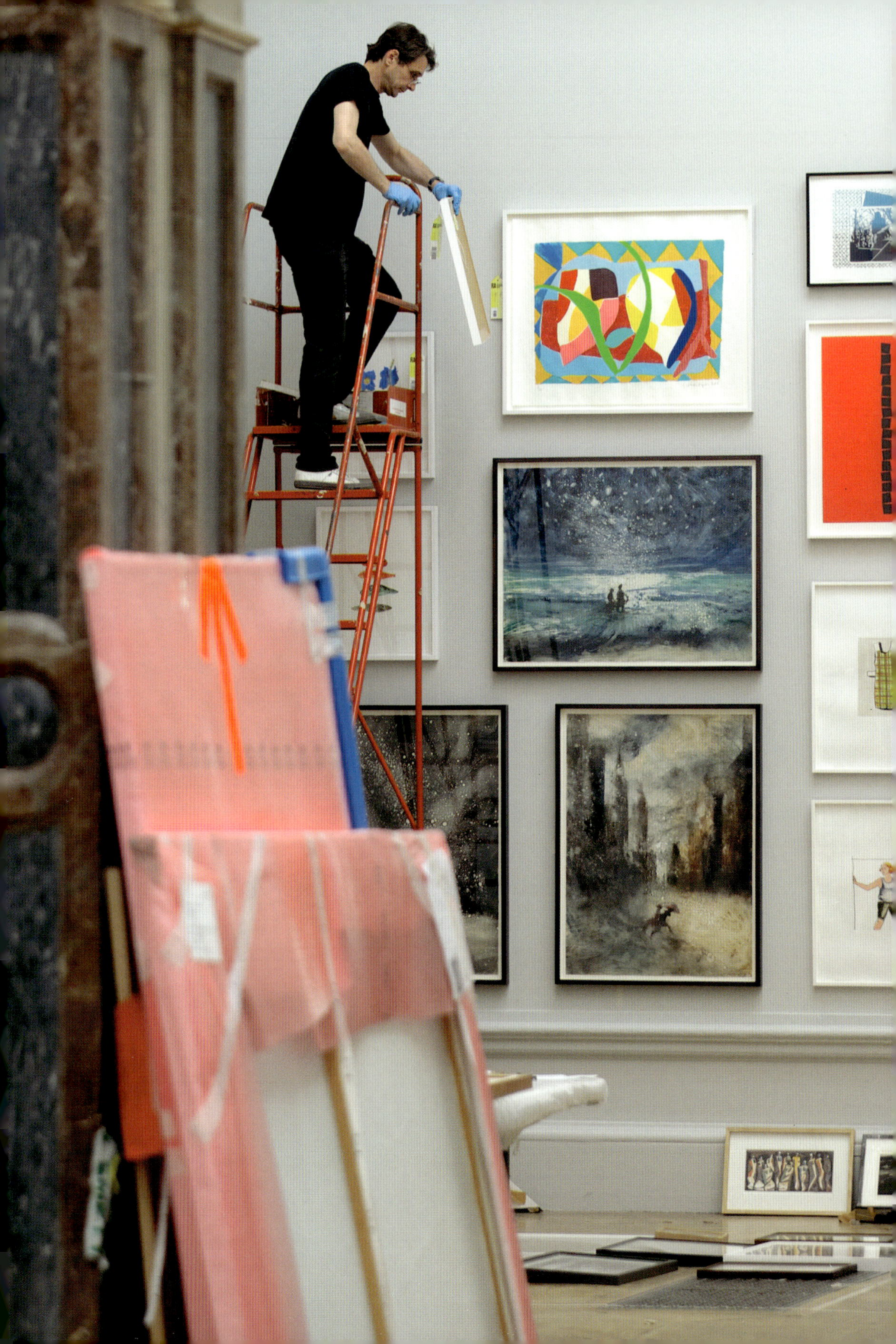

President's Foreword

We are fortunate at the Royal Academy to have members as generous and imaginative as this year's Summer Exhibition Co-ordinator, the sculptor Richard Wilson RA. An artist of international standing with many claims on his time, he was sufficiently intrigued to divert considerable amounts of his creative energy to this intellectually and aesthetically demanding process.

Richard decided early on to invite a selection of artistic duos whose work he admires. Spread across the entire Summer Exhibition, their work provides an opportunity for us to see how the conception, development and execution of a work can be achieved by imaginative minds working in close concert. In particular it raises the question of authorship - the privacy, silence and subjectivity of the solitary maker set against both a much older craft and workshop tradition and the recent flourishing of artistic duos and partnerships. The results demonstrate the creative richness that successful partnerships can yield.

Other themes have emerged within this year's exhibition. Ron Arad RA's monumental work in the Annenberg Courtyard – elegant and serene in its upright, static position – becomes playful, disturbing even, when in randomly choreographed motion. It films Burlington House and its surroundings, giving us remarkable views from impossible angles on a large screen. As its title suggests, *Spyre* (pp. 8-9) also refers to mass observation. The visual documentation of people is a major component of the celebrated Turkish artist Kutluğ Ataman's ambitious work *The Portrait of Sakıp Sabancı* (pp. 4-5). Ataman presents a technologically contemporary portraiture, acknowledging the collective and individual memories of each person who has come into contact with the work's subject, and how, together, these might 'describe' him. Another central theme is the critical relationship between man and the environment, exposed in Jane and Louise Wilson's haunting photographs of Chernobyl and the abandoned city of Pripyat, and Fumiaki Aono's work, whose subtle poetry gives new life to the frail debris of the 2011 tsunami in Japan.

In this year's visual celebration we also sadly mark the passing of three celebrated Royal Academicians. The expansive oil paintings of the late Albert Irvin RA, who died in March last year, sing on the wall, bringing joyful colour to Gallery III. We remember too the late Ellsworth Kelly Hon RA, who died in December, through the exquisite economy of his drawings in Gallery II; and we recognise the considerable achievement of the late Zaha Hadid RA by showing her 1994 work *Cardiff Bay Opera House, Aerial View.*

On behalf of the Royal Academy and Council, we give heartfelt thanks and congratulations to Richard Wilson, for his vision, enthusiasm and diplomatic skills, and equally to the Royal Academicians on this year's Summer Exhibition Committee, who have supported and worked with him throughout: Stephen Chambers, Louisa Hutton, Bill Jacklin, David Mach, Jock McFadyen, Cathie Pilkington, David Remfry, Ian Ritchie and Bill Woodrow. Our thanks also go to Insight Investment, supporting the Summer Exhibition (with immaculate judgement) for the eleventh consecutive year.

Christopher Le Brun PRA
President, Royal Academy of Arts

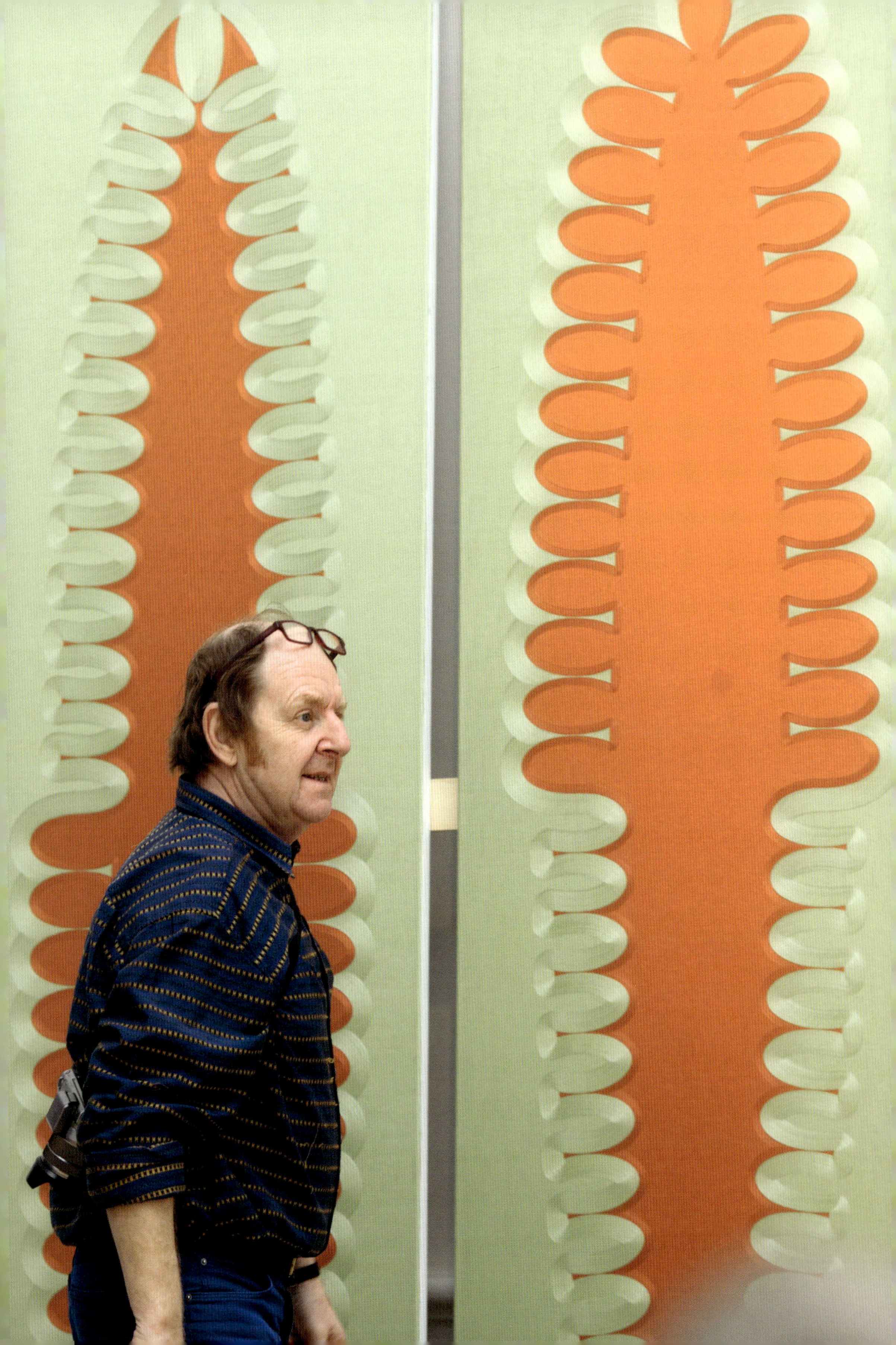

Richard Wilson

At 1.23 am on 26 April 1986, Reactor 4 of the Chernobyl Nuclear Plant experienced a massive power surge during a planned equipment test. The resulting explosions and fire destroyed the reactor core and sent a plume of radioactive particles into the atmosphere. The full impact of the disaster was not initially realised, but by the next day the Soviet authorities had decided to evacuate the neighbouring city of Pripyat, which housed the plant's workers. Within a few hours, all 49,400 residents had left their homes and businesses. Believing that they would be gone only for a few days, they left most of their possessions behind. Thirty years later, a 30-mile exclusion zone still exists around the plant, preventing their return. The 'atomic city' of Pripyat is now a ghost town left to decay.

Almost exactly 25 years later, at 2.26 pm on 11 March 2011, a 9.0 magnitude earthquake was registered 43 miles off the eastern coast of the Oshika Peninsula in Japan. This triggered colossal tsunami waves that killed 15,891 people across twenty prefectures and left more than a quarter of a million people homeless. The tsunami also inundated the Fukushima Daiichi Nuclear Power Plant, causing meltdowns in three of the reactors and the release of radioactive material into the atmosphere. Residents within twelve miles of the plant were evacuated and an exclusion zone was imposed.

This summer, the continuing aftershocks of these disasters, one man-made, one natural, ripple through the Summer Exhibition. Richard Wilson RA, this year's Summer Exhibition Co-ordinator, has selected large-format photographs from Jane and Louise Wilson's series *Atomgrad (Nature Abhors a Vacuum)* (2010, see p. 70) to frame the Entrance Staircase. These haunting, dystopian images reveal the current state of Pripyat's abandoned public buildings with striking clarity. Spaces which once bustled with life are now given over to nature. Light streams in through shattered windows, exposing a scene of falling plaster, peeling paint, broken tiles and collapsed ceilings. Furniture lies tumbled and smashed, desks are strewn with open books, torn curtains hang from their collapsed rails. Chaos has replaced order. Trees and shrubs push through the very walls and windows intended to keep the natural world at bay. Dust and debris cover every surface, transforming previously bright colours into a mottled camouflage of greens, browns and greys. This once-solid world has begun to disintegrate, slowly returning to the constituent parts from which it was built.

When the tsunami hit Japan in 2011, the destruction was not gradual, as it had been at Pripyat. In a single moment, shops, offices and homes were transformed into a shattered heap of wood, concrete, glass and abandoned personal effects. When the Japanese artist Fumiaki Aono wandered through the ruins of Sendai, he collected some of these objects, inspired by the potential he saw in their broken forms. Describing himself as a 'fixer' rather than a maker, Aono took what he had salvaged and sought to heal it. He mended sake bottles with books, cassette tapes with plywood, and notebooks with plastic vessels and acrylic paint. For Aono this was an act of reincarnation as well as restoration, giving these smashed and splintered materials new life and meaning through an artistic flesh.

By placing Aono's work in Gallery VI (pp. 76-77), directly opposite the Staircase and the Wilson twins' photographs, Wilson has established an axis of ruin and regeneration, of wonder and amazement, that runs straight through the centre of the Summer

Exhibition. We travel from a decaying world, reduced to its raw materials, to one healed and reconfigured through art. In these evocative works, we encounter the underlying flux and flow of life, the cosmic cycle that sees solid objects turned to dust and dust become a solid object. They remind us that the broken can be made beautiful, and find renewed potential.

The twisting and turning forms of Wilson's own works reflect the dynamic reality of the world. Although static, they imply movement: a fruit machine with its countless permutations, the slipstream of a stunt plane tumbling through the air, a ship's wheelhouse rotating and spinning around a circular track. Wilson takes familiar forms and reimagines them, curious to find new meaning in them and to discover what they might become. In *City Block*, his precise laser scans of building façades are turned into three-dimensional building blocks which, when jumbled together and reassembled, transform hollow architecture into solid sculpture, and make specific places universal. Wilson's reinventions are deliberately startling. He spins us, disorientates us and turns us upside down so that we emerge blinking into a new world, filled, he hopes, with wonder at the familiar made strange.

The versions of *Wheelhouse* (p. 141) and *Slipstream* shown here are both models for larger sculptures, and whereas *Wheelhouse* is still a proposal, the full-sized *Slipstream* (2014) now hangs from the ceiling of the new Queen's Terminal at Heathrow Airport. A 70-metre, 77-tonne leviathan of shimmering stainless steel, Slipstream, like all Wilson's site-specific sculptures, required him to work with a team of engineers, designers, builders and fabricators, without whom it would not exist.

The modernist model of art history celebrates the Romantic ideal of the lonely artist sitting alone in his or her studio: the sole creator of an original vision. But although the process of making art certainly can be solitary, it is not a lonely activity. The moment artists translate their curious gaze into a physical mark or a sculpted form, they are by necessity reaching out beyond the confines of their individual selves. They embark on an act of communication with something or someone else; a dialogue with materials and sources of inspiration, sometimes with dealers, galleries and a viewer, and occasionally with another artistic collaborator.

Wilson is particularly fascinated by the collaboration that occurs when two artists operate as a duo, and he has invited several artistic pairings to show this year. Challenging the enduring belief that an original vision can only come from a single hand, the works of artists such as Gilbert & George, the Chapman Brothers, Dalziel + Scullion, Noble and Webster and the Singh Twins capture the multifaceted viewpoint of the Cubists. They present us with a single creation woven from two perspectives, demonstrating how the fluid connection of creative dialogue can merge into one.

We find the same fluid dialogue at the heart of both the Royal Academy and the Summer Exhibition, in a community of artists and architects who come together to talk, share, select and inspire, and in an exhibition where there is no hierarchy, only visual exchange. They remind us that, far from being a selfish or self-contained act, the process of creating art is one of empathy, whether we work alone or in a team. As Edith Stein argued in her doctoral thesis *On the Problem of Empathy* (1916), we are all individuals seeing the world from our own

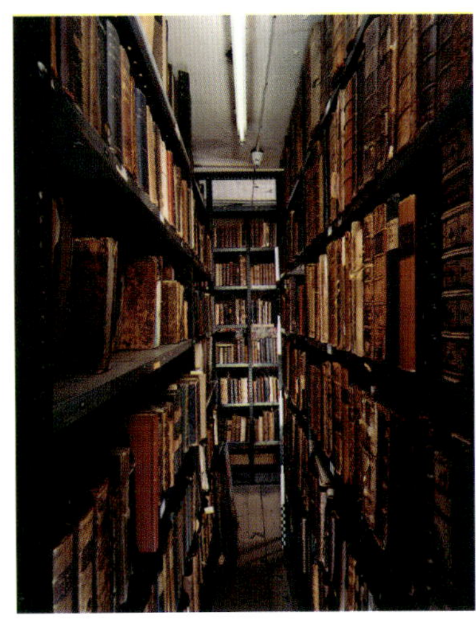

Jane & Louise Wilson
Oddments Room IV
C-type print on aluminium
218 × 180 cm

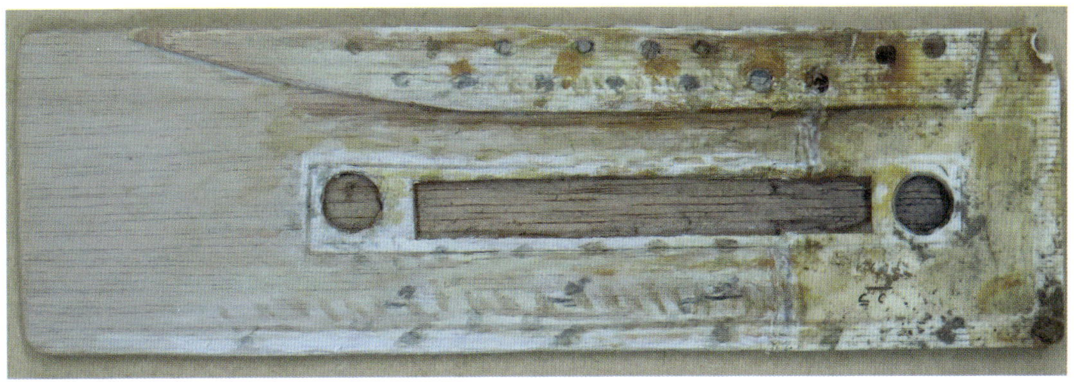

Aono Fumiaki
Mending, Restoration – Restoration of Cassette Tapes Collected in Yuriage, Miyagi, Japan, After the Great East Japan Earthquake and Tsunami
Cassette tape, plywood and acrylic
7 × 20 cm

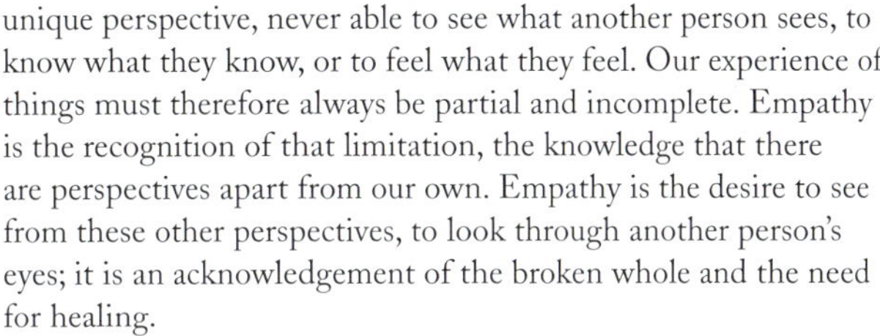

unique perspective, never able to see what another person sees, to know what they know, or to feel what they feel. Our experience of things must therefore always be partial and incomplete. Empathy is the recognition of that limitation, the knowledge that there are perspectives apart from our own. Empathy is the desire to see from these other perspectives, to look through another person's eyes; it is an acknowledgement of the broken whole and the need for healing.

Aono's sculptures demonstrate that art can heal the shattered materials of a broken world. The duos on display here show us how art can heal the artist and viewer as well. They show us the possibility of moving out of our necessarily one-sided view of reality to see a perspective that is not our own. Artists present viewers with new sights and new thoughts; viewers can show artists things in their work they may never have intended.

Each artwork in the Summer Exhibition reaches out to us, clamouring for our attention, a unique voice offering a unique vision of the world. When we respond, a connection is made, a moment of empathy occurs and we see another point of view. Sometimes we are shown the familiar from a slightly different perspective, sometimes we notice things we have never seen before. But whether recognisable or strange, each of these encounters is for Wilson an opportunity for wonder, a chance to be amazed. And in those moments of amazement, as our eyes open wide and we feel a shiver down our spine and our skin tingles, art not only reaches out to our minds, but simultaneously seizes our bodies and emotions. In each of the exhibition's galleries, as we look into into the unique world of each artwork and see all these different perspectives, Wilson wants us to be uplifted and inspired. We may not like everything we see, and we may find some perspectives difficult to grasp, but each is an essential part of the whole.

Wilson's vision for this year's Summer Exhibition invites us to walk along its axis of destruction and regeneration, from the ruins of Chernobyl to the reformed bottles of Sendai. He shows us the role of art in bringing healing, empathy, wholeness and wonder. As a result, wandering through the galleries, each with its own distinct identity, we encounter the possibility of a world reincarnated and made whole by art.

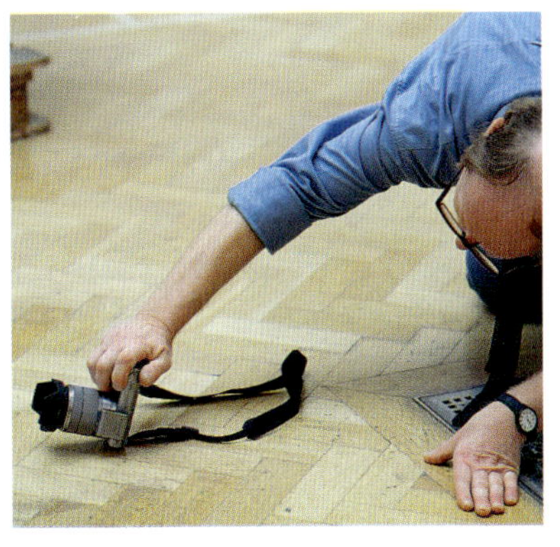

Richard Wilson photographing the installation in progress

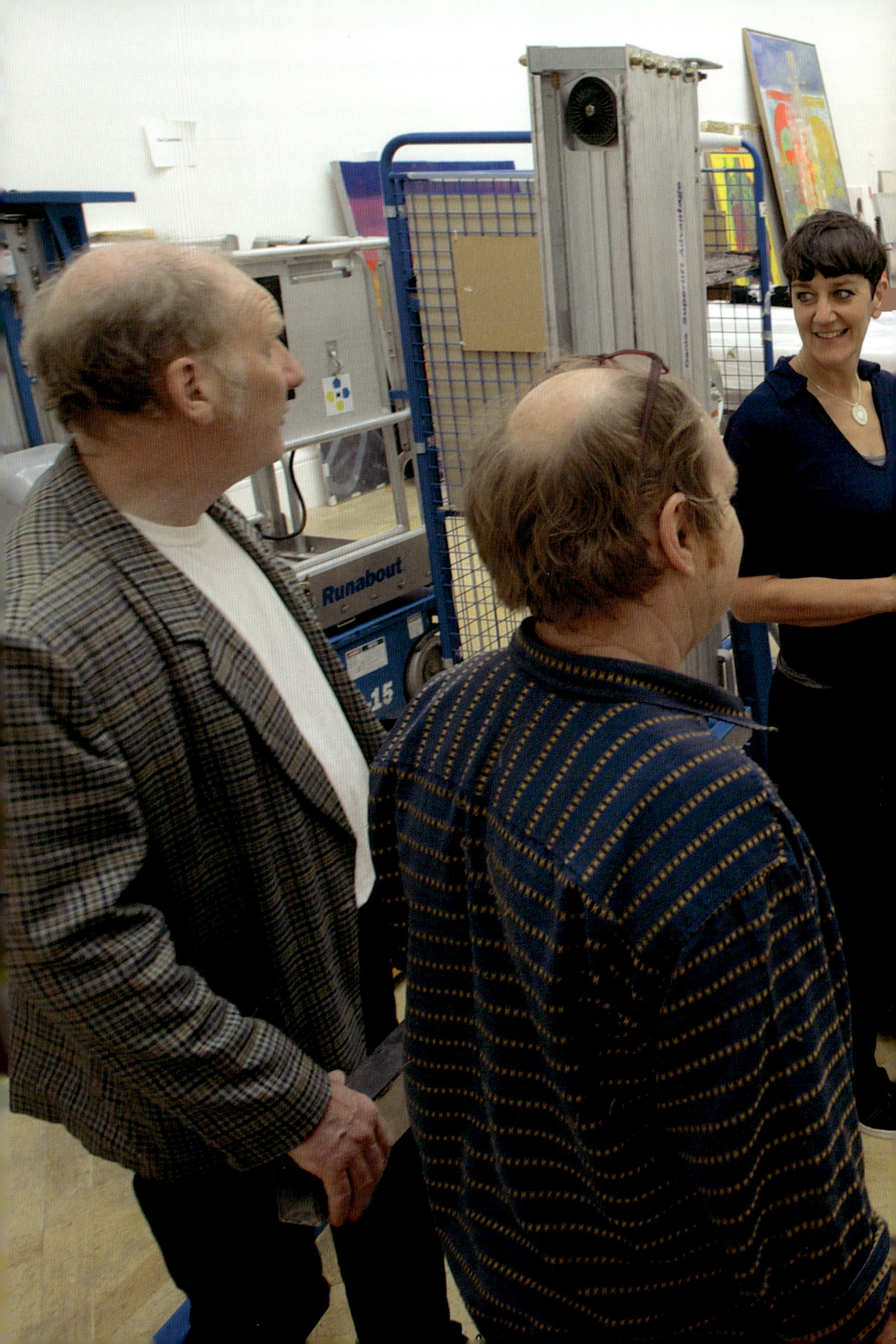
Runabout

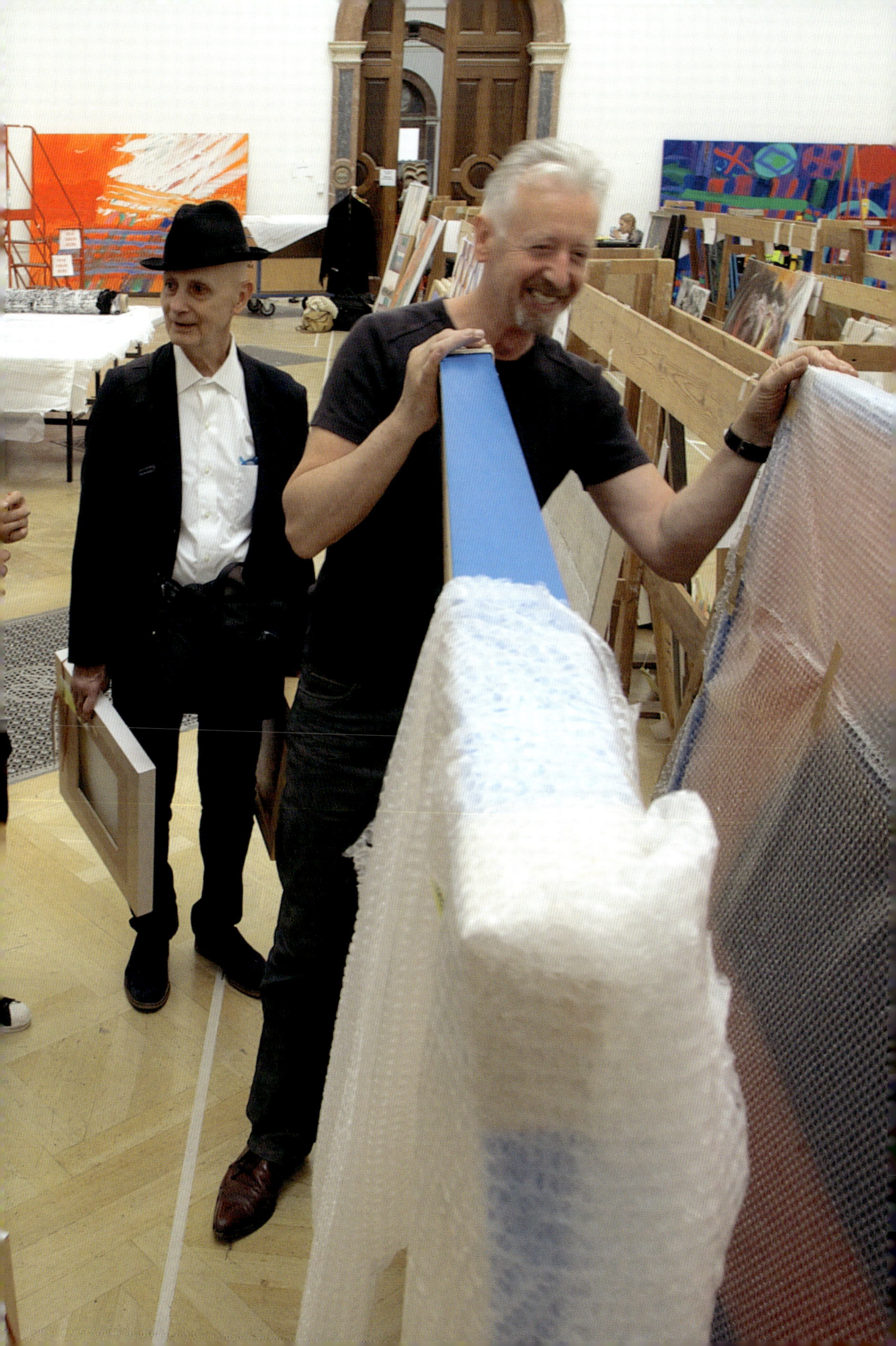

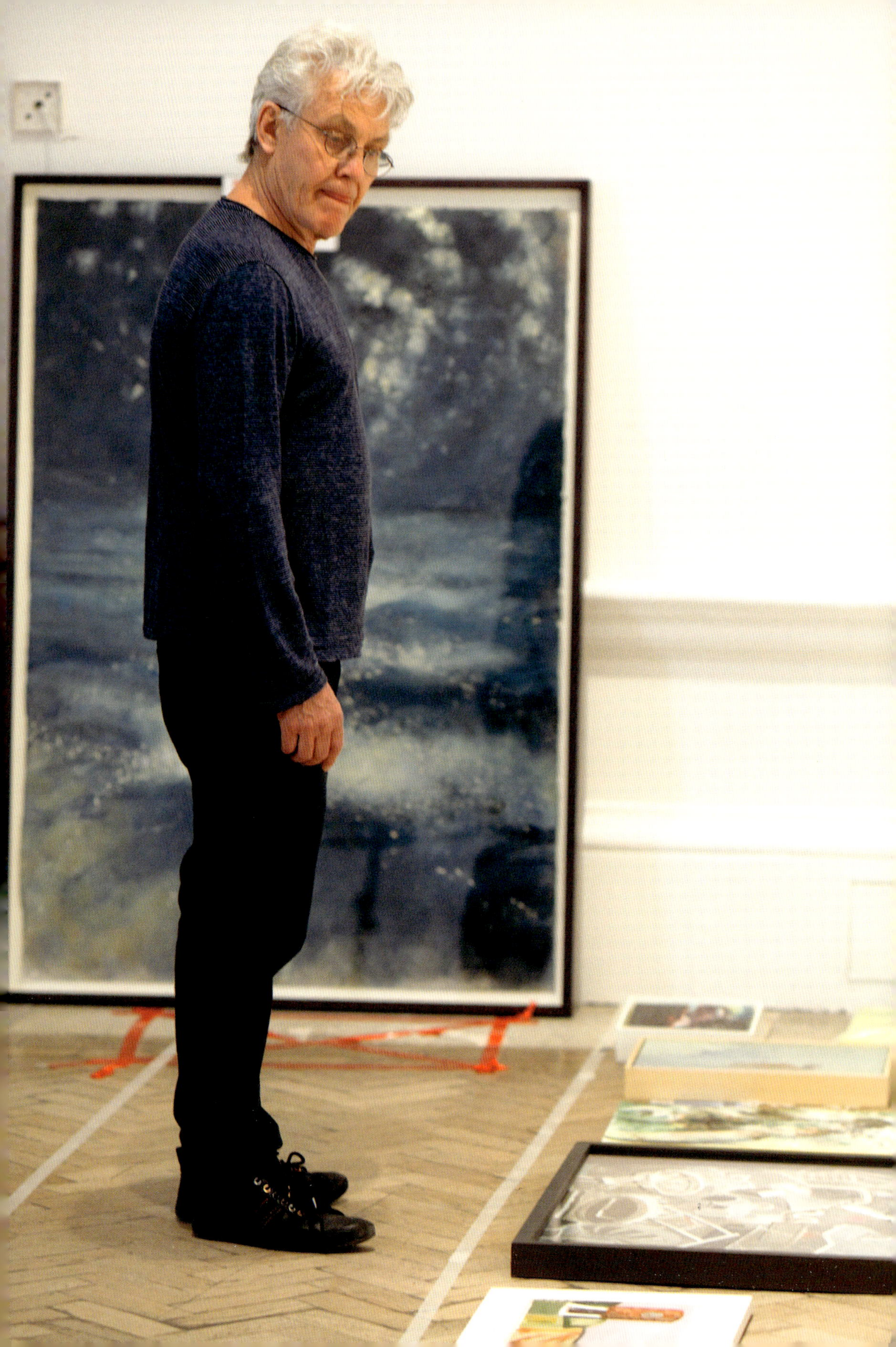

Bill Jacklin

Manhattan rises like a volcanic island out of the Hudson, East and Harlem rivers, its industrial canyons of steel, concrete, and glass absorbing the city's 1.6 million residents and 3.5 million commuters, and the 60 million tourists who visit each year. Defined by the grid plan that was laid out in the Commissioners' Plan of 1811, Manhattan is divided into distinct districts and villages, each characterised by differences in architecture and culture. Central Park lies at its heart, a green lung that softens the harshness of rigid lines and busy lives.

Bill Jacklin has lived in Manhattan since 1985, inspired by the energy that flows through its streets and public spaces. For 30 years he has wandered through its neighbourhoods, returning again and again to Grand Central Station, Central Park and The Shore, a flâneur, watching the world go by. With pencil and sketchbook in hand he translates the people, places and things he sees into dots and marks that provide a direct connection with the place. These dots and marks establish his presence and allow him to capture something of the essential, unseen truths of this world.

As with all cities, Manhattan's architecture has a tangible personality that affects the flux and flow of the place. Not only do these diverse buildings contain space on the inside, but they also create a negative space between their façades, where the natural forces that shape this urban environment become sensible. Jacklin has pursued the eddying crowds as they go about their daily business since he first visited New York in the 1970s. *In the Square* captures this quicksilver murmuration of humanity as it passes through Times Square, a soft, abstract swirl of colours darting in unconscious rhythms, with brief bursts of individuality emerging from an amorphous whole.

But it isn't just people who fascinate Jacklin. Despite his urban subject-matter he is a painter of natural history, studying the invisible forces of nature that flow through these built-up streets. He is drawn to the movement of light as the sun crosses buildings and pierces the shaded depths of these man-made canyons, the wind blowing down long thoroughfares, smoke rising out of cracks in roads and pavements, and the fog rolling off the sea, seeping into buildings, insinuating its damp tendrils through cracks and windows, to dissolve hard edges and blur what we see. He wants to catalogue the feeling of air on our skin, the warmth of the sun on our faces. He shows us cause and effect as these forces impact on each other to create the unconscious heartbeat of the street.

In *Storm Over the City II* (p. 157) and *Tempest in the Square IV* and *X*, Jacklin's natural history of Manhattan conveys in graphic form the impact of these forces. Buildings, people, trees and sky dissolve into a swirling, interconnected whole. Splatters and smears of paint and ink reduce reality to its atomic constituents, shot through with momentary outbursts of solidity that anchor us against the raging storm. We are able to be present in this vibrant metropolis because Jacklin was present, translating these feelings into a vibrant language of colour and light.

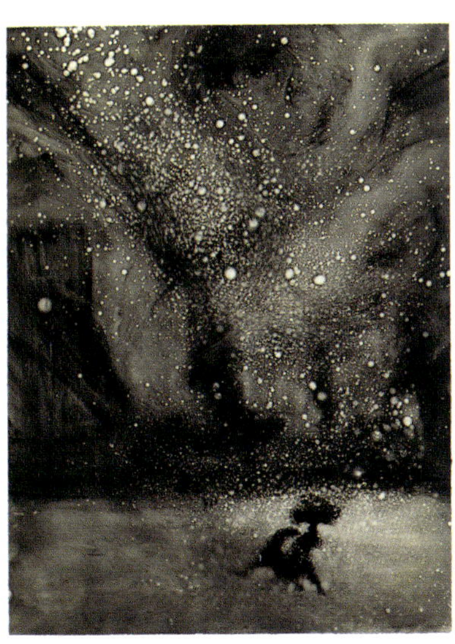

Bill Jacklin RA
Tempest in the Square IV
Monotype
100 × 74 cm

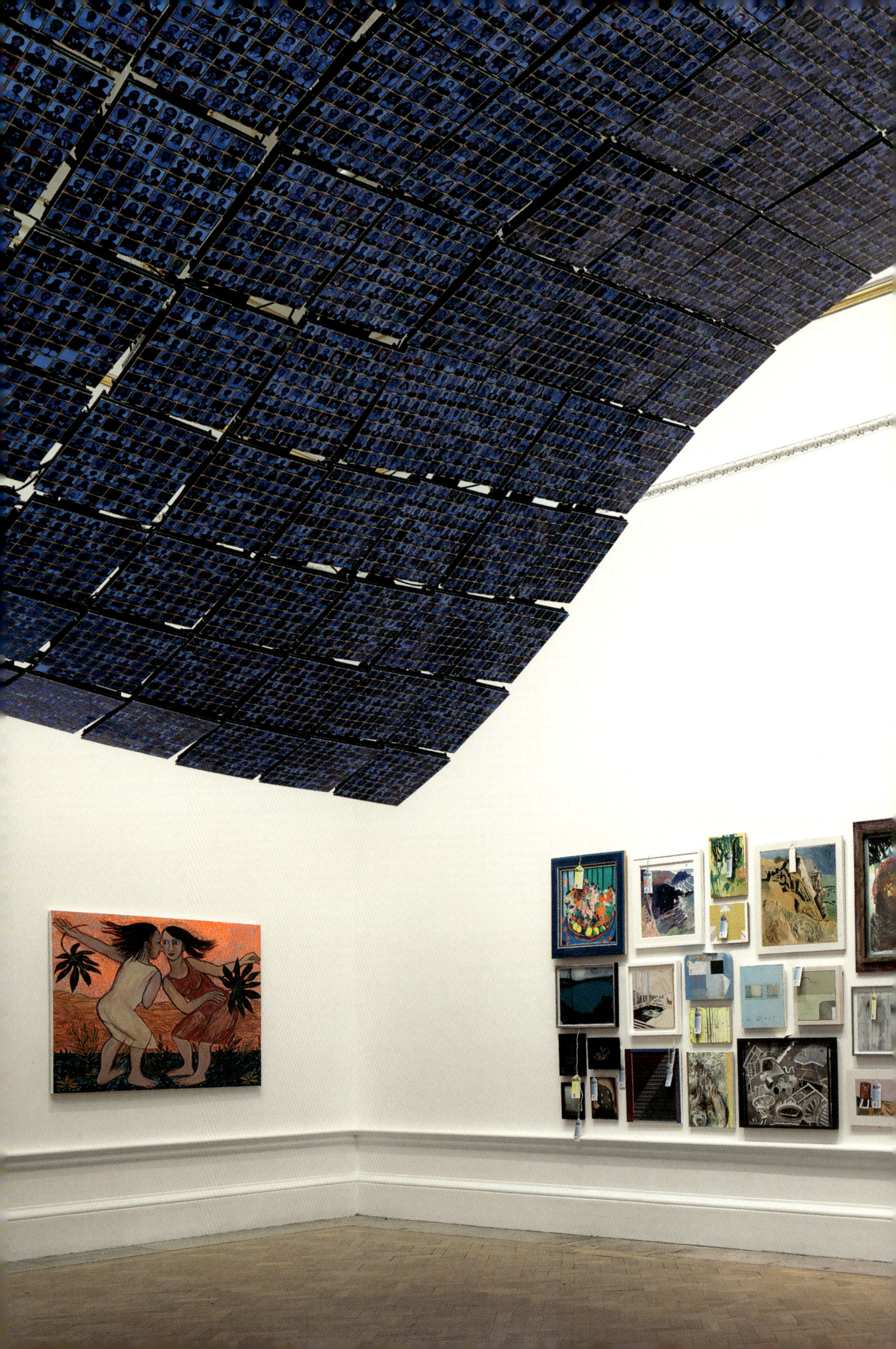

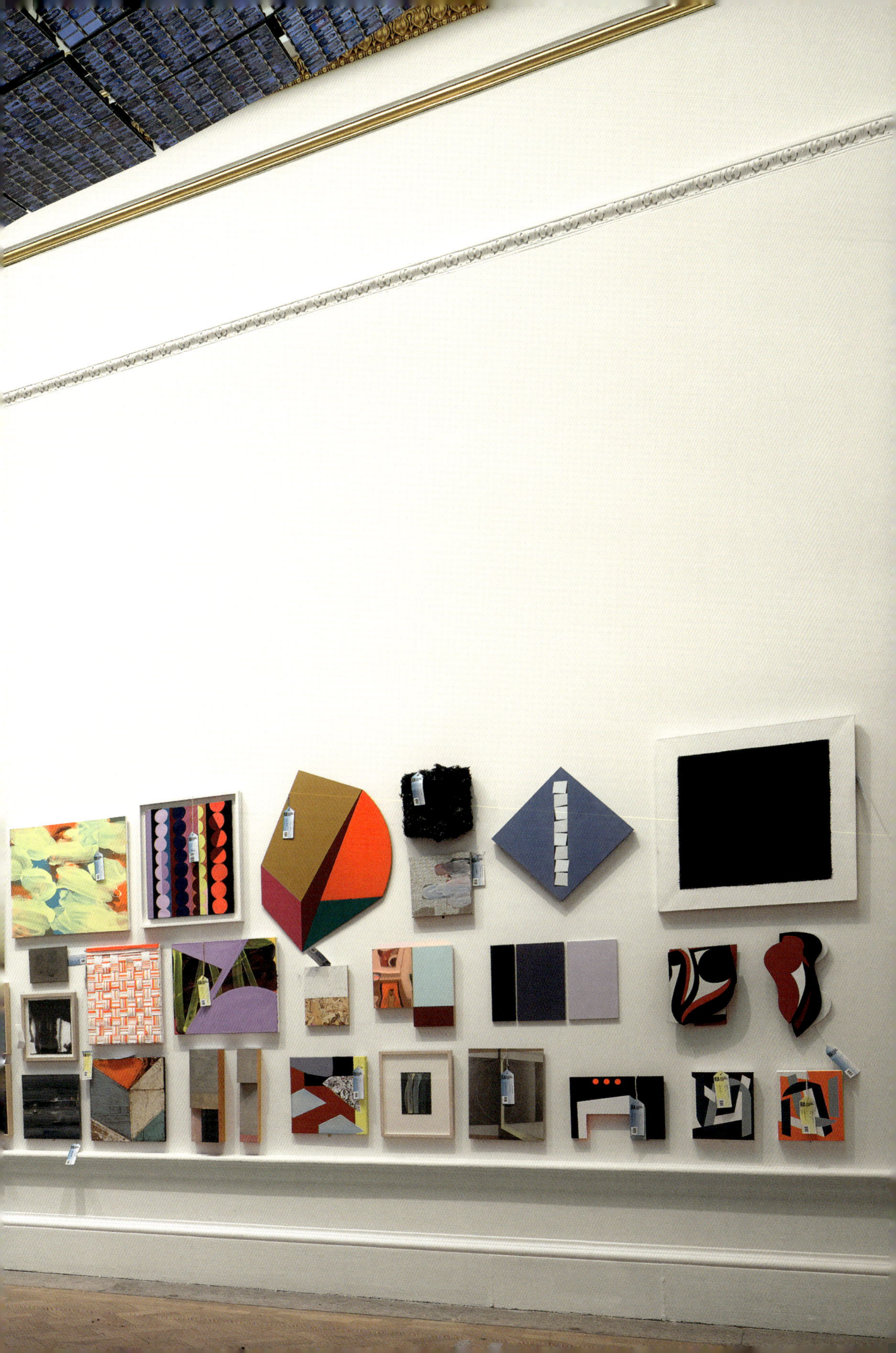

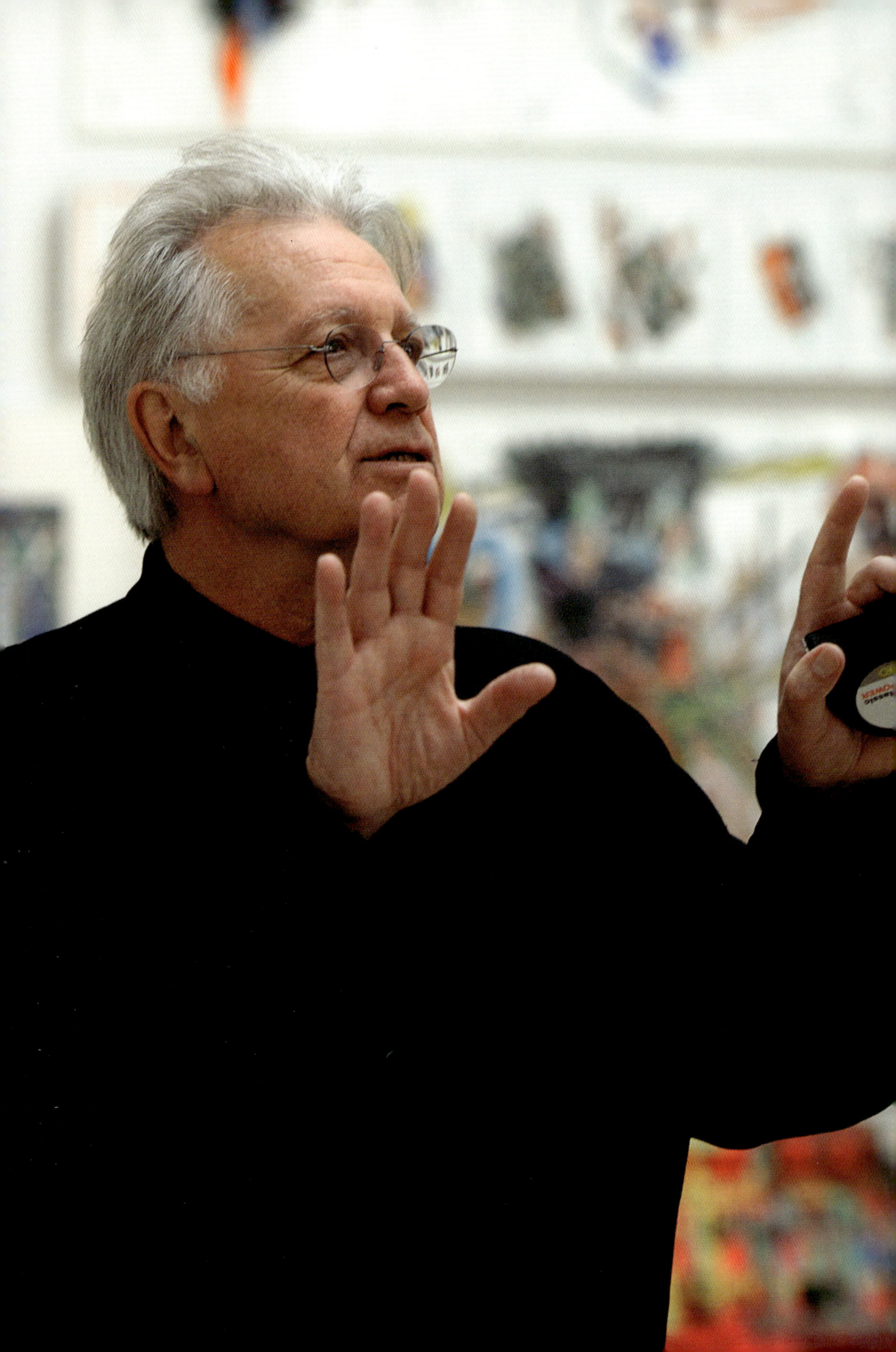

Ian Ritchie and Louisa Hutton

The first bridge was probably a fallen tree straddling a stream, put there by nature or hunters needing to cross. Then came beam, Roman arch, cantilever and suspension, each offering architects and engineers a different solution to the same problem: how to span a void.

In 2006 Ian Ritchie CBE RA won a competition to design a river bridge for Stratford-upon-Avon. As someone who first imagines his buildings in verse, he wrote a poem responding to the brief, setting out his intention to create a 'floating arc of light'. In profile, the Shakespeare Avon Footbridge certainly seems to disappear at its centre, as Ritchie combines cantilever and arch and pushes both to their extremes. Like a fishing line cast across the water, the bridge was intended to hover imperceptibly above the river surface, reduced to nothing more than a line, an architectural metaphor for Shakespeare's words, their gossamer thread of imagery and ideas connecting past, present and future. Like many architectural designs, particularly for bridges, the Shakespeare Avon Footbridge was never built. It remains just an idea, realised only in a model, some plans and a poem.

Rather than crossing something tangible, some bridges reach out into the unknown, a line thrown out into the heavens: Bifröst, the rainbow bridge leading to Valhalla; or a church spire connecting heaven with earth. Ritchie's proposal to place a tower next to the Grande Arche de la Défense in Paris, expressed in his etching *Triangle de la Folie, La Défense, Paris*, transforms secular offices into sacred architecture. Here we see the silhouette of a church and campanile, or a mosque and minaret. The tower rises, a symbol of prayers ascending towards heaven in a cloud of incense, ready to echo with the noise of bells announcing worship, or the voice of the muezzin calling Muslims to prayer, bridges of smoke and sound reaching out in devout hope.

In his model for the Abbey Theatre in the GPO, Dublin, Ritchie provides a reminder that architecture not only contains space but it also frames the shared experience of the people within that space. Here is an auditorium in which actors, audience and author are united by a bridge of words. The coloured walls in the middle of this transparent model, echoing the Hague Blue of the Architecture Room, also signal invisible connections, their pale translucent shades, like a prism, momentarily revealing the unseen architecture of light that criss-crosses the Universe, allowing us to see that we are not alone.

Louisa Hutton RA likewise relies on light and colour to serve as a bridge between individuals and the world. Her architectural practice uses colour to create a 'corporeal, kinetic' relationship with buildings as people walk around them. Light and colour can often seem intangible qualities, and yet photons are substantial, with minute masses that have an impact on our retinas and bodies. They are not mere products of the mind but physical bridges that connect us to the world outside, as our reflection in the glossy surface of Hutton's *Homage to the City* (p.125) reminds us. The vivid colours of this print, rippling across our retinas like a gust of wind, simulate in two dimensions the sensory experience of our three-dimensional engagement with architecture.

As architects working with others, Ritchie and Hutton rely on words and drawings to bring together the disparate ideas of those involved in a project. The tangible things express the interior thoughts of each individual, building a creative bridge that allows ideas to be born.

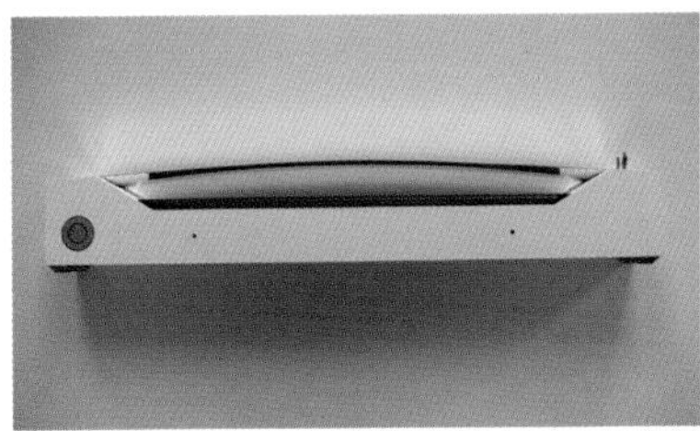

Ian Ritchie CBE RA
Shakespeare Avon Footbridge
Acrylic
H 18 cm

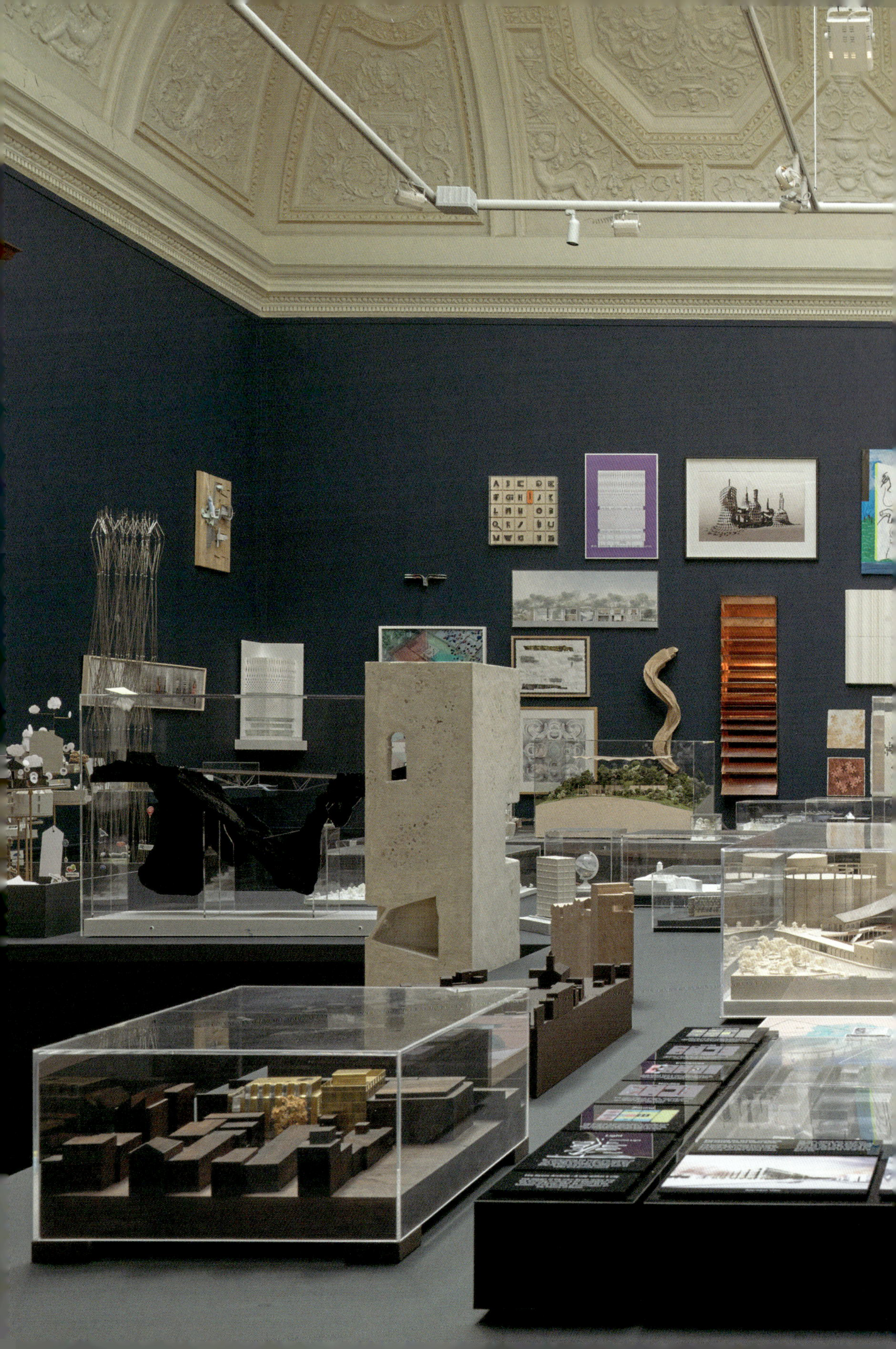

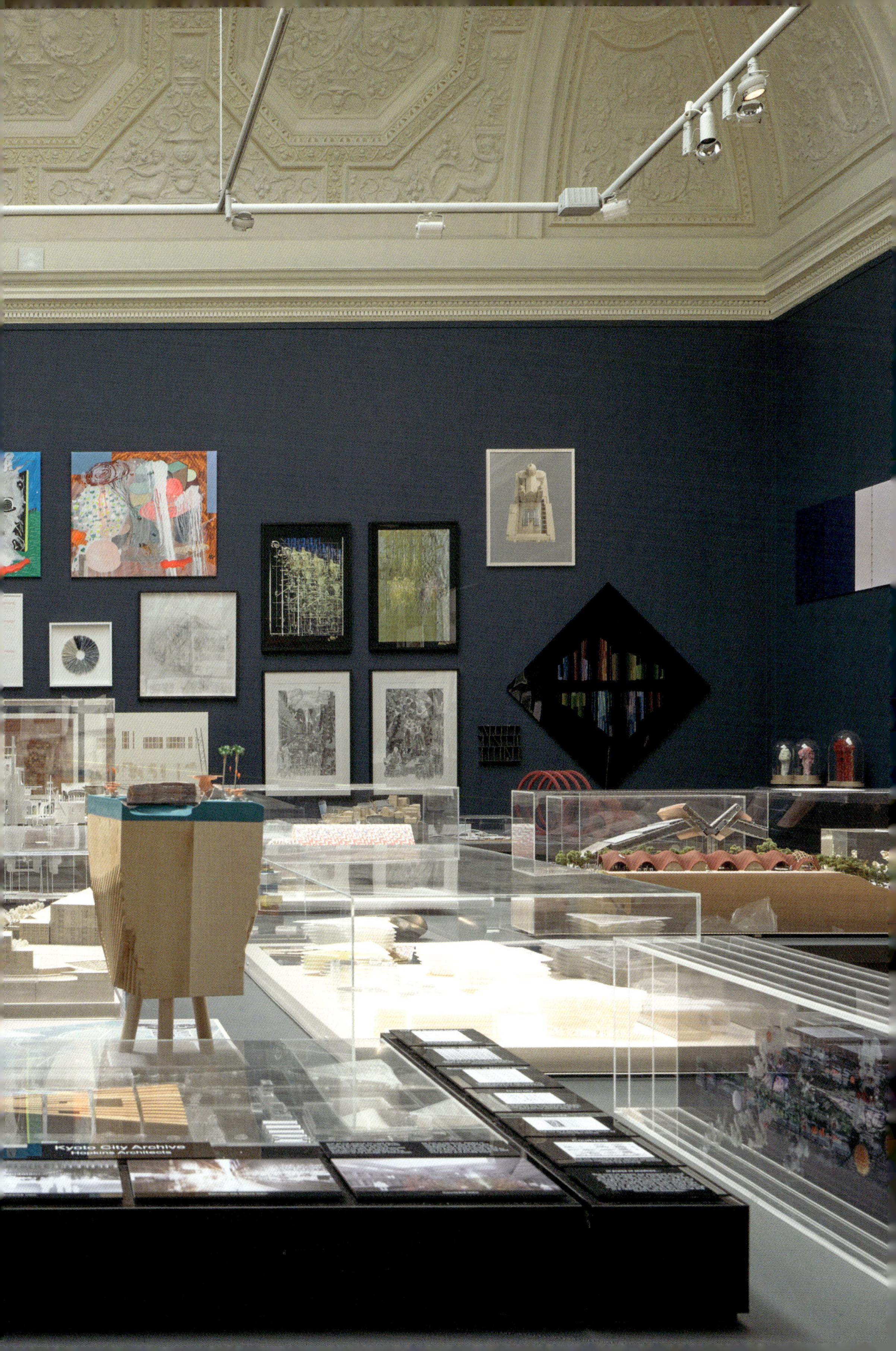
Kyoto City Archive
Hopkins Architects

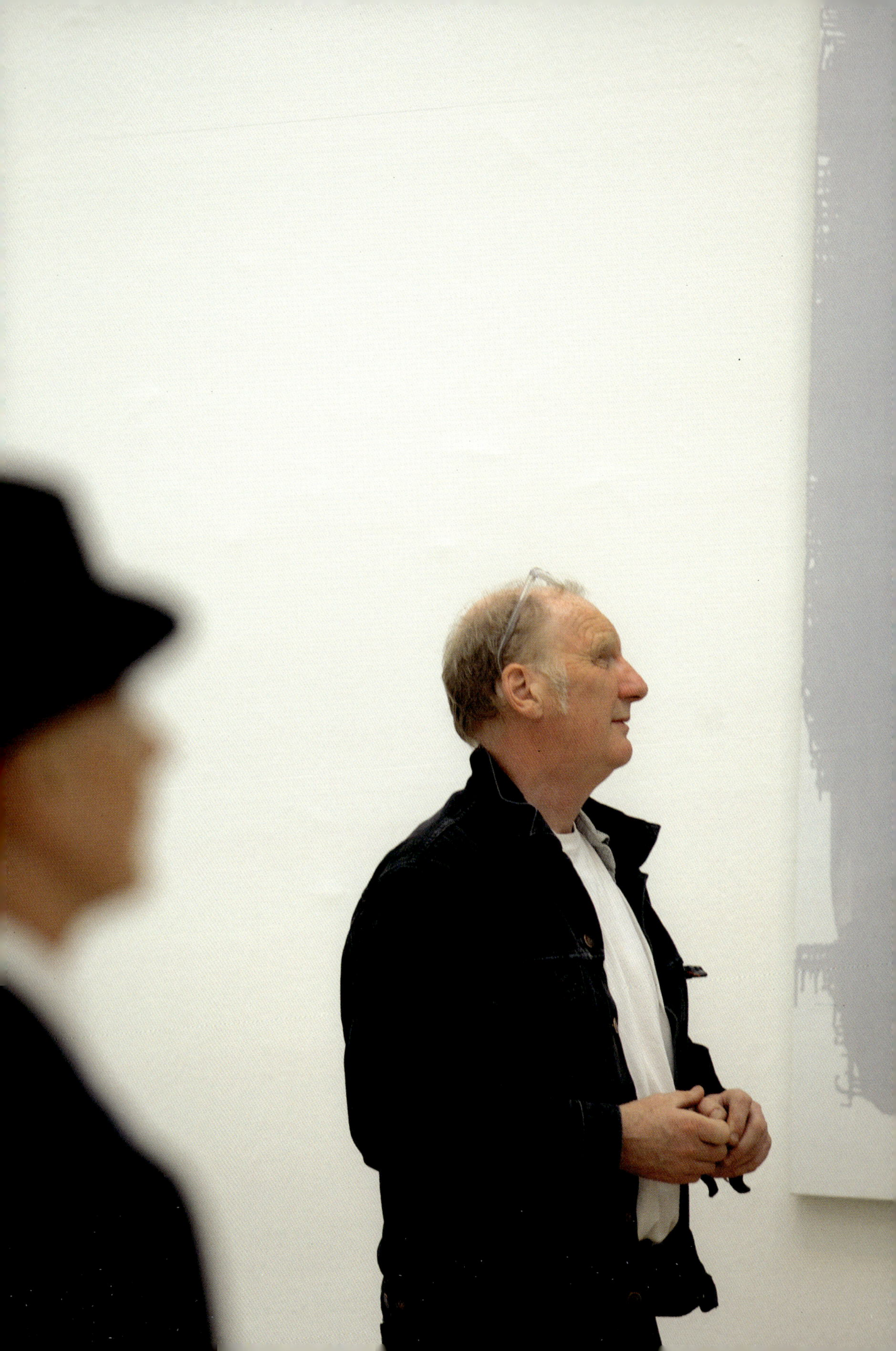

Jock McFadyen

By the mid-nineteenth century, landscape painting had firmly emerged from the backgrounds of Western art. Even the classical and historical veneer that had once made landscape a suitable academic subject had largely been removed had largely fallen away, so that when Constable and Turner exhibited at the Royal Academy's Annual Exhibitions of the 1830s and 1840s they could celebrate the countryside as they saw it, rather than having to reimagine it.

But then, as modernism challenged the academic foundations of art, landscape painting underwent the most radical of its reinventions. Artists no longer felt tied to a single perspective, or struggled with the constraints of portraying picturesque scenes; instead they sought to capture the landscapes of daily life and the experience of walking through an increasingly industrialised world. From the steam-filled railway stations of the Impressionists to the limitless space and enveloping light of Rothko's colour fields, artists have consistently pushed at the boundaries of the genre. They have made faithful replicas of landscapes, dissolved them into an expressive, abstract blur of brush-marks and colour, and even used the landscape itself as their canvas, walking across it or re-arranging its elements to change our perception of things.

For Jock McFadyen RA, landscape painting is a radical activity that allows him to be truthful to the world as he creates fictions that allow us to see it with fresh eyes. In *Libra-y* and *Pink Flats 2* (p.166) he transplants buildings from one location and puts them in another: a Portakabin library from Scotland finds new life in a Bethnal Green park, while a block of flats leaves its crowded urban location to find itself in splendid isolation. Libra-y could almost be seen as a self-portrait of the artist himself, a Scot living and working in East London, but it is also a Claudian image, a ruin set amid a grove of trees in the electric half-light of dusk, turning an inner-city park into a nocturnal pastoral idyll. *Pink Flats 2* finds beauty in the overlooked, too, with angular brutalist architecture transformed into a symphony of subtle colour.

McFadyen loves to play with paint, using differently sized brushes, including a broom, to turn his surfaces into a dynamic visual experience. From a distance his scenes have the postcard familiarity of panoramic views, but as we are drawn into individual passages of detailed, impasto brushwork, or bathe in limpid washes of realistic skies and water, we find ourselves in a more nuanced, multifaceted environment. Here is a painted equivalent for the experience of walking through the world, in which blurred impressions from the corner of the eye mingle imperceptibly with the close-up details of our central vision.

In *Quarry 2*, McFadyen shows us his local surroundings from a very different point of view. This painting re-creates part of his garden in France, dug up and cast in wax, a homage both to Boyle Family and to the aerial glider paintings of Peter Lanyon. We look down on a miniature world complete with toy cars and a textured paint surface embedded with found materials. But this is not the theatrical realism of a train set or an architect's model; it is a real place made fantastic and extraordinary, tilted up and edited, to show us the world anew.

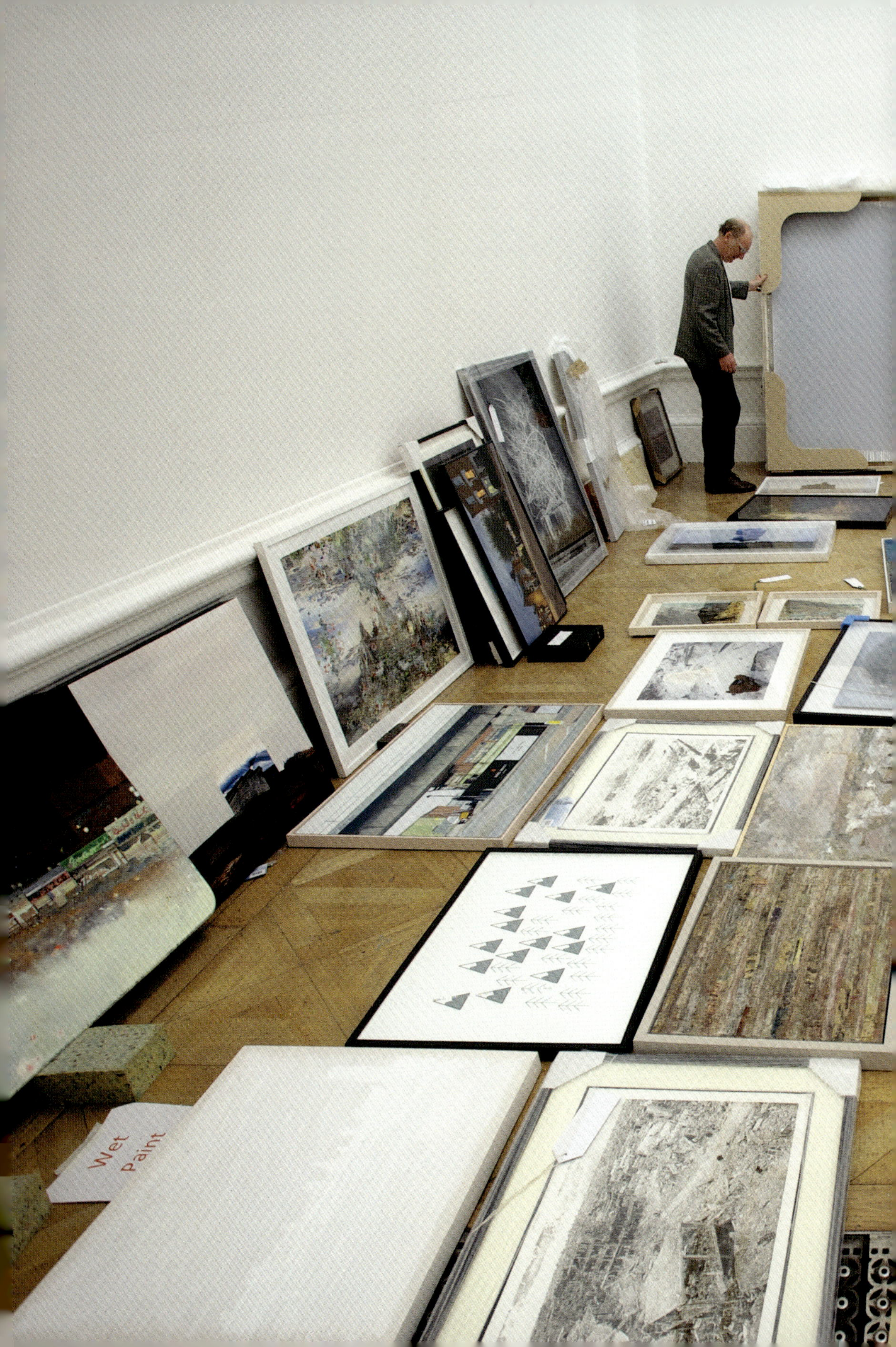
Wet
Paint

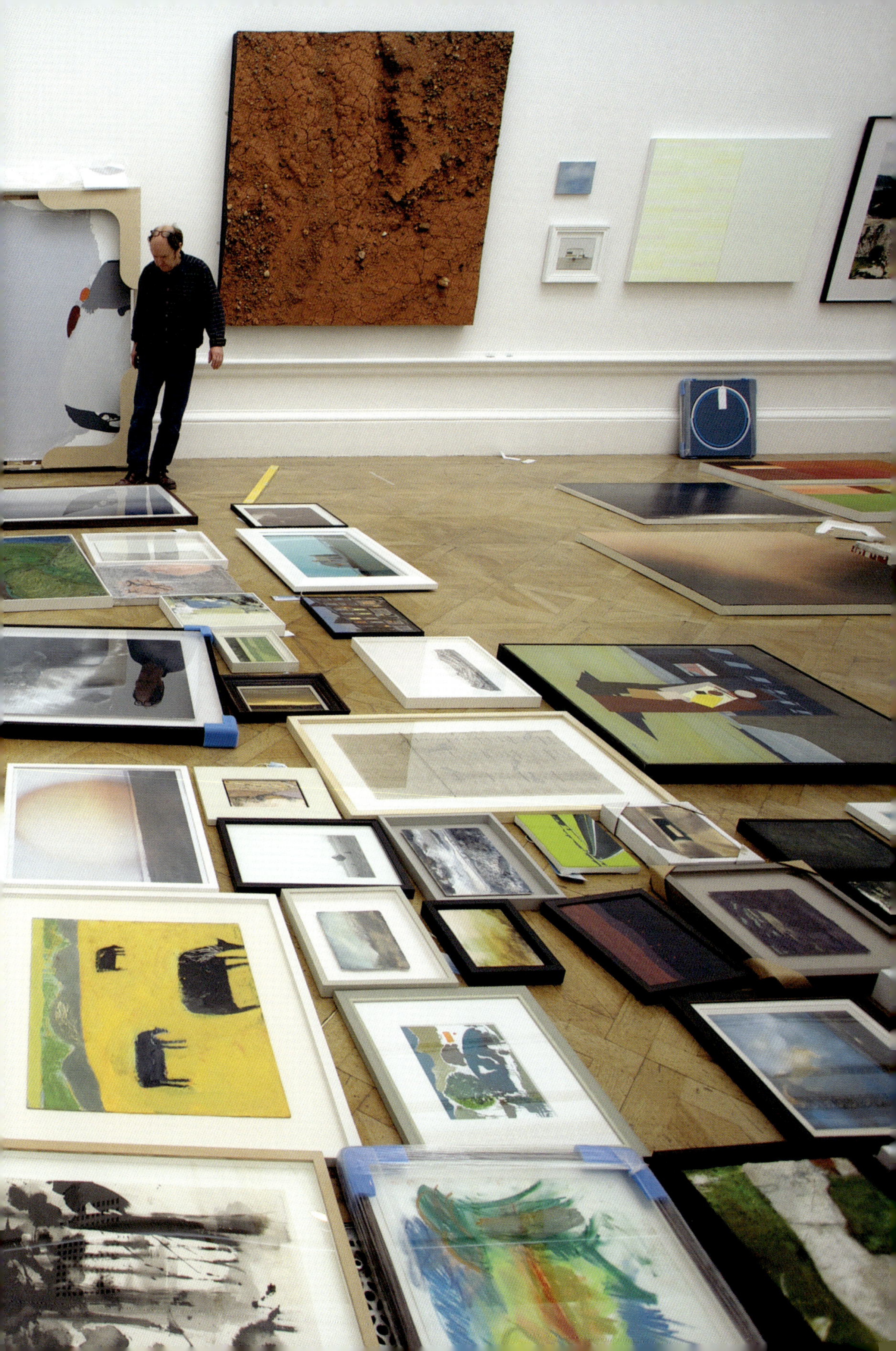

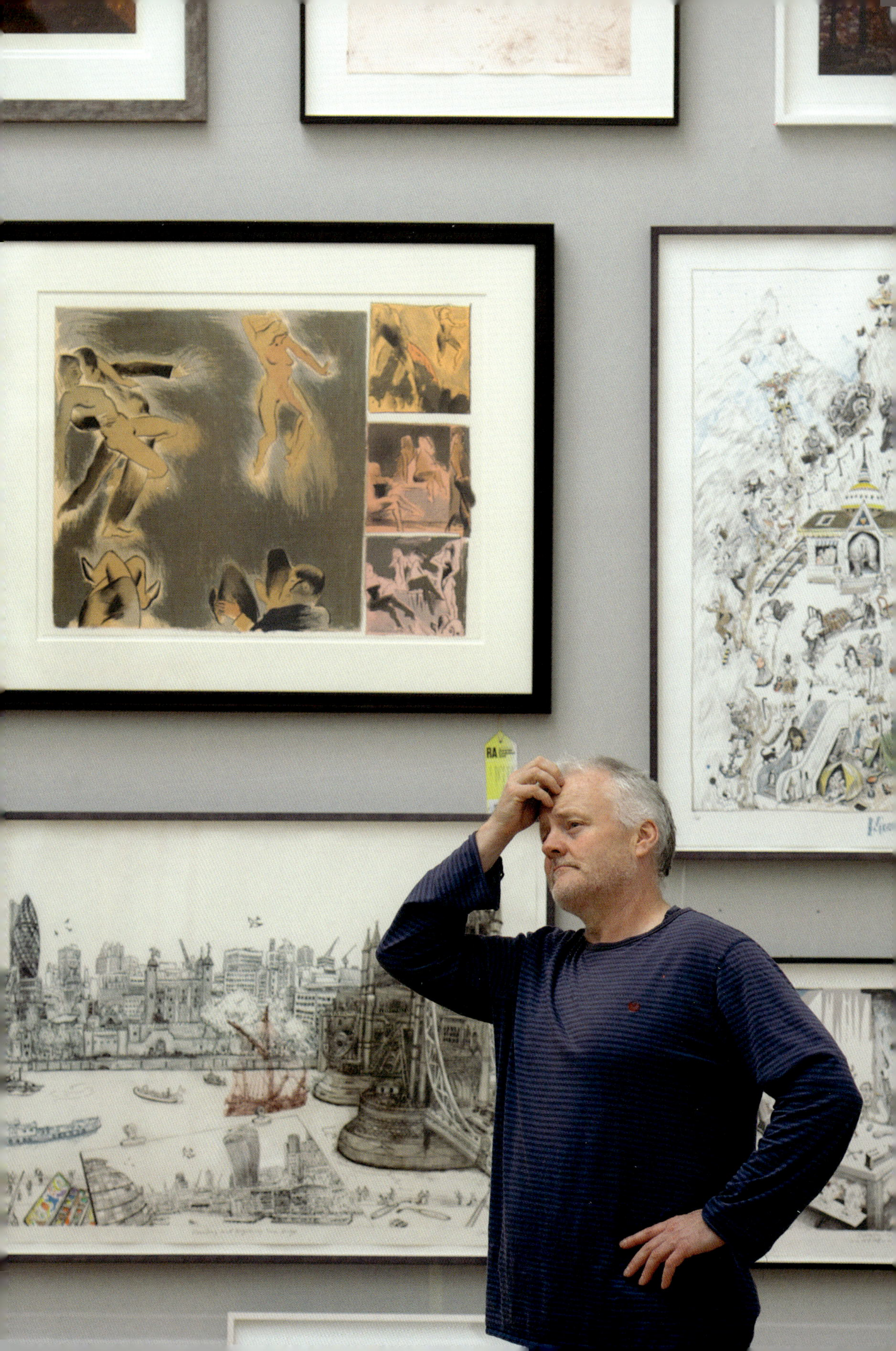

Stephen Chambers

In 1894 Herman Casler invented the Mutoscope, a large 'Rolodex' of silver photographic prints that generated an early form of moving image. Until decimalisation rendered them obsolete in 1971, these devices could be found at the ends of piers and in amusement arcades surrounded by groups of young boys eager to pay their money to see 'what the butler saw'.

Stephen Chambers is intrigued by this act of standing with an eye pressed to a keyhole, hands cupped around the face, furtively peering into another world, yet vulnerable to being caught unawares. It is so different to the way we usually engage with art, admiring it from a distance and first with our minds. For Chambers, the act of looking should be riskier and should require us to be more engaged; there should be an essentially voyeuristic aspect to it, which can reveal hidden realms and uncomfortable scenes. Although frequently seductive, art can also be chilling, confronting us with cannibalism on Géricault's *Raft of the Medusa* or the horrors of the Chapman brothers' *Hell*.

Chambers wants his work to draw us in, slow us down, make us look up close, and feel. His enigmatic figures, which seem both familiar and strange, emerge from the world of the unconscious. Here are the archetypal, mythic forms of children's book illustrations: Jack leading the cow to market, or the tree-like Ents from Tolkien's *Lord of the Rings* – possibly. For Chambers's narratives are only fragments, enticing snapshots but nothing more complete or tied down. They are a reminder that looking through a keyhole can only ever reveal to us part of the room. The rest is speculation, a narrative that must be constructed in the imagination of the viewer.

The Door transforms us into Jack looking through the giant's keyhole, tempting us with a golden, otherworldly space beyond, in which such mundane objects as tins of baked beans and a bunch of flowers seem extraordinary. But a flex hangs down from the ceiling like a noose and a chair is covered with lamps, preventing anyone from sitting on it. Suddenly this apparently tempting space becomes slightly sinister. Pulling back from it, we become aware of the area of flat, warm grey that frames the keyhole, and only then do we realise that we don't know what lies around the corner, behind the door, hidden out of sight. We find ourselves on the outside again, peering guiltily through, caught out and embarrassed by the possibility of someone standing behind us who might have seen what we were doing. We may be drawn in to become part of the painting, but we are also clearly observers. The boundary between fiction and reality has been blurred: the painting leaches into our reality and vice versa, and we stand on the border between two worlds that have briefly merged.

The backgrounds of Chambers's *Stupid Stupid* series of etchings (p.185) are complex scaffolds of repeating patterns and enticing colours. Like the roundels of gothic architecture or the gilded backgrounds of Renaissance art, these diaper patterns of shimmering colour show the no man's land between here and there; intangible spaces of infinite possibility, they are the effervescent birthing pools in which images are born into this world, emerging from the artist's unconscious thoughts and unprompted ideas.

These intriguing works are portraits of the artist, an unintentional autobiography shaped by Chambers's daily life and rich imagination. They are each, in their way, *Self-portrait (as a Shed)*: collections of unconnected ideas and familiar objects sent out into the world in an explosion of paint and ink.

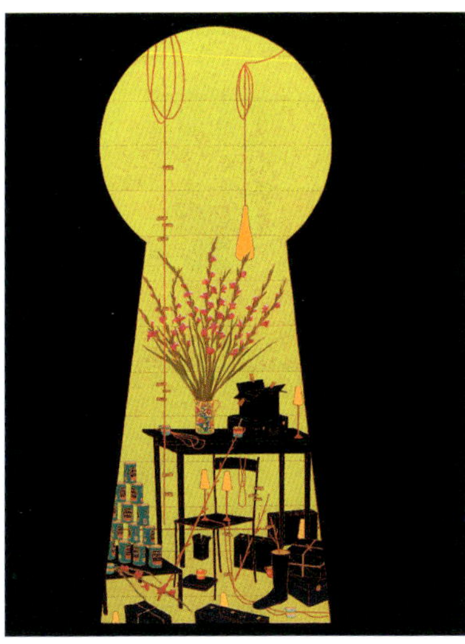

Stephen Chambers RA
The Door
Oil on linen
210 × 160 cm

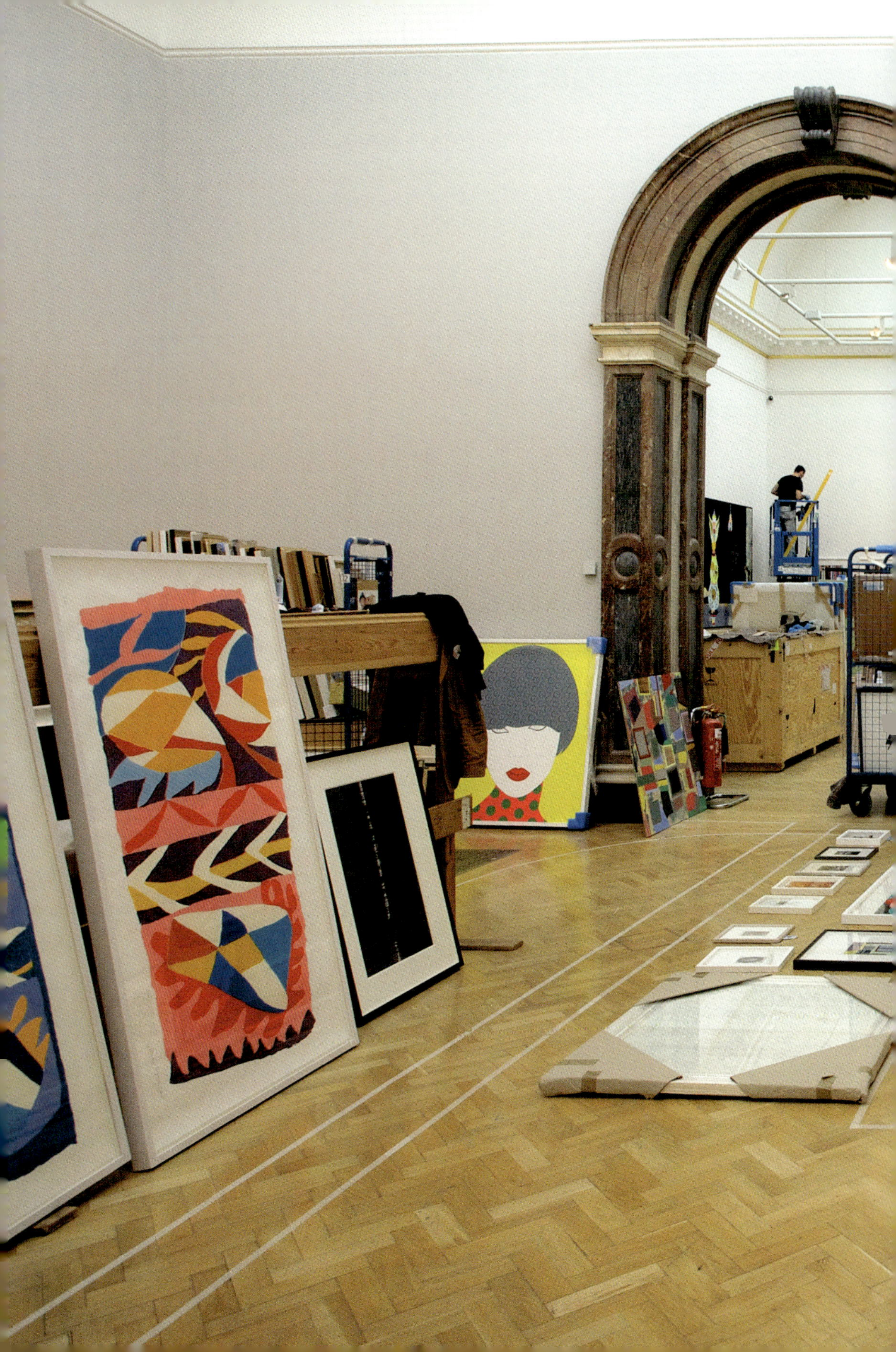

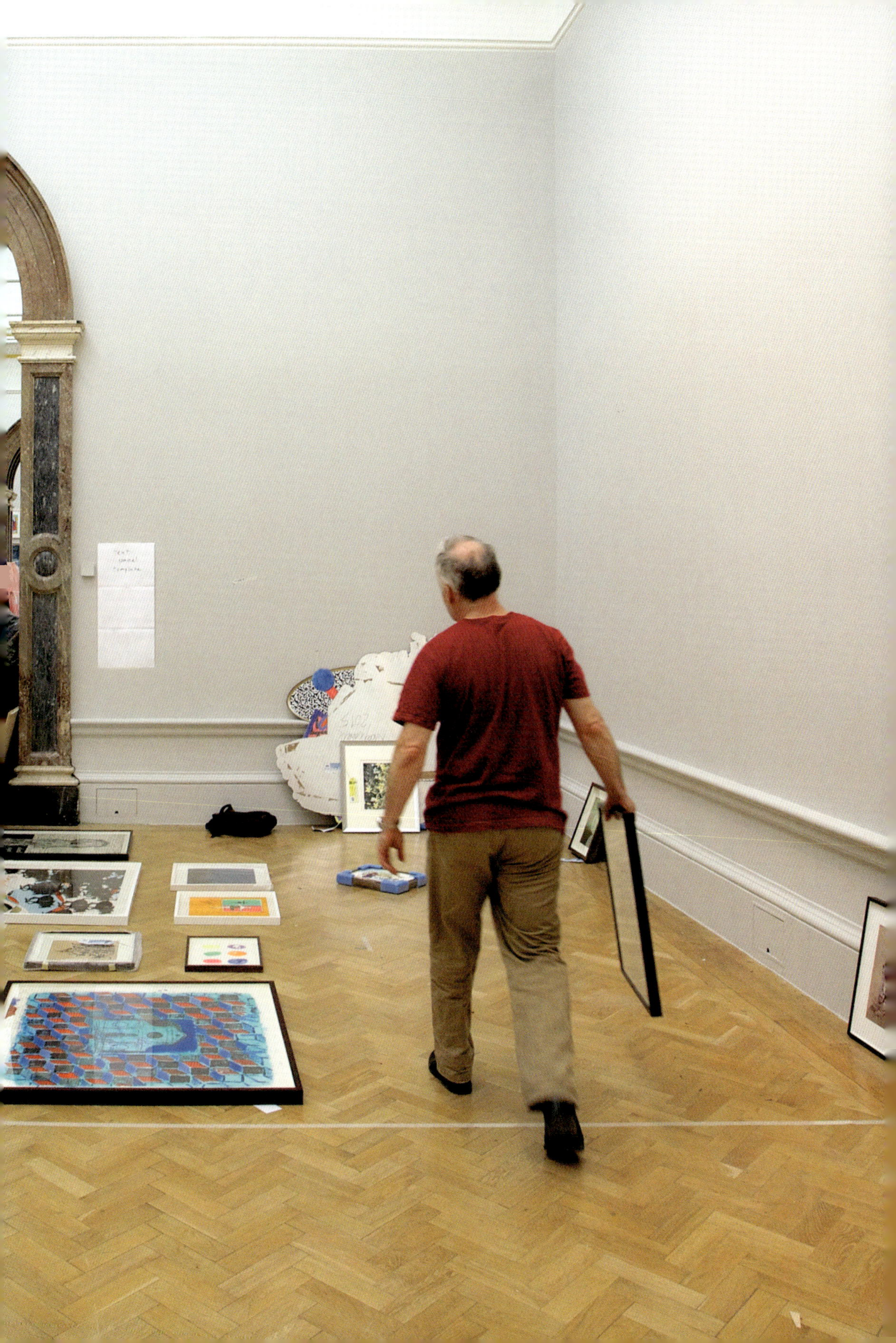

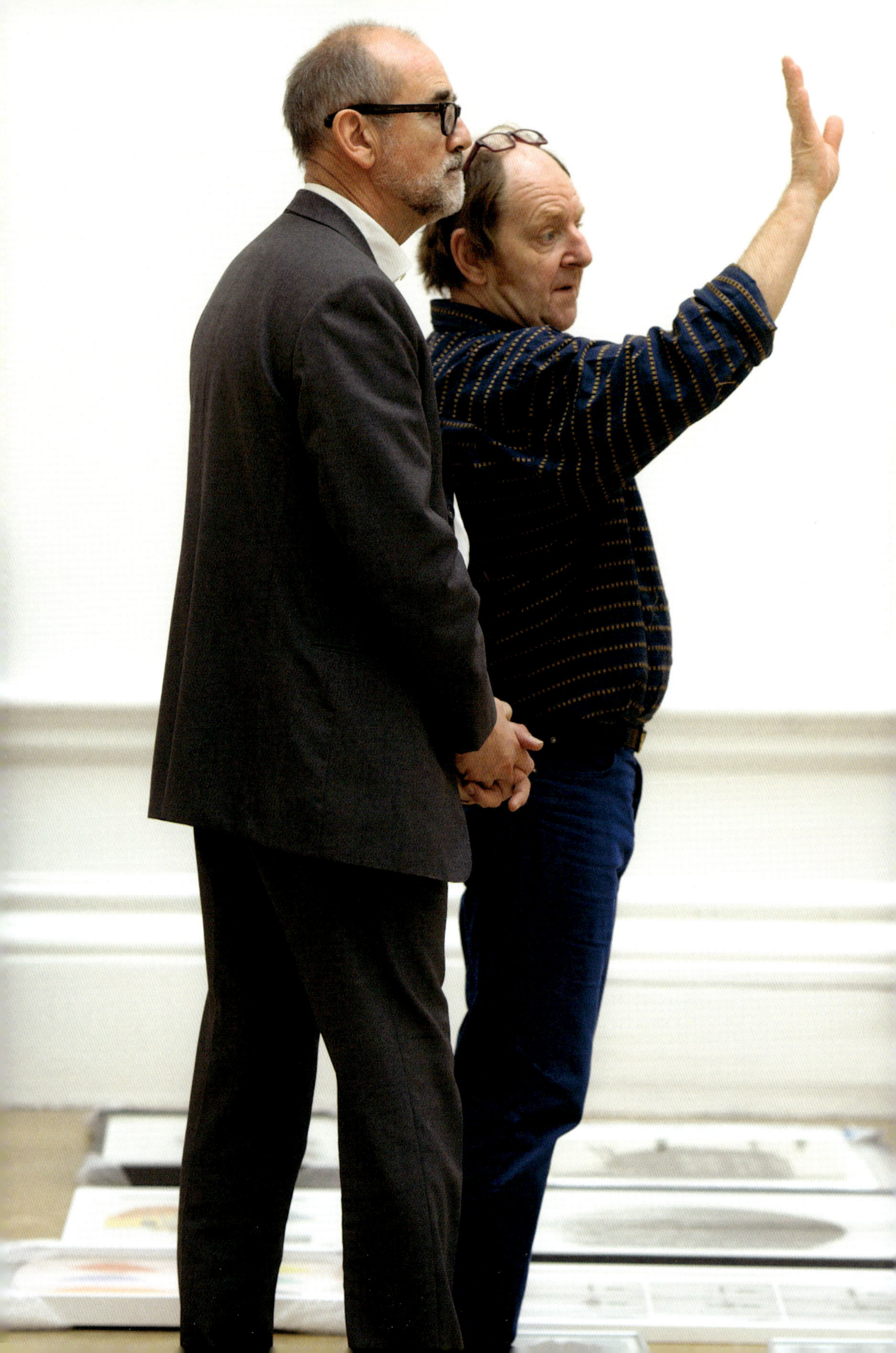

Christopher Le Brun

In the vaults beneath the Main Galleries is the series of corridors, studios and offices that houses the Royal Academy Schools. Established in 1769 as a national school of art to rival the French Académie Royale de Peinture et de Sculpture, the Royal Academy Schools continue to provide the oldest and the only free postgraduate art education, thanks to funds raised by the Summer Exhibition. Between 1769 and 1790, Sir Joshua Reynolds, first President of the Royal Academy, delivered fifteen *Discourses* to the institution's first students, in which he set out the principles of an art education capable of producing works of a high moral and artistic worth. For Reynolds, this was to be grounded in copying the Old Masters, drawing from casts of antique sculpture and making observations from life. Not only did this repetitive practice teach students how to represent the appearance of things, it also trained them to see with an innocent eye and to look without prejudice or preconception, so that they might then perceive the beauty they had discovered in their studies in the world.

This innocent recognition of beauty was achieved by looking and thinking. But the repetitive drawing of these ideal forms also brought students an embodied knowledge, an intuitive response to the world learnt from the repeated translation of gaze into gesture, into mark. *Goldengrove* (p. 182), a large diptych in oils entered by Christopher Le Brun, the current President of the Royal Academy, seems far removed from the life drawings made by the Schools' first pupils, but it is, like them, a search for innocence and enigmatic wonder involving a repetitive, physical act and intuitive knowledge. A dense flurry of Cadmium Red and Naples Yellow looping and scrawling across the canvas expresses Le Brun's belief that colour is 'a property of the world we delight in for itself'.

In his essay *Concerning the Spiritual in Art* (1911), Wassily Kandinsky described the way yellow spreads out and radiates towards the viewer. We find this quality in Le Brun's yellow, which seems to fill the space around it, erupting off the canvas, impacting on our retinas and exploding in our minds as a concussion of colour. The red and orange that surround this explosion appear more stable, but as we look at them they too begin to glow with an intensity that burns into our being. Although these colours dominate our gaze, they only exist because of the linear strokes that hold them, barely visible calligraphic gestures that bring them into existence and contain them.

Lines are normally used to define objects or give shape to ideas. But Le Brun's lines, dancing across his canvases, do nothing more than emerge. They represent the boundary between formlessness and form, nothingness and being, the moment when the invisible becomes visible and beauty is born. Artists once represented the platonic ideal of beauty through images of gods and classical heroes, which the students in the Academy Schools then copied. Le Brun represents it in a waterfall of Cadmium Red and Naples Yellow, making ecstatic lines and vibrant colours the new symbols for that state of innocence and possibility that existed when the world was new and its forms had not yet been born.

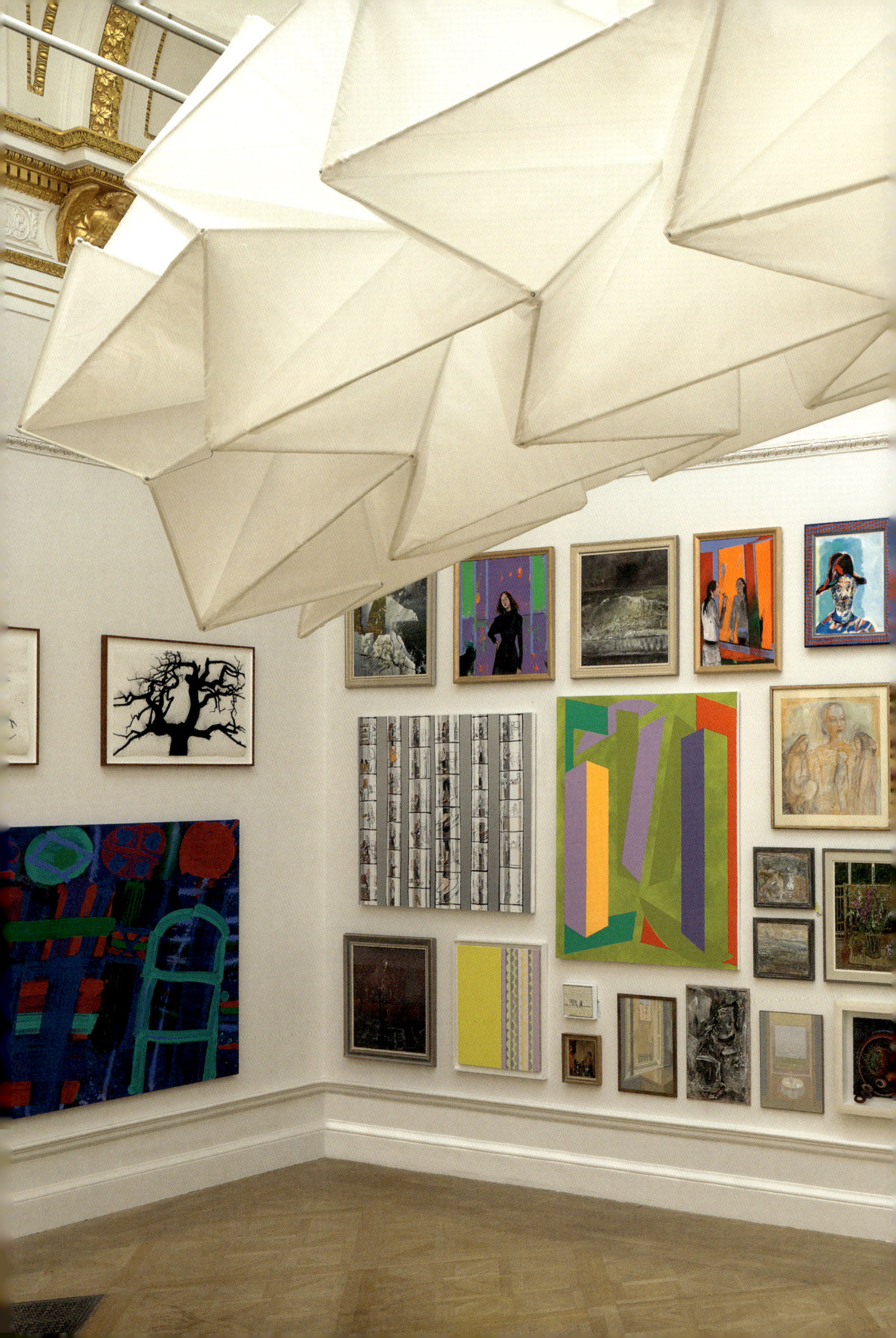

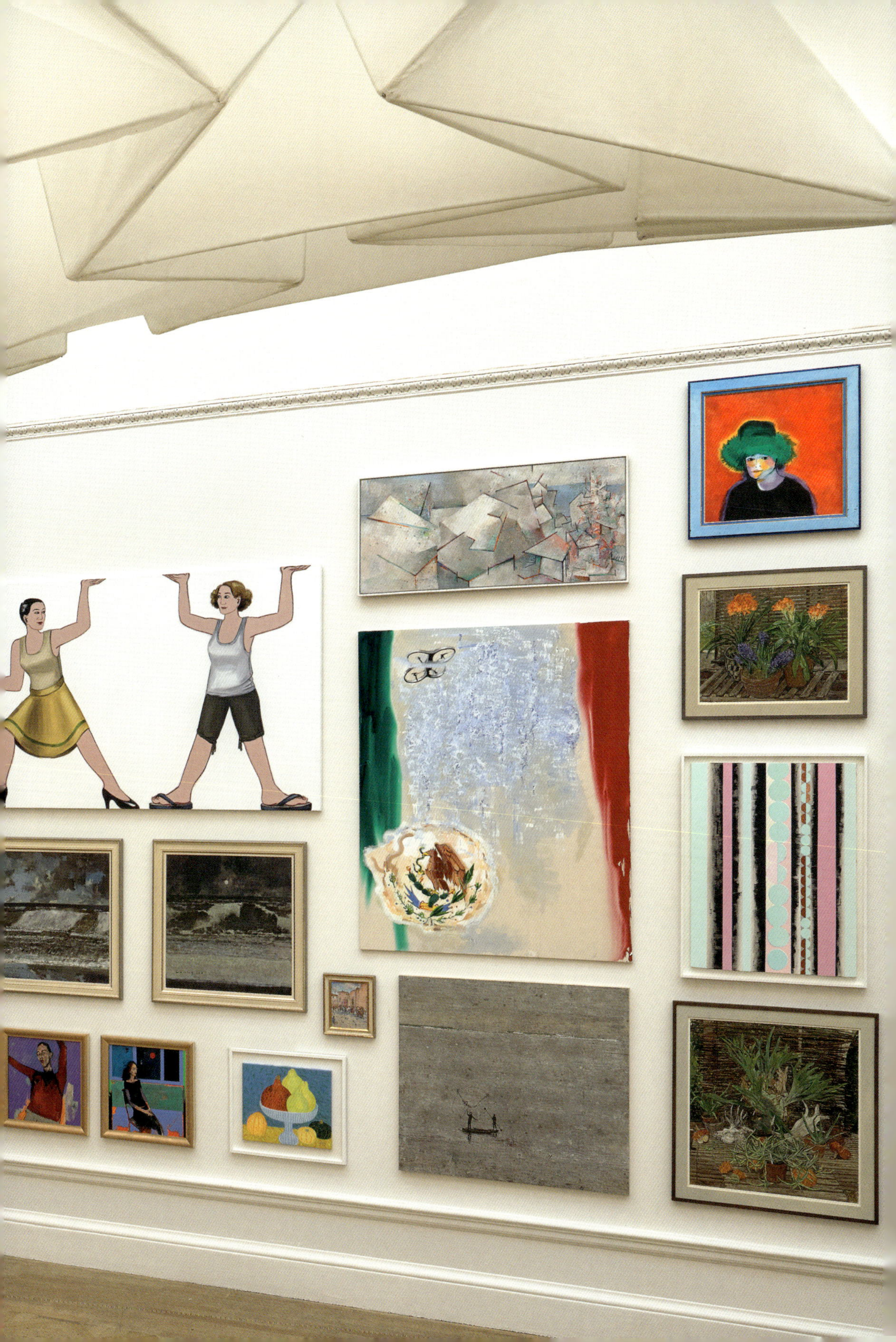

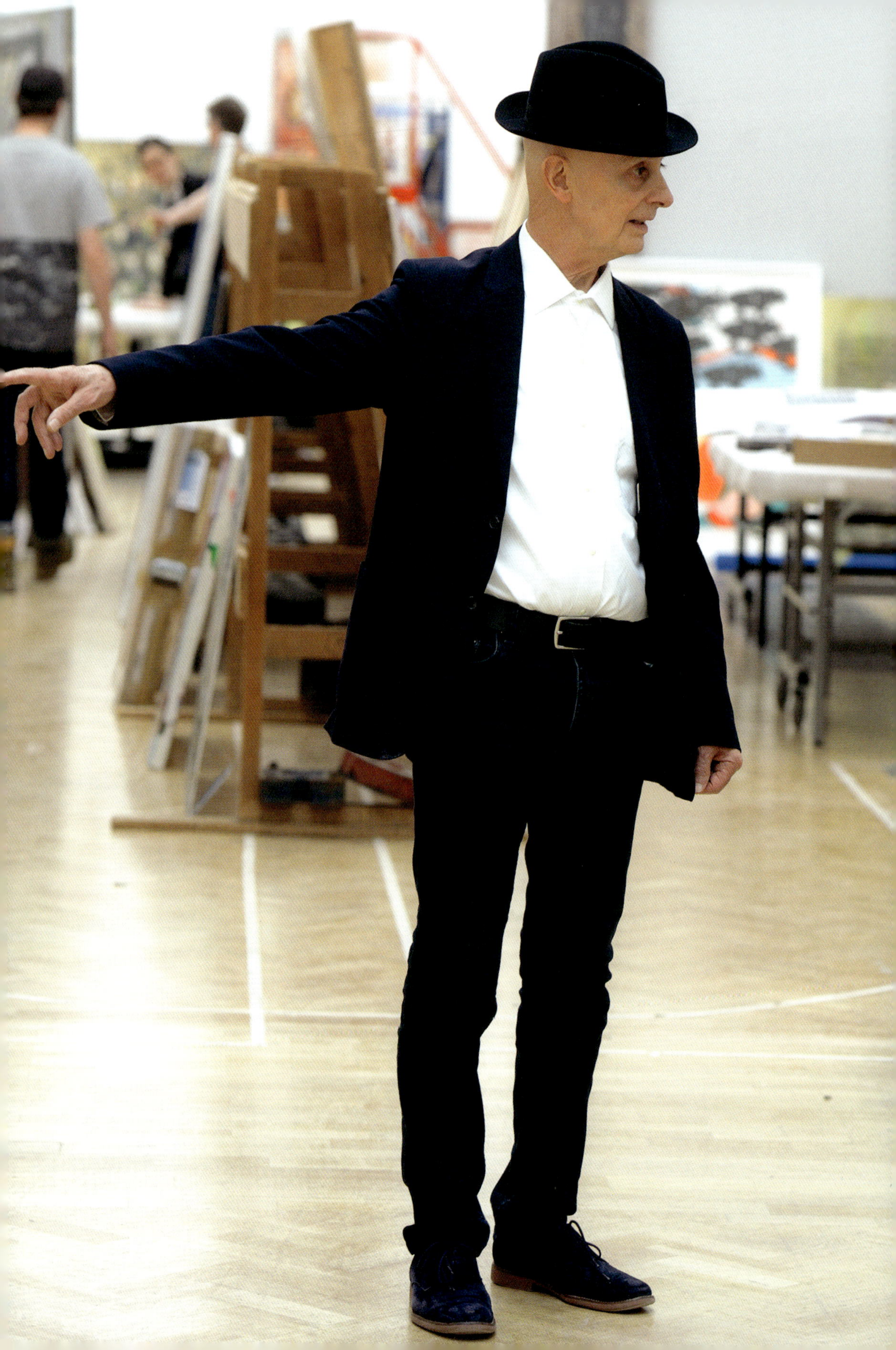

David Remfry

In 1995 David Remfry and his wife Caroline arrived at the legendary Chelsea Hotel in Manhattan with seventeen pieces of luggage and the conditional promise of an exhibition in New York. He stayed to make the work, and is still, technically, a resident of the Chelsea, although a change in ownership and a flood in his hotel studio saw the couple return to London in 2011. Remfry was inspired by New York, finding in the people he met, the dancers he observed, and the colourful residents of the Chelsea an endless source of subject-matter. He has never tired of watching the human predicament played out in the lives of those around him, using quick pencil sketches and fluid watercolour paintings to capture the intimate relationships that overcome human loneliness.

Remfry has never really seen himself as a landscape painter, feeling that the topography of where we live is less important than how we live. Yet over the years he has made a number of paintings and sketches of the famous Manhattan skyline. These long, aqueous works eschew the over-familiar silhouette to find an alternative view. In 2011, preparing to return to London, he painted the view from the Chelsea looking west towards the Hudson River. Beneath purple clouds, an orange sunset dissolves the city into a warm grey haze that seems indistinguishable from the sky. Although buildings can be picked out, they seem insubstantial, a watery reflection of the clouds rather than solid structures.

Remfry's elegiac *Hudson from the Hotel Chelsea* may seem atypical of his practice, but it captures many of his overriding concerns. He omits more than he includes, dissolving solid forms into an incorporeal pattern that swirls and eddies across the paper. We may think of Remfry as a figurative artist who upholds the representational traditions of life study and portraiture. But even a cursory glance at his submissions this year reveals an artist wrestling creatively with the intangible boundary between abstraction and figuration.

Remfry has returned to oils after spending 35 years painting in watercolour because of an illness, and his subjects hover on the cusp of dissolution. He is fascinated by how much can be left out before a figure disappears and only abstract blocks of colour remain. In *Woman with Imaginary Dog I* and *II*, based on a series of works exploring the relationship between dogs and their owners, Remfry leaves out the dog completely. The woman stands in a slightly contorted posture, reduced to a yellow dress, pink flesh, and red Afro hair. In *It Begins Again* (p. 80), a portrait of long-term Chelsea Hotel resident Susanne Bartsch, her torso is implied rather than present. She is surrounded by broad strokes of pinks, greys and greens that balance the exuberance of her presence, providing a scaffolding of colour from which she seems to emerge like Venus from the sea.

Remfry is attracted to tiny details: big hair, bright lipstick, false eyelashes, tattoos and stilettos. These absorb the eye in their intricacy. They pause time and focus our minds, ushering us towards that numinous threshold between being and nothingness, the solid and the unformed.

David Remfry MBE RA
Woman with Imaginary Dog II
Oil
61 × 50 cm

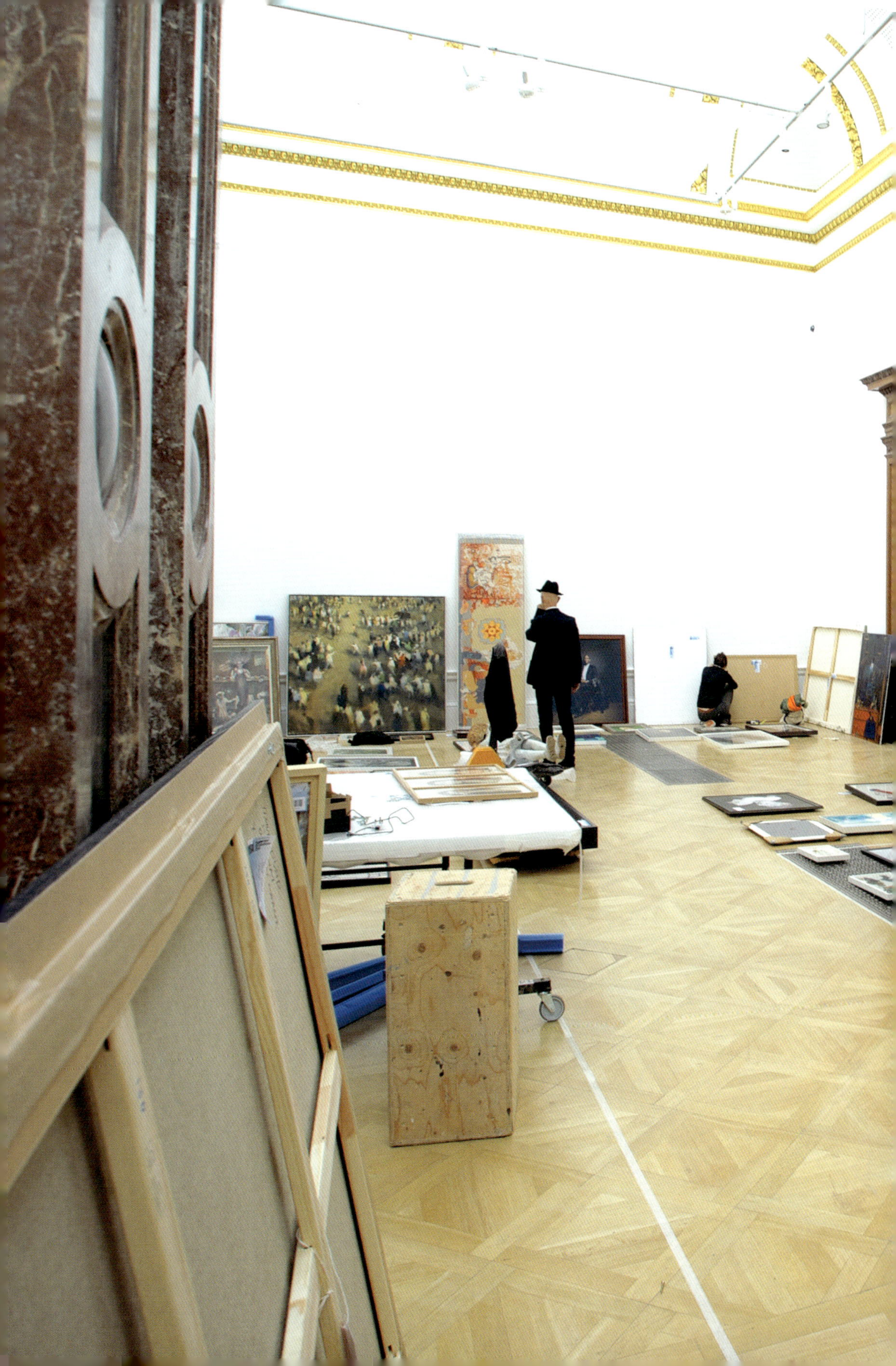

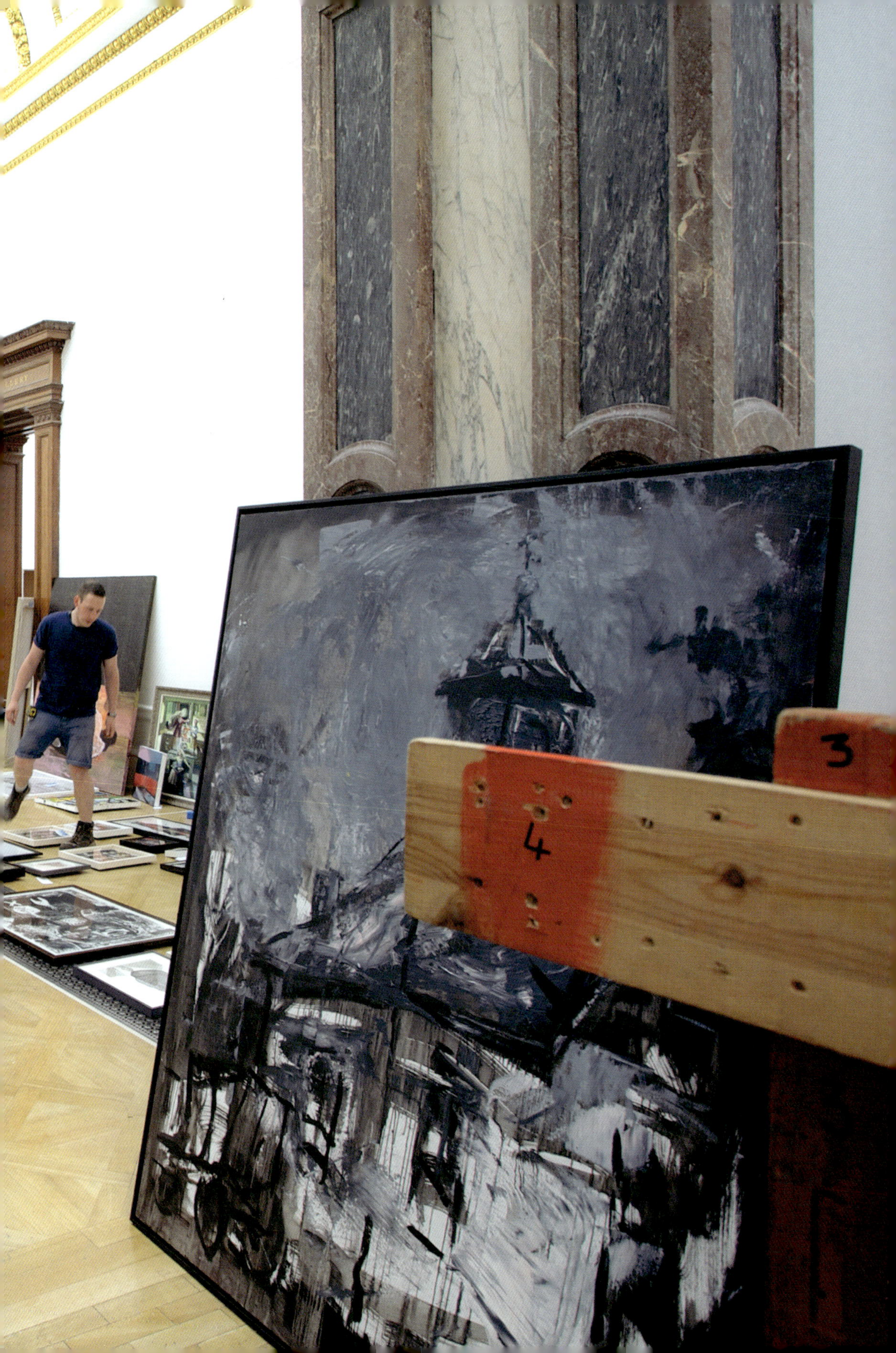
3
4

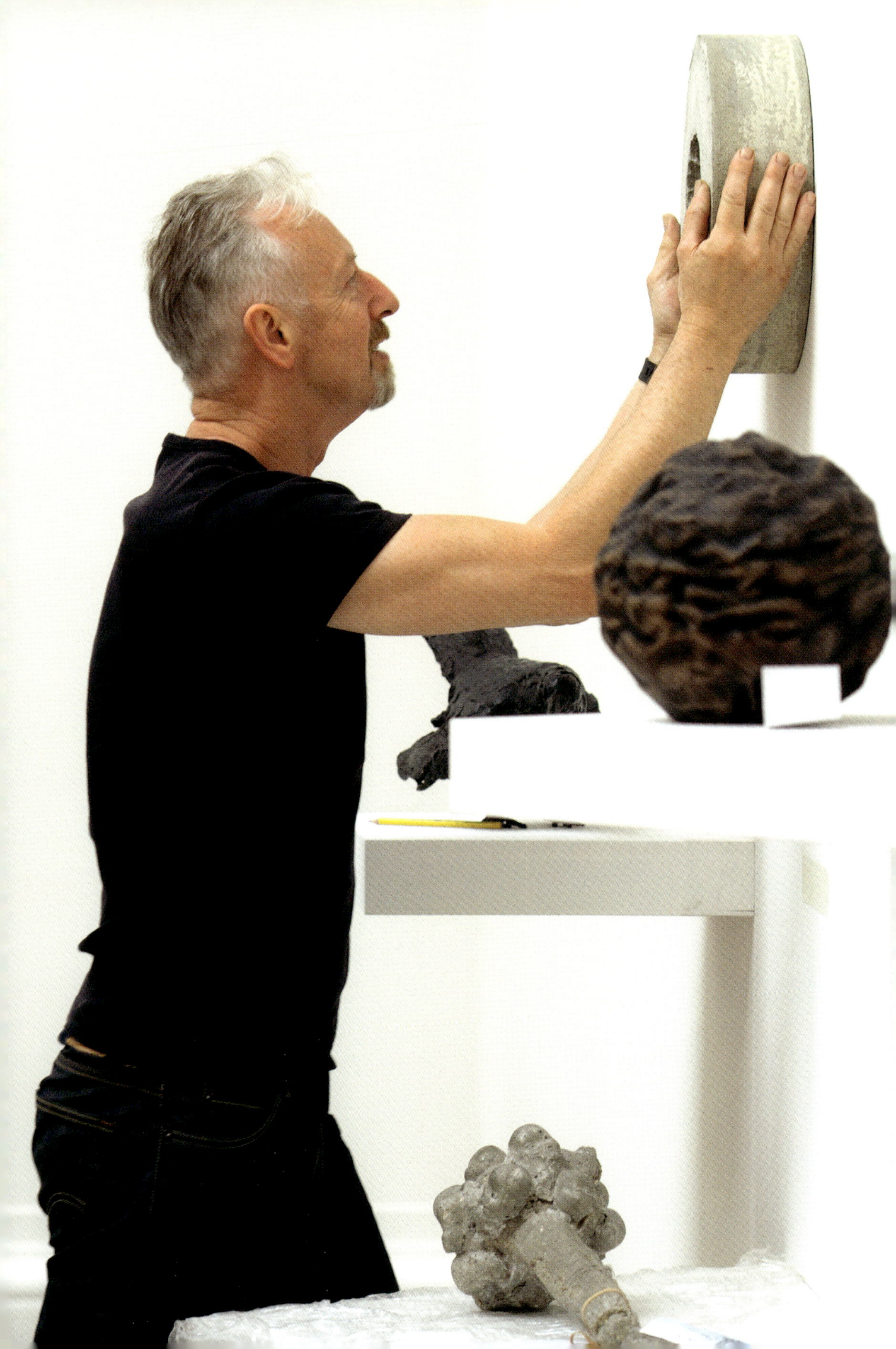

David Mach

When Sir Edwin Landseer RA painted *The Monarch of the Glen* (1851; National Museum of Scotland, Edinburgh), his famous study of a red deer stag, he was not only capturing the likeness of a magnificent animal but reflecting the Victorians' fascination with the Scottish Highlands. Here was the Romantic vision of Sir Walter Scott: an image of violet-tinged mountains and majestic nature that sanitised reality and made it sublime. His intimately observed portrait celebrates the physical presence of the wild beast, standing alone, surveying its domain, a serene symphony of golden browns that seem to glow beneath a glowering sky.

David Mach RA's *Silver Hart* (p. 138) hangs, in contrast, as a trophy on the wall of the Lecture Room. This is no image of regal serenity, no celebration of nature or animal form. Instead, Mach focuses on the red stag's roar, his rutting cry of desire and defiance. Made, like a number of Mach's works, from metal coat hangers, and bristling with metallic energy, this intensely physical sculpture thrusts out from the wall into its surroundings, demanding to be noticed. It's a brash, confident statement of authority that grabs and holds our attention. Look at me, it seems to say, in a declaration of intent that not only serves for Mach's sculptures but for all the sculpture in this year's Summer Exhibition.

Yet as we look, the substance of the work dissolves, dissipated into the atmosphere in a shimmering haze of metal points. Each point is like a simple antenna, broadcasting and receiving, wanting to make contact, curious to see what is out there, and eager for someone to respond. The mysterious form of Mach's *Dark Matter*, on the other hand, pulls us in. It sits there immobile, daring us to engage with its undulating, contorted mass. Unlike *Silver Hart*, with its recognisable identity, the form of *Dark Matter* was, and remains, unknown. Having retrieved a massive tree root that he had found half buried in the sand of a Scottish beach, Mach began to gouge out the rotten wood from it, contributing his own process of erosion, until he was left with an indeterminate shape. Then he began to probe its interior, screwing over fifteen thousand screws into the surface, each twist and turn a moment of tactile discovery and an act of repetitive contemplation, allowing him to reach into the invisible, solid depths of this mysterious material, to feel its give and take, and its untapped possibility.

The identity of this tree was lost when it fell. For years, half buried in the sand, it waited to be rediscovered. But then, just as pieces of plywood breathed new life into Fumiaki Aono's broken video cassettes, Mach's probing screws reincarnated this ancient, wave-tossed wood, giving it a metallic skin, and the opportunity to become something new. Like the identical vases he transformed through multi-coloured pins into *All the Fish in the Sea*, he has turned this lumpen wood into a meteor travelling through space, a strange creature covered in shimmering scales, or just a shape, intriguing and compelling, which draws the eye in and holds it within its depths.

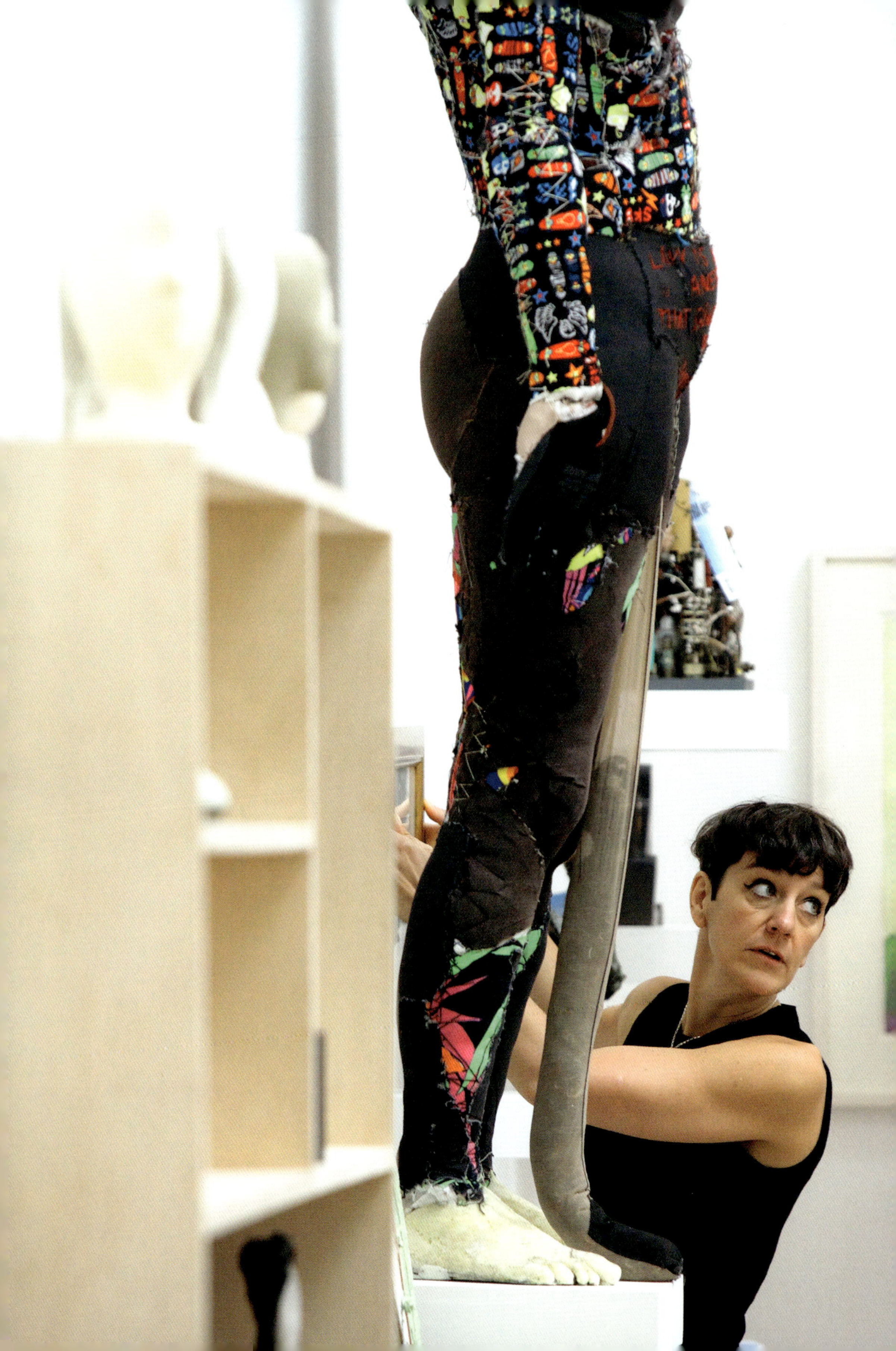

Cathie Pilkington

There is something uncanny about Cathie Pilkington's sculptures. Familiar forms are made oddly unfamiliar. Thrown-away objects are recast and reassembled, given a new life that both attracts and repels. There are shelves of artistic doppelgängers: Magritte, Moore, Meret Oppenheim; and strange reassemblings and reimaginings that see paintings become sculptures, and sculptures turned into dolls.

Pilkington is a collector and hoarder. Drawn to the discarded and broken, she rummages through car-boot sales and junk shops. Her studio is filled with the dolls and ornaments she finds, mingled democratically with her own work. Stacks of fabric lie next to her sculptures and prints, with a pile of disassembled dolls' heads and legs nearby. In the silence of the space they talk to each other, and to her, suggesting new lives and playful possibilities, looking for healing and new purpose.

Pilkington's works echo these unexpected studio conversations. They are a bricolage of chance encounters and tangential links, an assemblage of fascinating objects and separated parts whose visual narratives both draw us in and rebuff us. She teases us with ideas without filling in all the gaps, leaving the rest to our imagination. These are images of beauty and childlike innocence shot through with the sinister and strange. Her *Degas Doll No. 5* is a concocted figure – a combination of the rounded, fleshy beauty of Degas's original dancer with a doll's leg, a Spanish dancer's hands and a Janus head – that brings the sexually ambiguous nature of the original into stark relief.

The uncanny is not something merely frightening or strange, as Freud noted in his 1919 essay of the same name, but a combination of fascination and repulsion, an Oedipal encounter with those inner desires from which we want to hide. In *Head Case*, Pilkington confronts us with a cabinet of artistic wonder containing three shelves stacked with small white sculptural heads that intrigue and compel. They tease us with memories of a Picasso sculpture or a child's rag doll, their fabric surfaces a siren call demanding a visual caress. On the right of the shelving unit, a figure hidden beneath a piece of red fabric forms a point of colourful punctuation; on the left, a sculptural double for Magritte's painting *Rape* (a woman's face recast as a naked female torso) teases and shocks with its libidinous desire. Although some of these heads stare back at us, the sightless faces of others offer an emotional, an uncommunicative emotional void. The sculptural elements of this work, however, are offset by a background that suggests a simple Mondrianesque grid painting and both flattens the space and pulls us through it. The white pegboard in the top half offers tiny black holes with a limitless void beyond; the bottom an intense black, with small mirrors attached to reflect our gaze and show us what we could not otherwise see.

Each element of Pilkington's sculptures is deliberately handmade. She is drawn to the physical process and craft of making, assembling soft fabric into bodies and then filling them with plaster to make them into hard sculptures. Pilkington's intimate relationship with her diverse materials shapes what she makes. She knows intuitively the forms that work together and those that don't, what may attract and what may disquiet. And over the years she has spent assembling the different constituents of her sculptures and prints, she has learnt how to take a broken world and make it whole by fashioning hybrid creatures of mysterious promise.

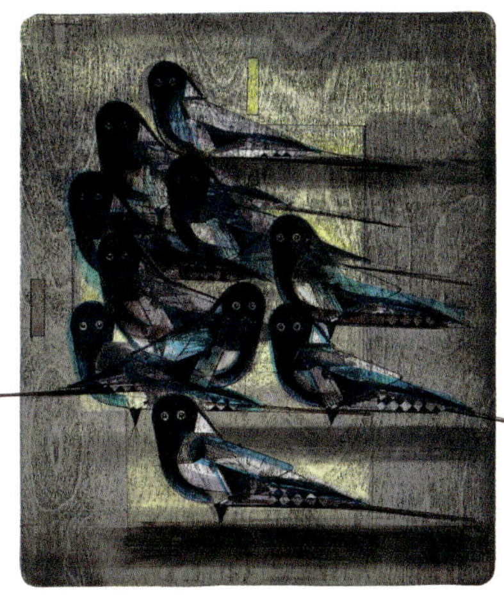

Prof Cathie Pilkington RA
Magpie Rhythm
Hand-coloured mokulito lithograph
45 × 38 cm

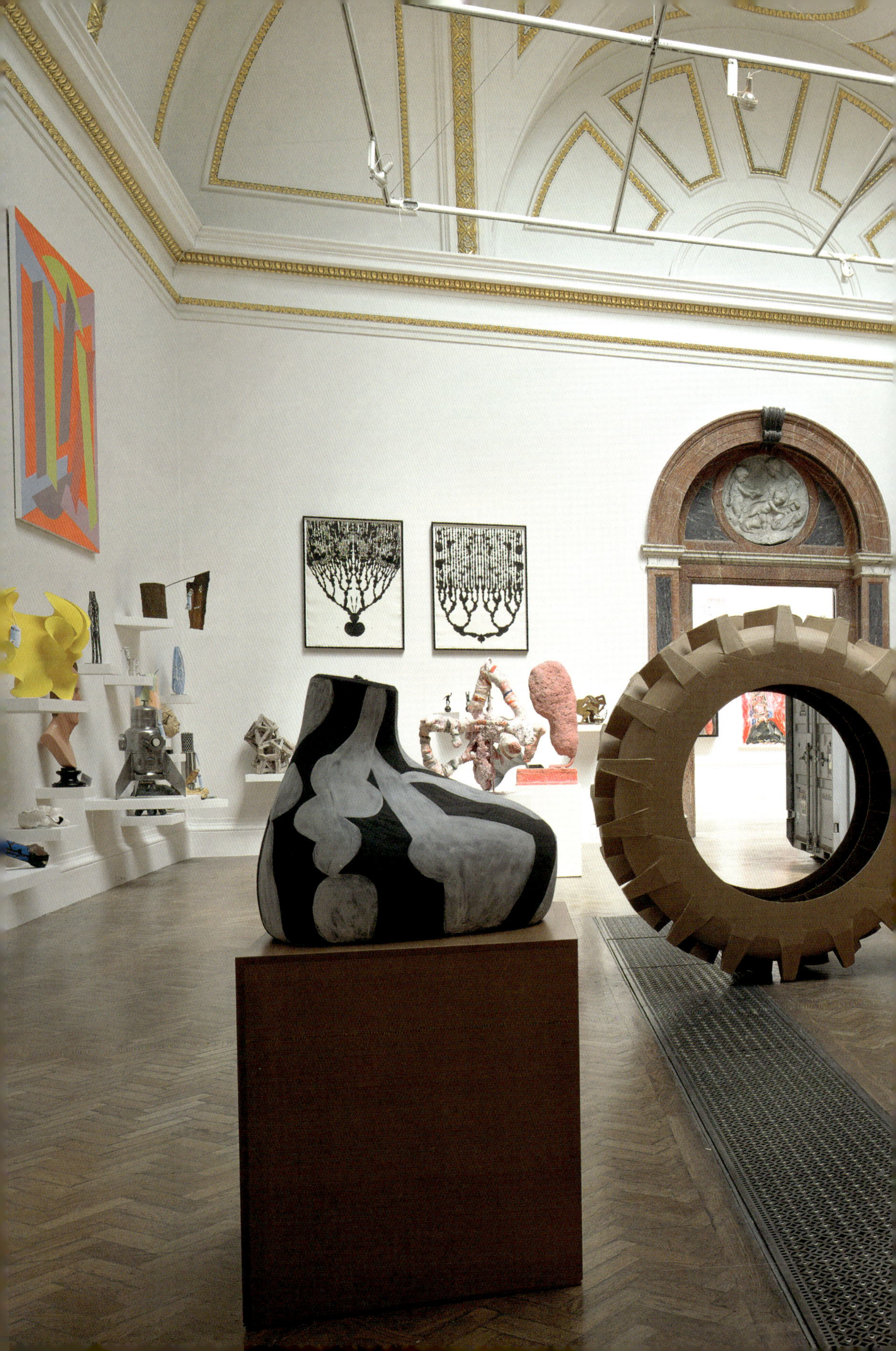

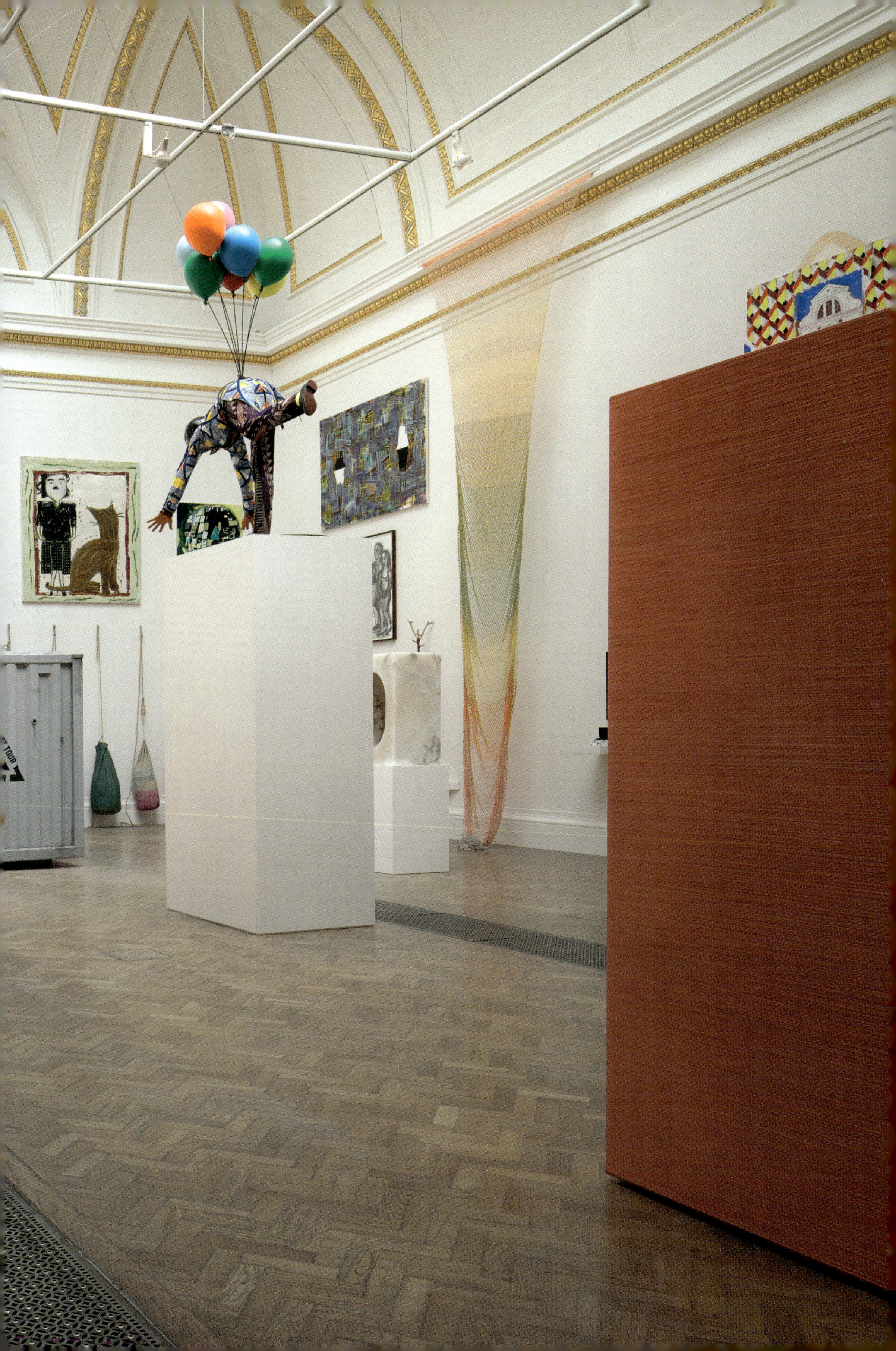

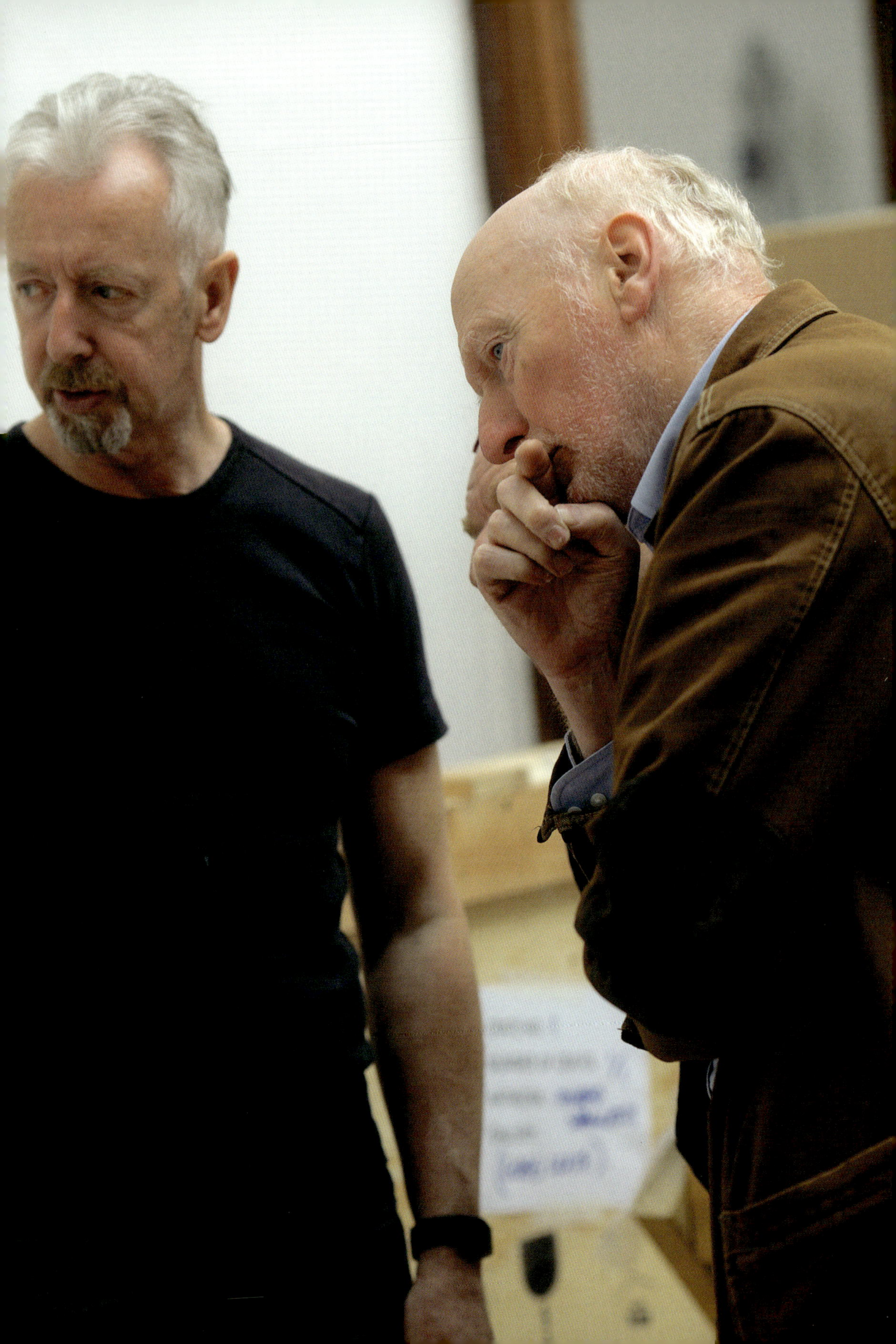

Bill Woodrow

When the French painter Paul Delaroche (1797–1856) saw his first Daguerrotype, an early type of photograph, he was supposedly heard to lament, 'From today, painting is dead.' His statement expressed the crisis of identity felt by many early nineteenth-century artists confronted with this new medium, which captured the world with a realism and immediacy that even the most skilful painter could never emulate. Yet now, we have come to realise that painting and photography are not in competition. Rather, each makes its own distinctive contribution to our visual knowledge and experience.

When Bill Woodrow RA came across a toad in his garden, he was fascinated. Toads are usually seen as part of nature's underbelly, something poisonous, lurking in the undergrowth, among damp, rotting leaves. But Woodrow saw something beautiful, so he photographed it. His camera allowed him to capture the visual information of that moment precisely, showing with undiscriminating accuracy the shadows and highlights, the colours and patterns of the scene. Woodrow's photograph of the toad stayed in his mind, and eventually he decided to do something with it. He could have stayed with the photograph, editing it, cropping it, manipulating its colours and lighting until he had transformed the image into something more than a factual record. He could have highlighted things, revealing hidden aspects. He could have offered a scientific record, accurate in every detail, or blurred things to convey a sense of emotion, mystery and wonder. But, instead he decided to paint the toad (p.184).

Using oil paint on paper, he captured the toad's mottled skin, a pebbledash of grey, green and blue. The original photograph might have shown this in more detail and with greater accuracy, but Woodrow relished paint's ability to give actual substance and texture to his depiction. For in laying a skin of paint onto the paper surface, he was using a physical material to represent the physical world, something that photography cannot do, since it paints with intangible light.

To move this image from the particular to the universal, Woodrow made another version and replaced the garden surface shown in the photograph with an abstract colour background. Even so, he felt that these two paintings of a crawling toad were too illustrative. They had the same aura of verisimilitude that a photograph often has, the sense of looking at something actual and real, however false, imaginary or abstract its content. They were images of a toad, nothing more. Woodrow wanted to show what a toad could be, to offer this overlooked, reviled amphibian the possibility of a new life through art. So he painted a red circle onto one, and a green one on the other. In an instant, the diptych was completely transformed. The circles seemed to press down on the three-dimensional solidity of the animal form and flatten it, and like a magnifying lens they focused the viewer's attention away from the whole, and created an area of isolated two-dimensional space in which the toad's skin could become an abstract pattern.

Woodrow still has the original photograph, his unique record of that moment of particular wonder, but he also has the diptych, which expresses his wonder at what a toad might be: the artistic duo of illustration and imagination, which celebrates what the world is like, and shows us what it can be.

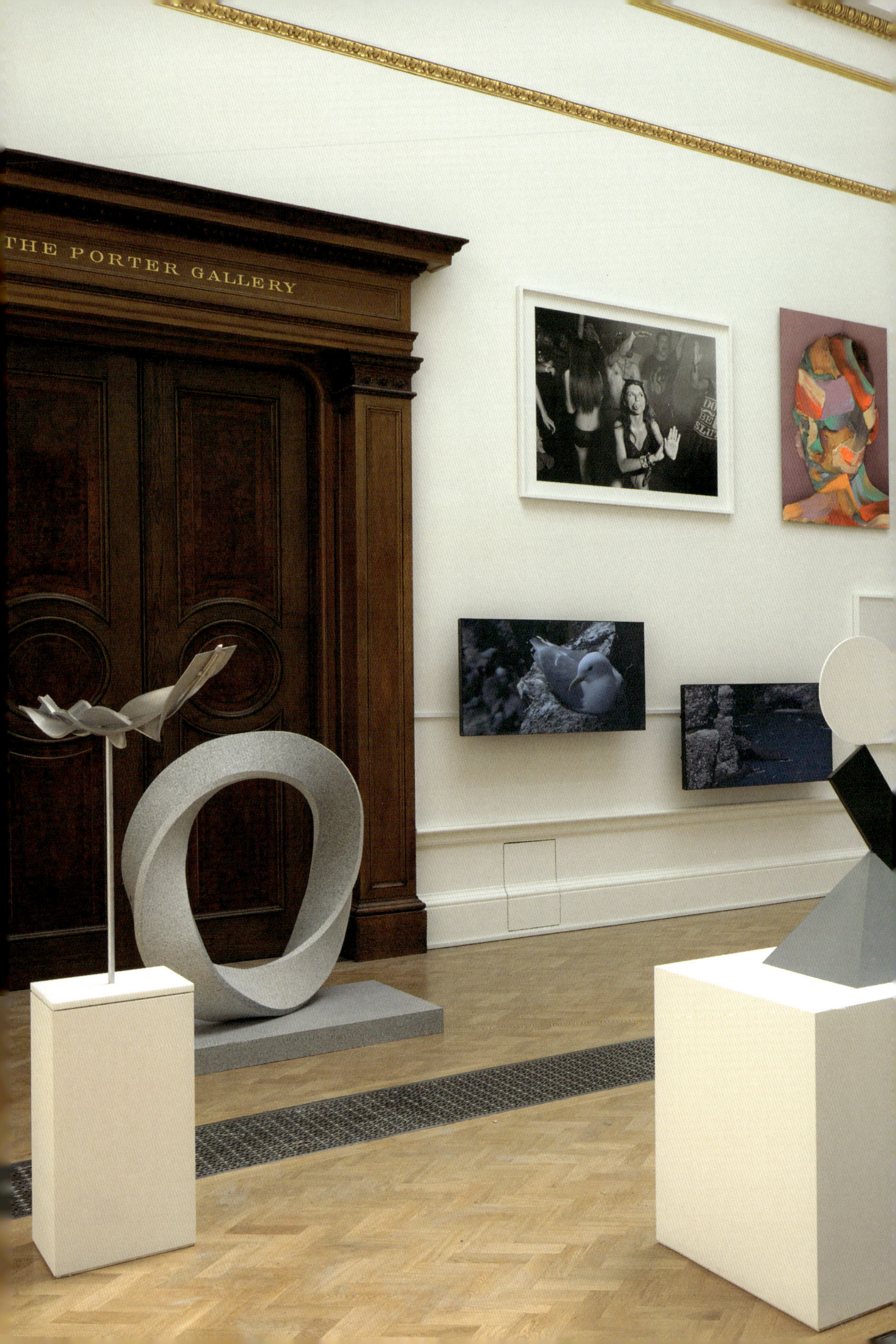
THE PORTER GALLERY

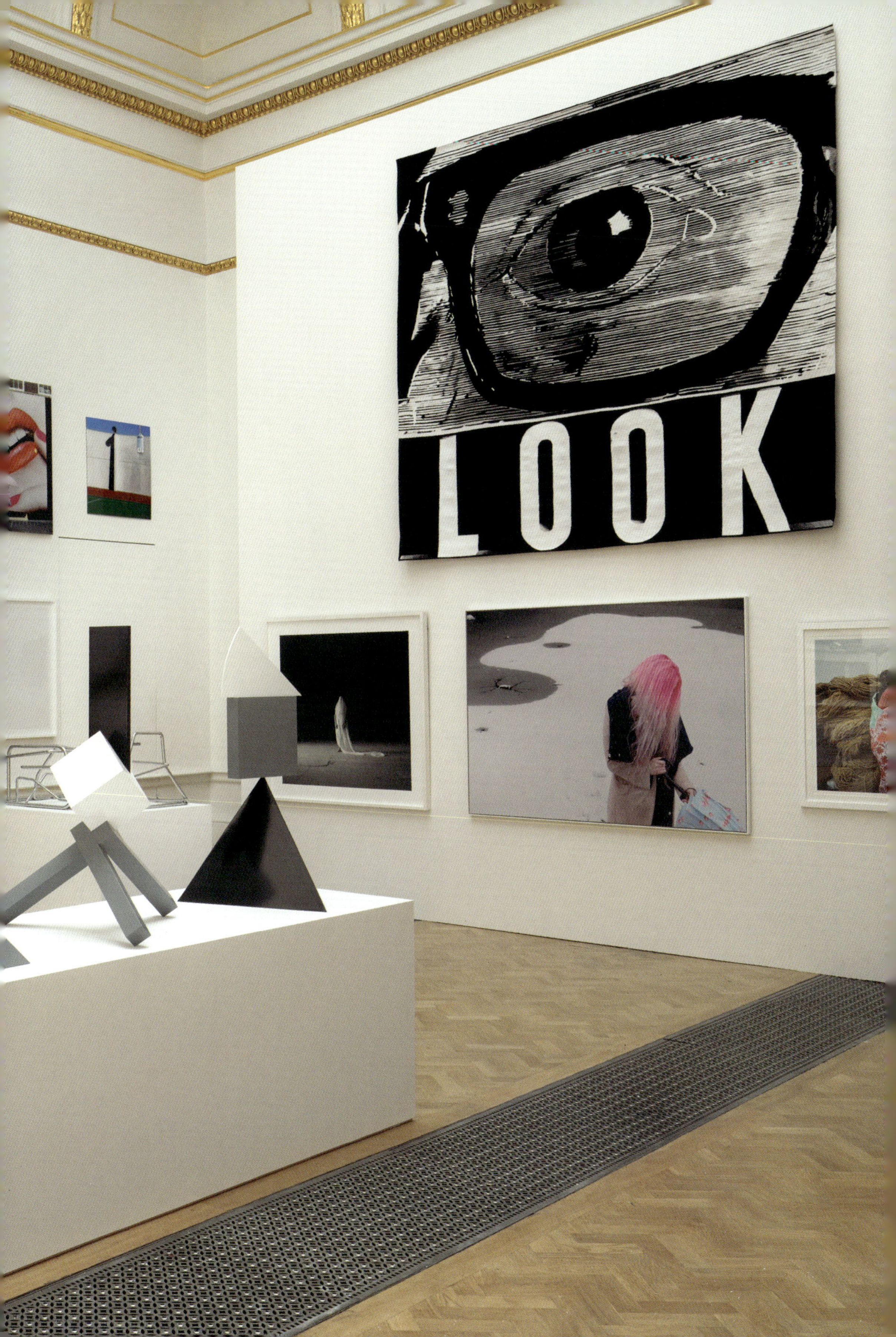
LOOK

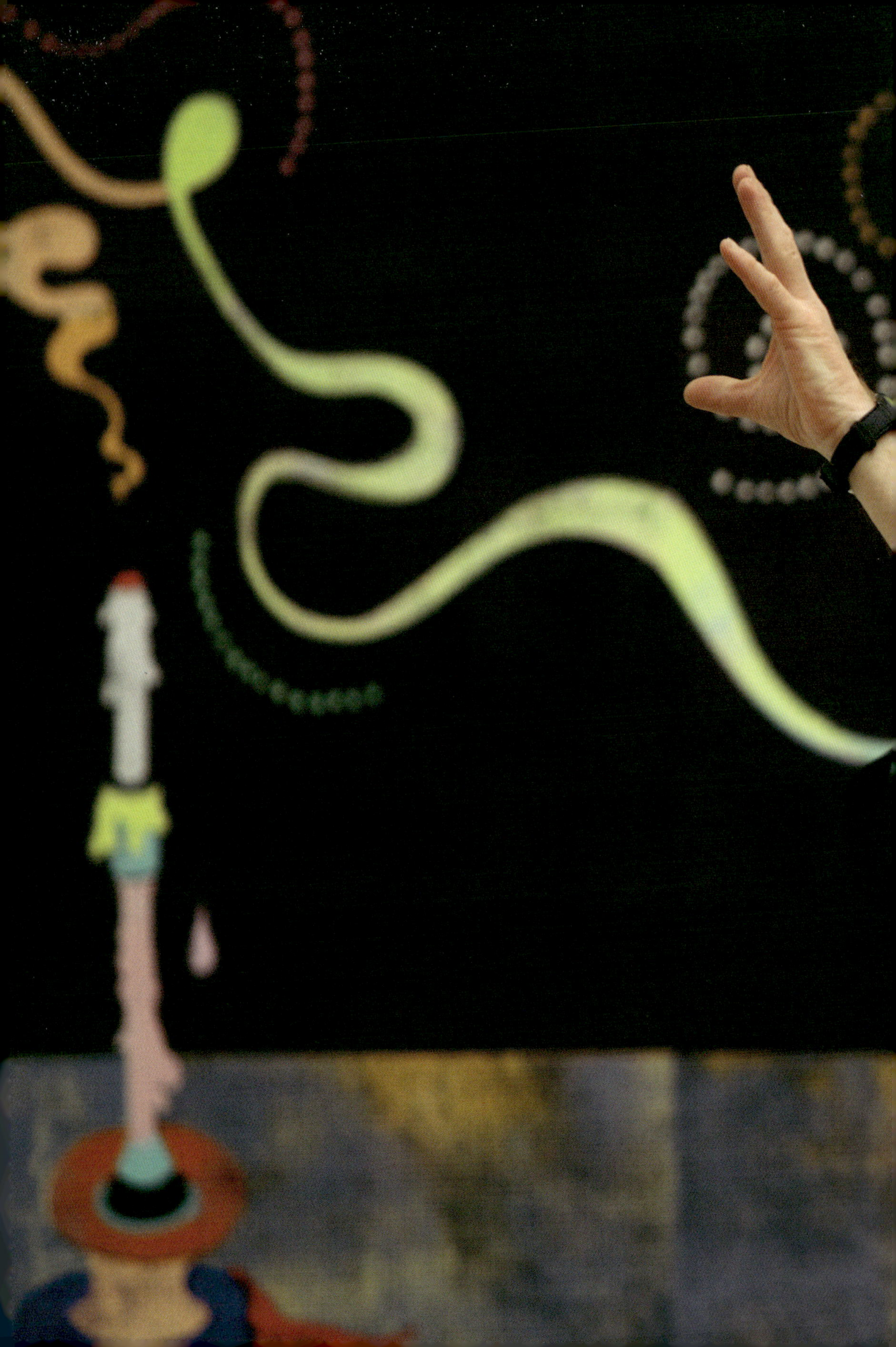

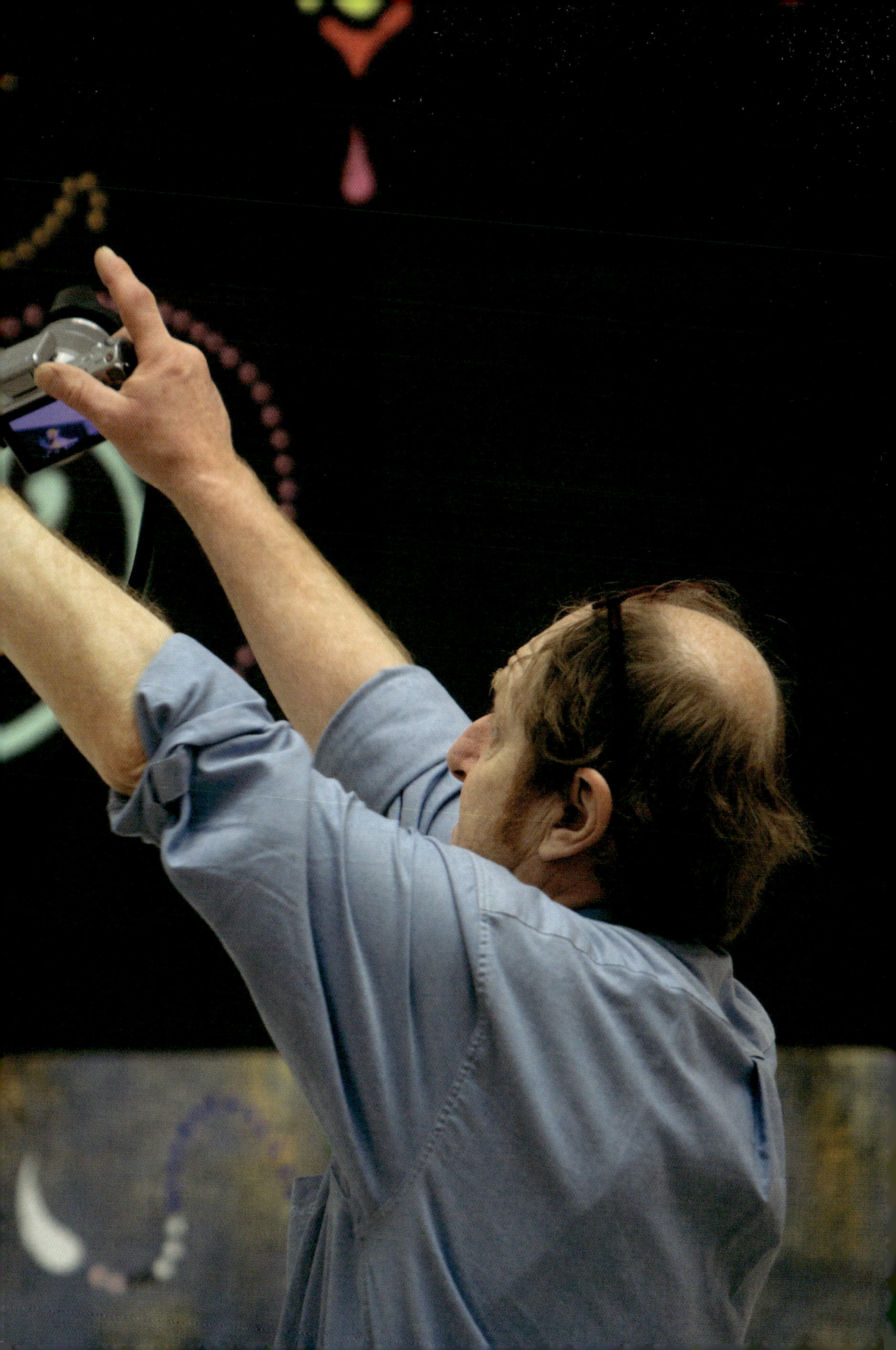

Boyle Family

Elemental Study for the Barcelona Site (Red Mudcracks with Rivulets, Green Mudstones & Shells), 2000–2016, World Series 1968

Mixed media, resin, fibreglass

183 × 183 cm

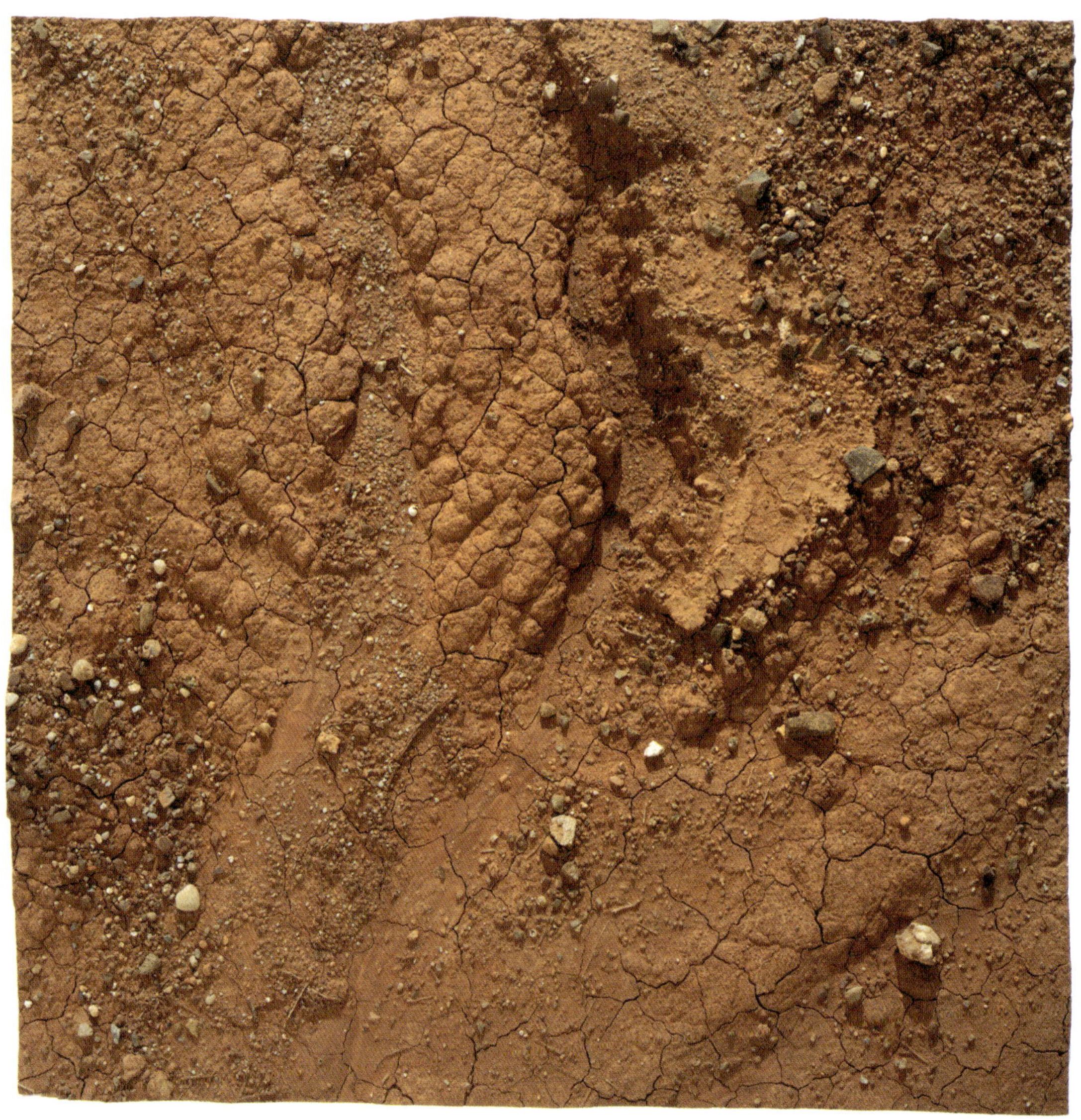

Boyd & Evans
Tonopah NV
Archival pigment print
120 × 120 cm

Ackroyd & Harvey
Beuys' Acorns
Archival digital print
46 × 35 cm

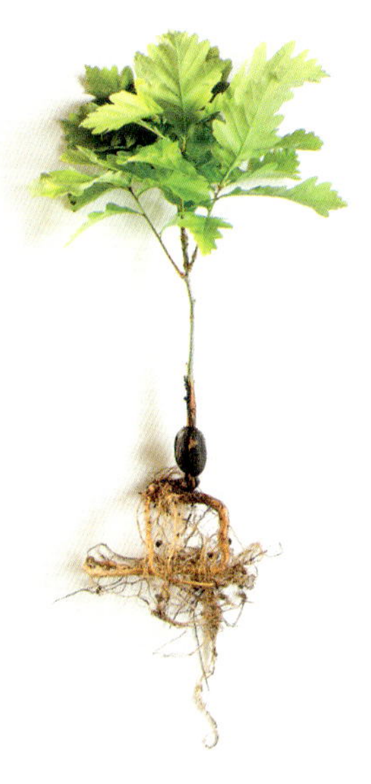

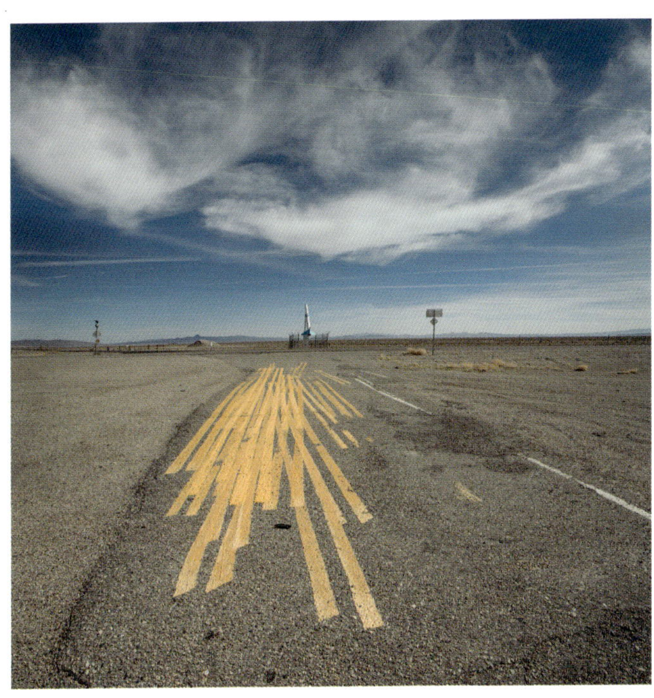

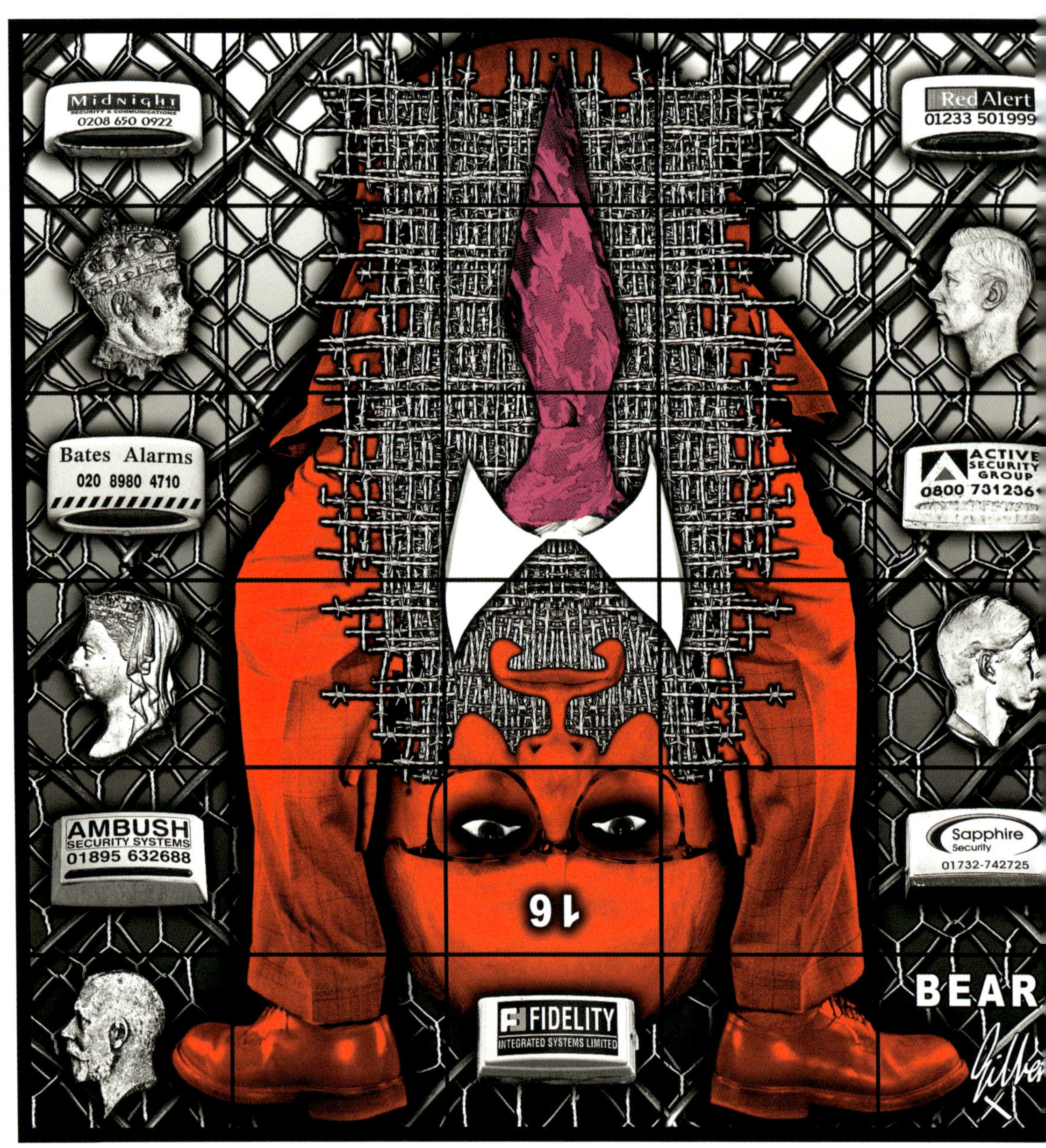

Gilbert and George
BEARD AWARE
2016
381 × 755 cm

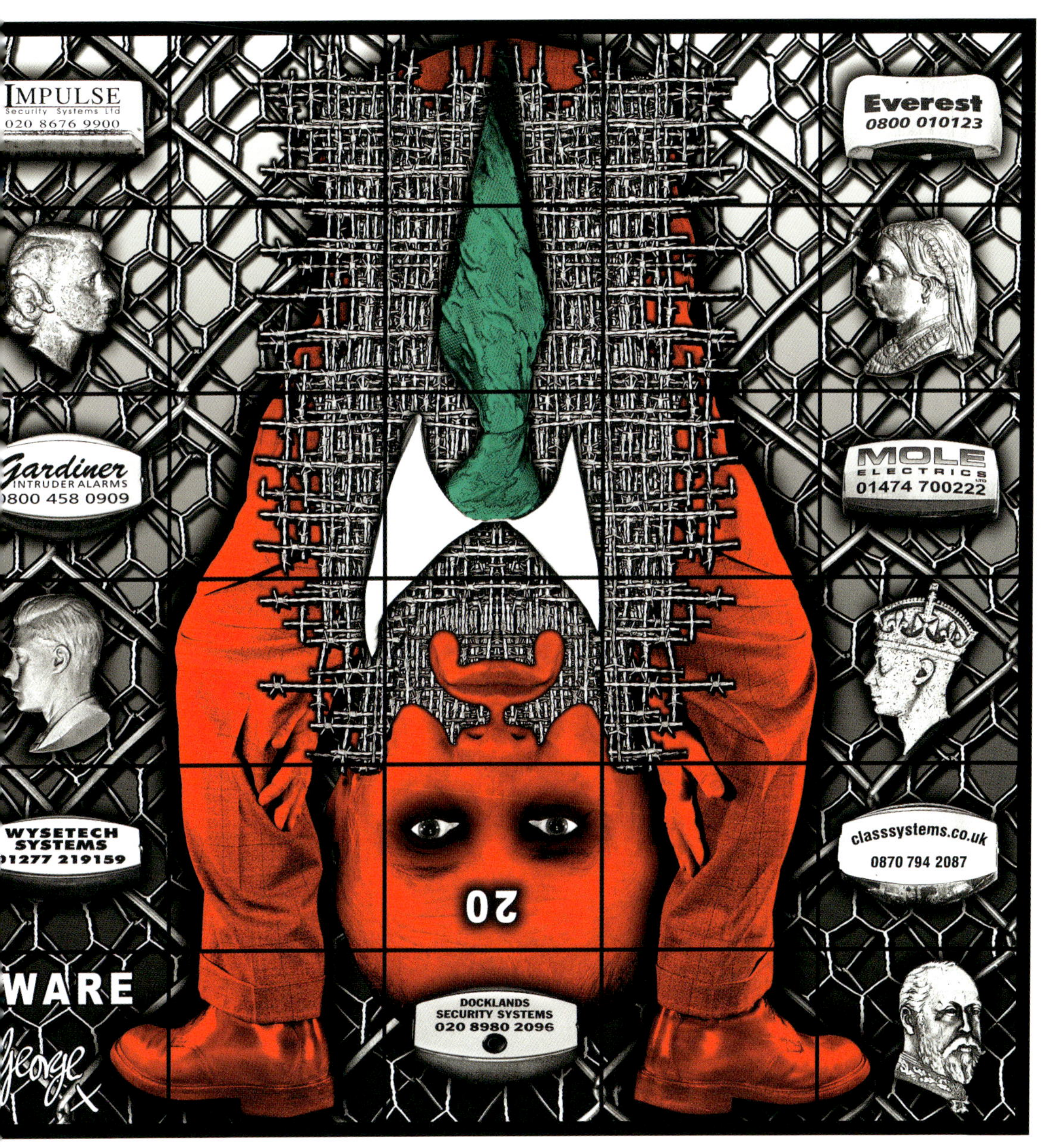
IMPULSE
Security Systems Ltd
020 8676 9900
Everest
0800 010123
Gardiner
INTRUDER ALARMS
0800 458 0909
MOLE
ELECTRICS
01474 700222
WYSETECH
SYSTEMS
01277 219159
classsystems.co.uk
0870 794 2087
WARE
DOCKLANDS
SECURITY SYSTEMS
020 8980 2096

Anna & Bernhard Blume
Triptych from the Series: De-Konstruktiv
Inkjet print
164 × 109 cm

Peter Fischli David Weiss
Büsi (film still)
Film

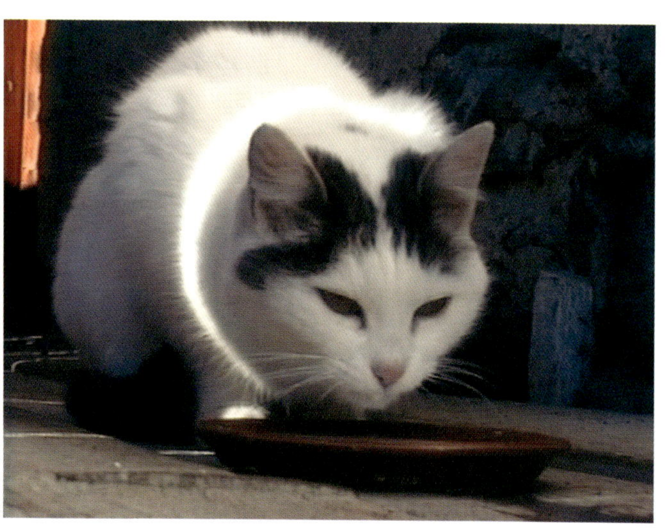

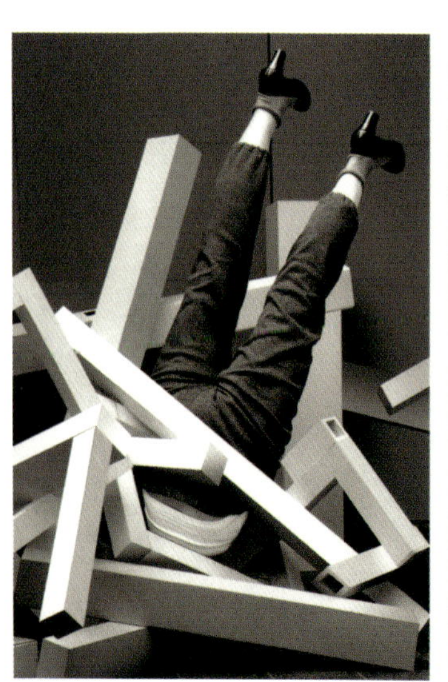

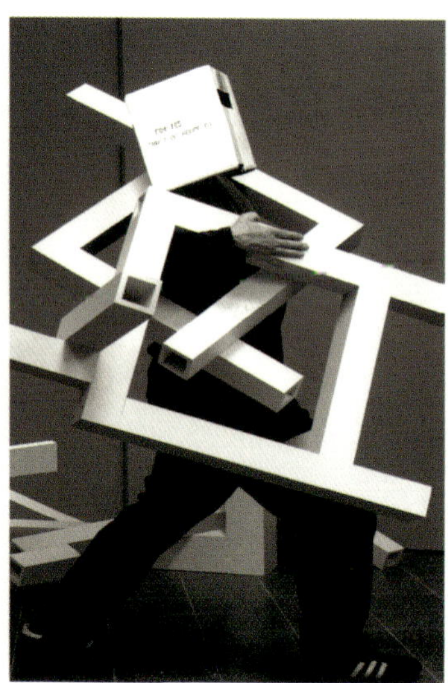

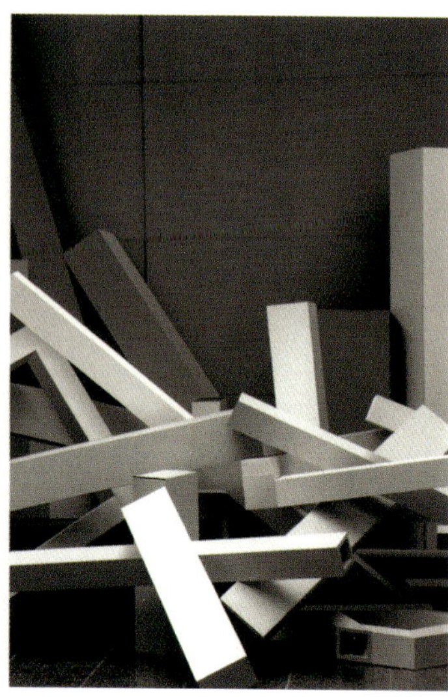

Allora & Calzadilla
2 hose petrified Petrol Pump
Stone
H 205 cm

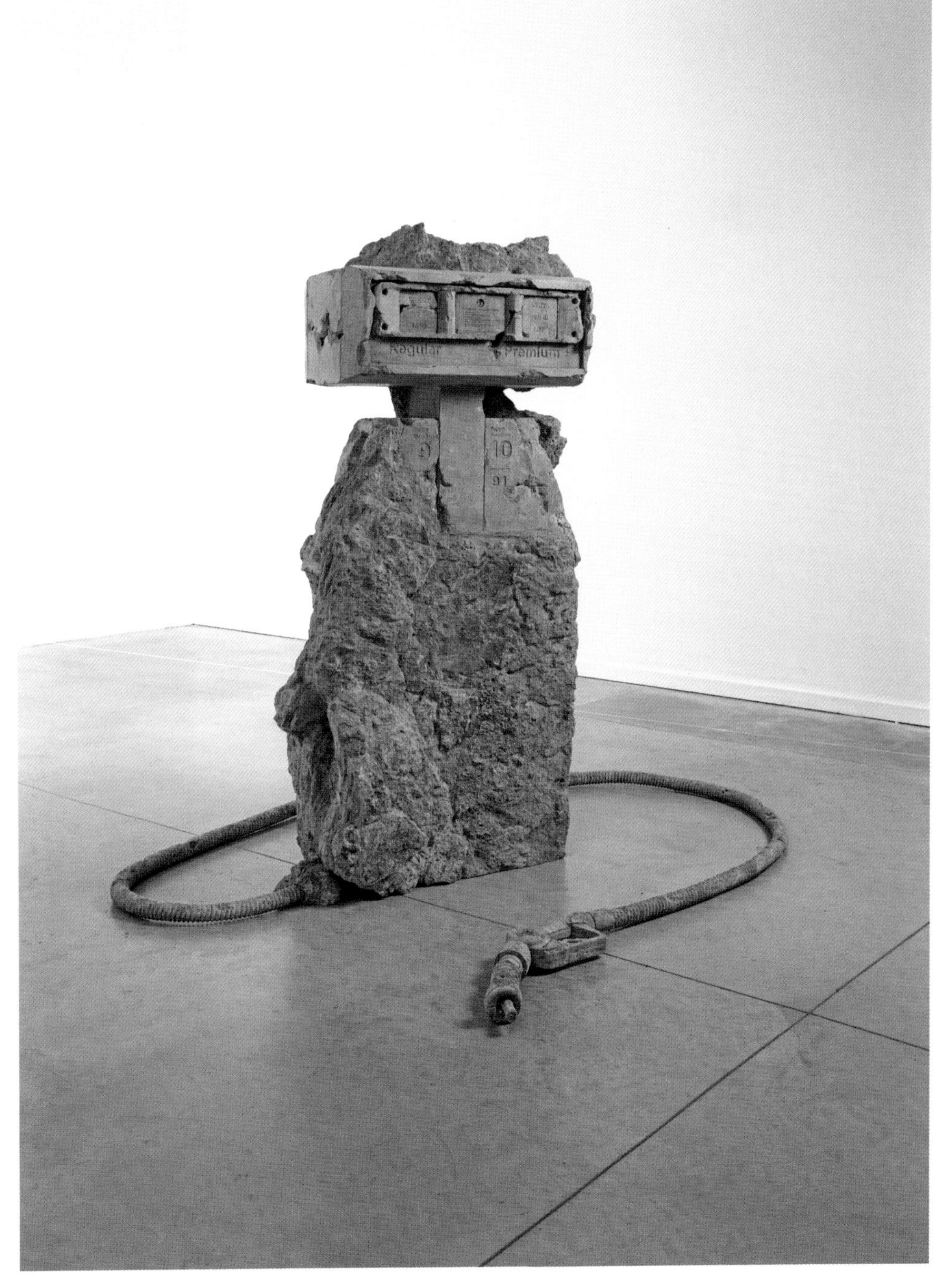

The Singh Twins
London's Burning: Read All About It
Mixed media
105 × 88 cm

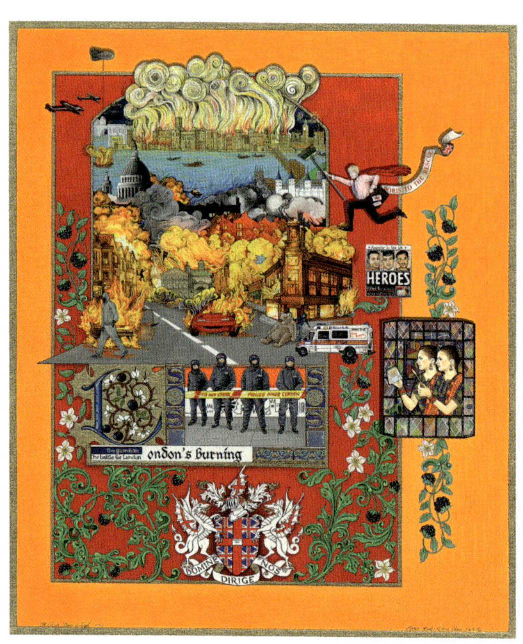

EVA & ADELE
Transformer-Performer Double-Act VIII
Mixed media
208 × 308 cm

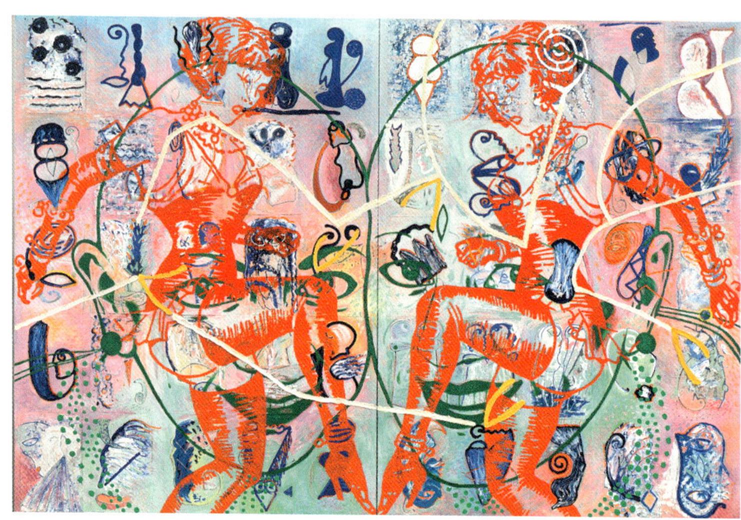

Emma Biggs & Matthew Collings
Face
Oil
152 × 152 cm

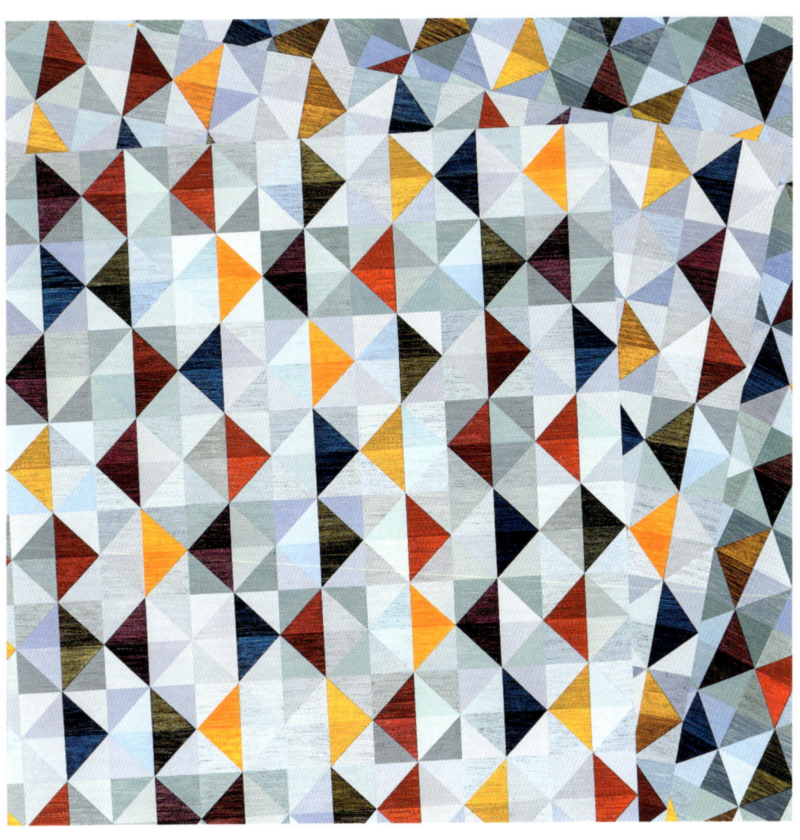

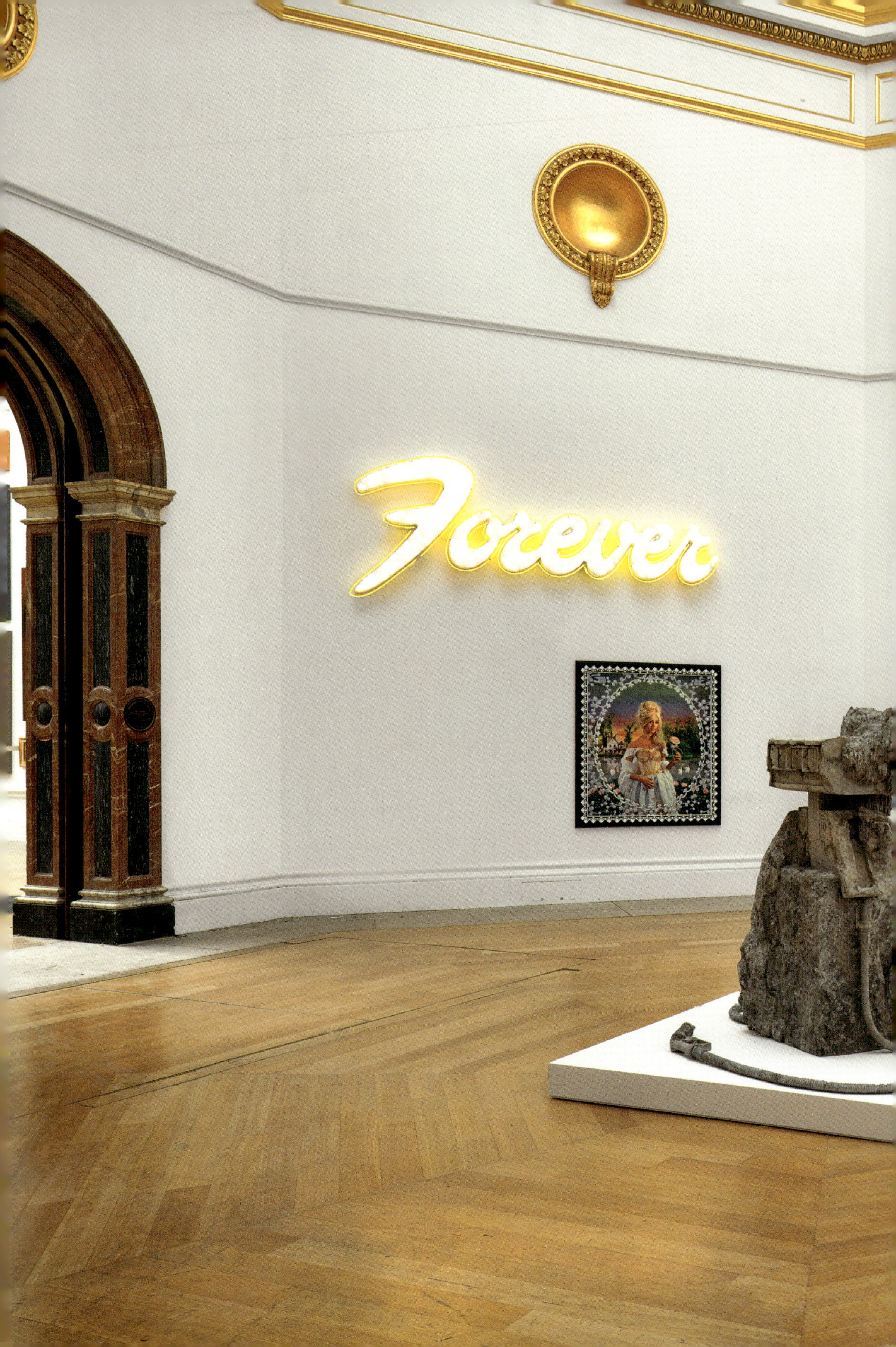
Forever

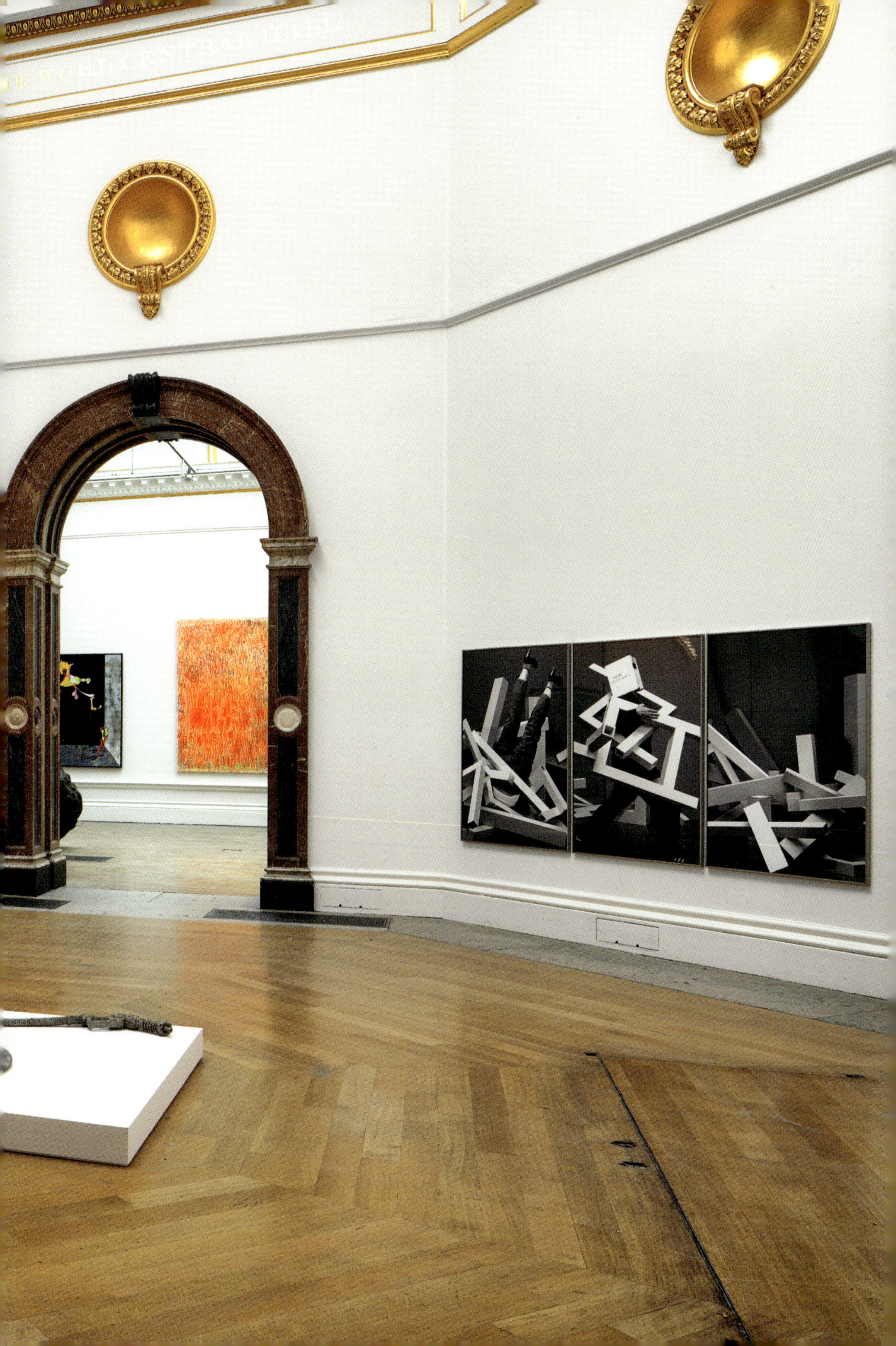
WOHL CENTRAL HALL

Jake & Dinos Chapman
Human Rainbow II (Coloured)
Hand-coloured etching
40 × 47 cm

Human Rainbow II (Coloured)
Hand-coloured etching
40 × 47 cm

The Kipper Kids
The Kipper Kids
Inkjet print
219 × 152 cm

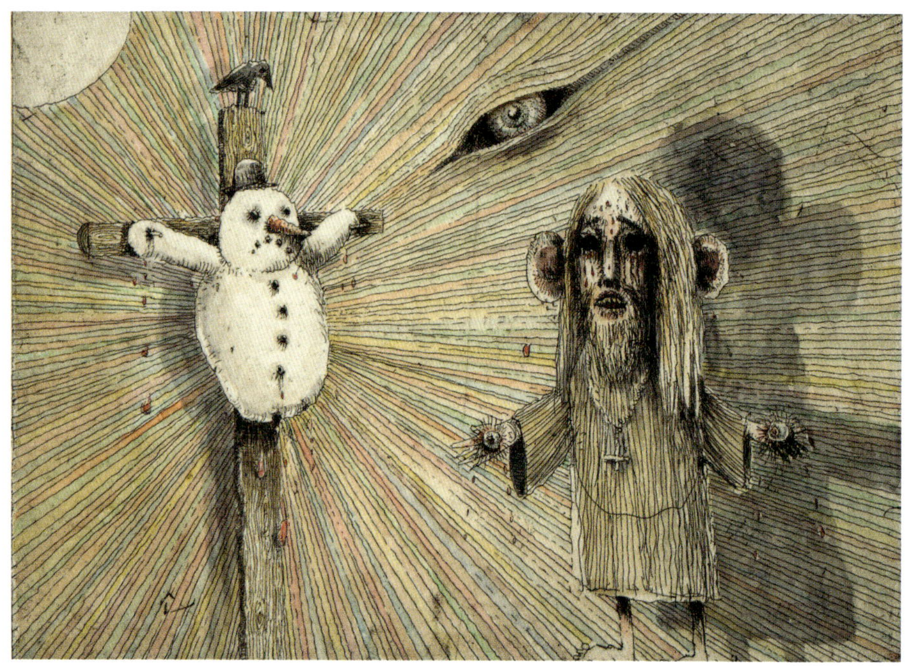

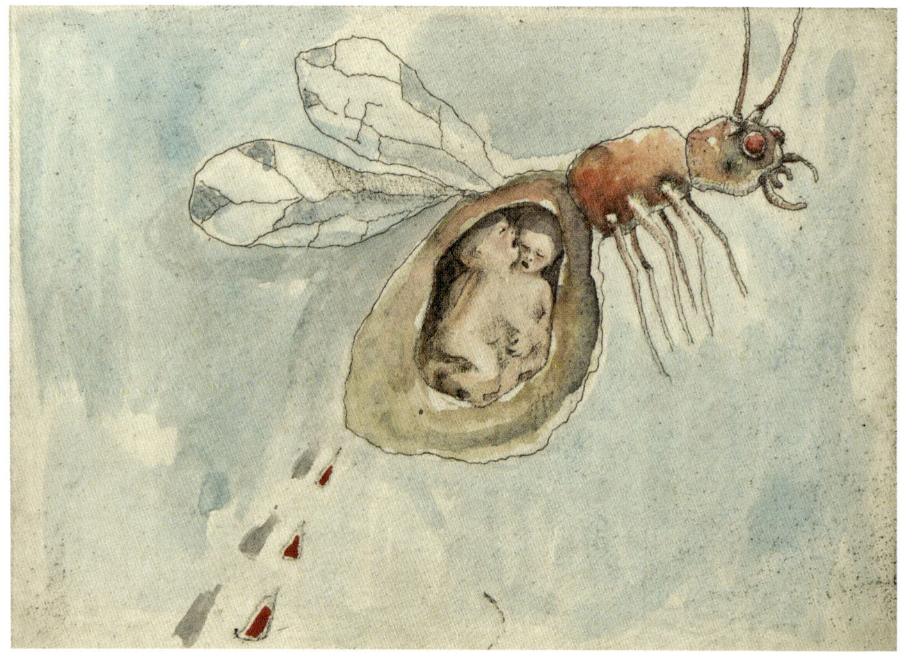

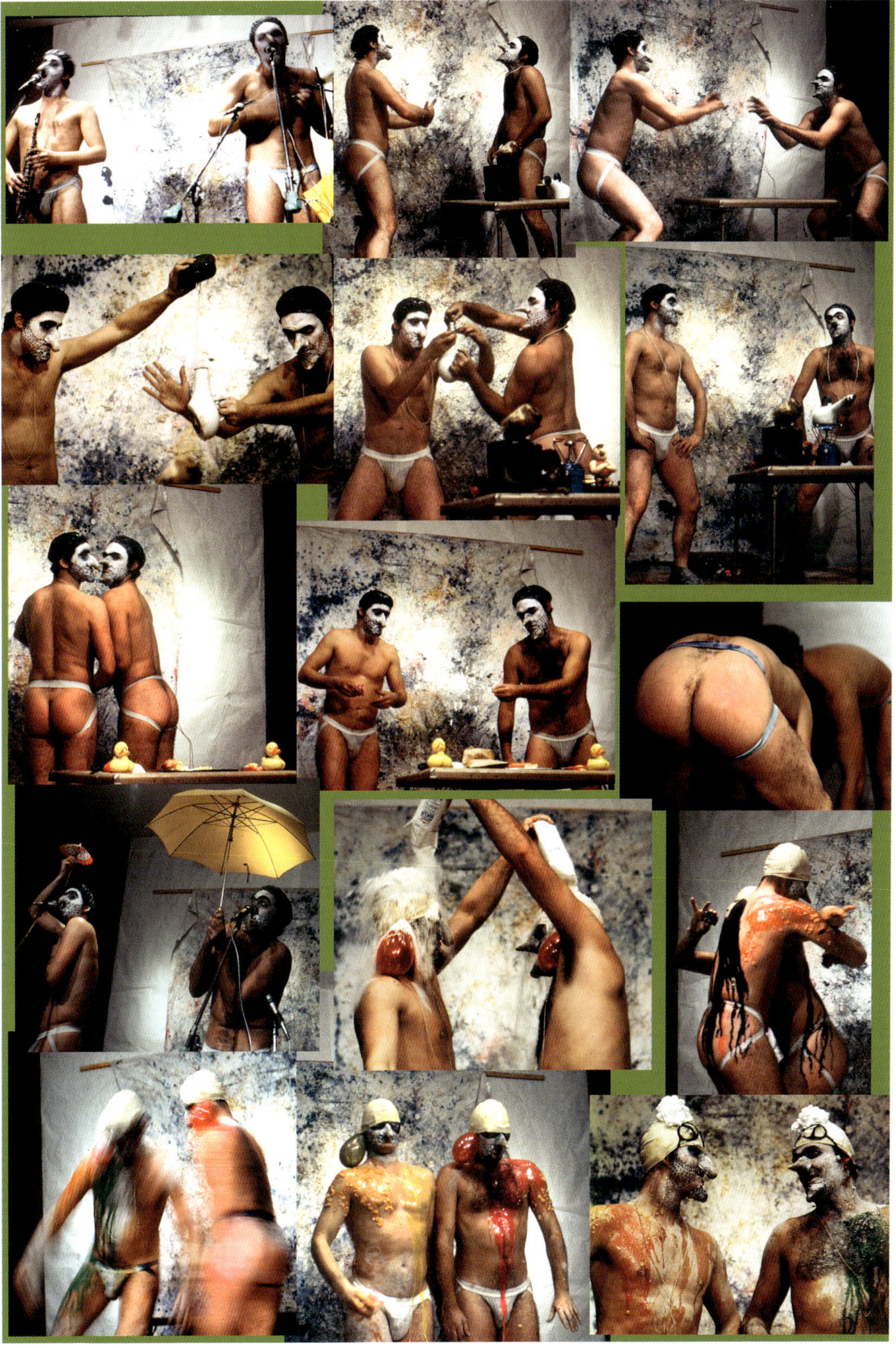

Bernd and Hilla Becher
Stoneworks
Silver gelatin print
173 × 239 cm

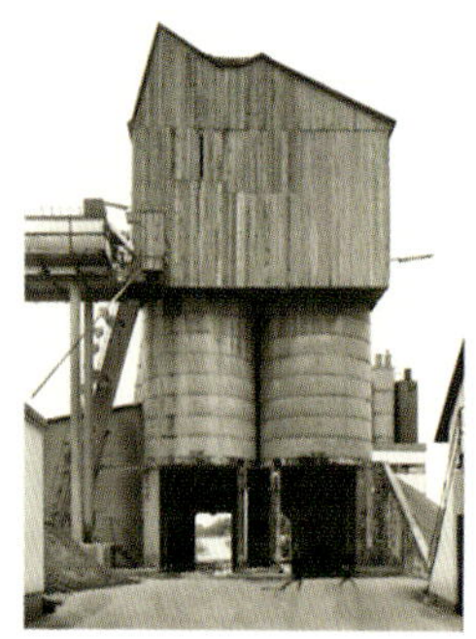
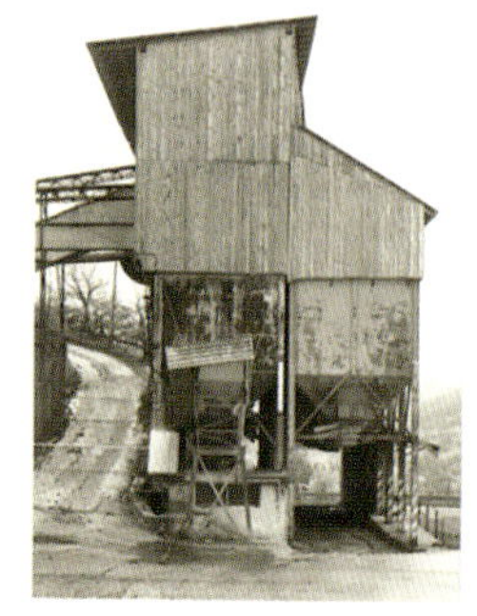
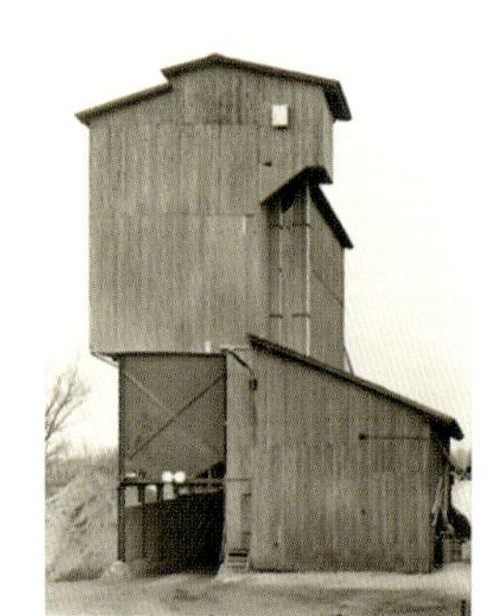
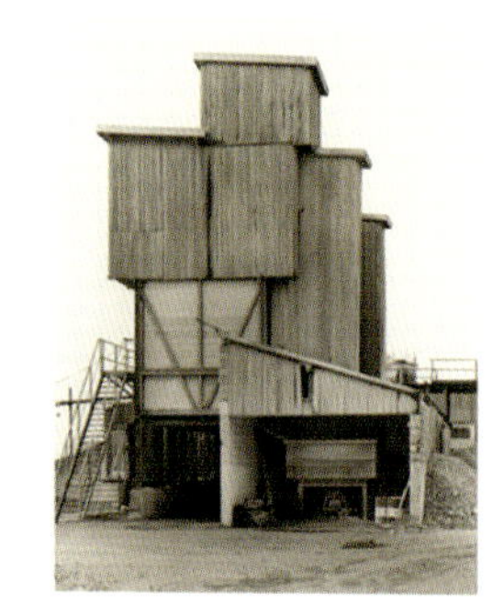
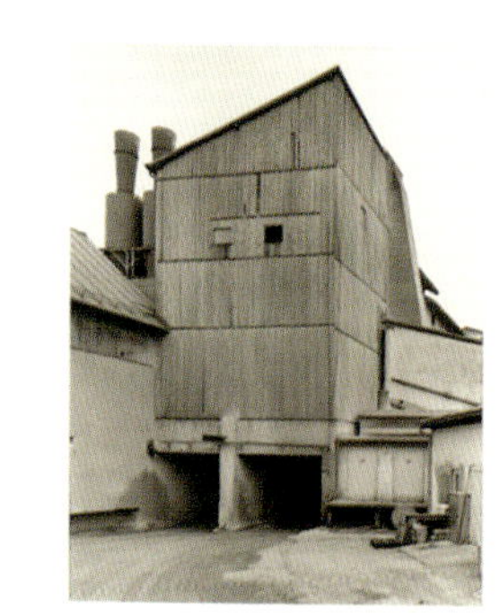
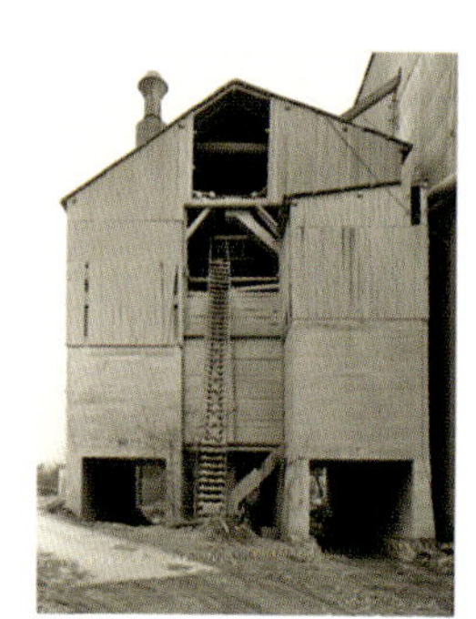

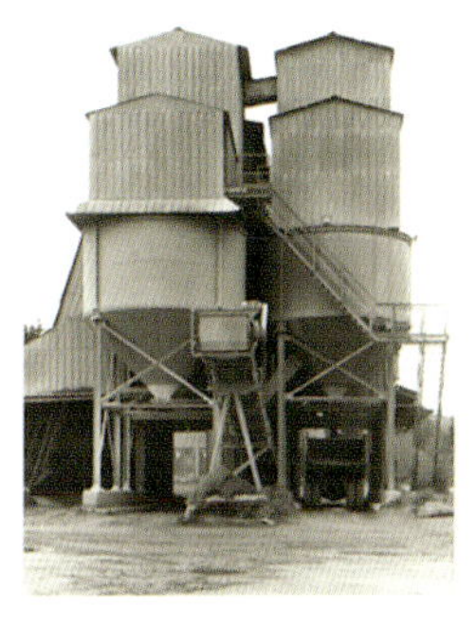
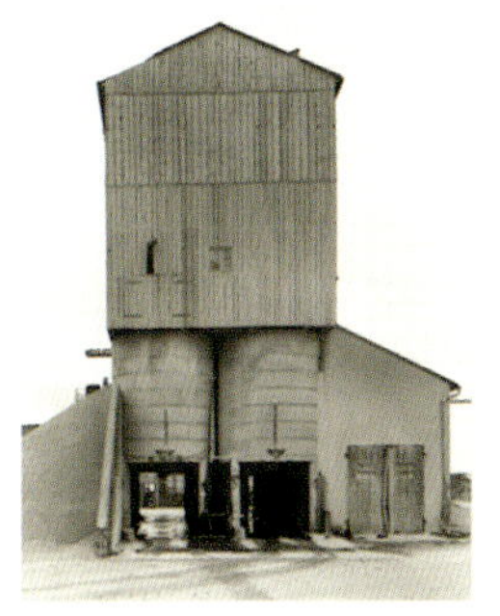
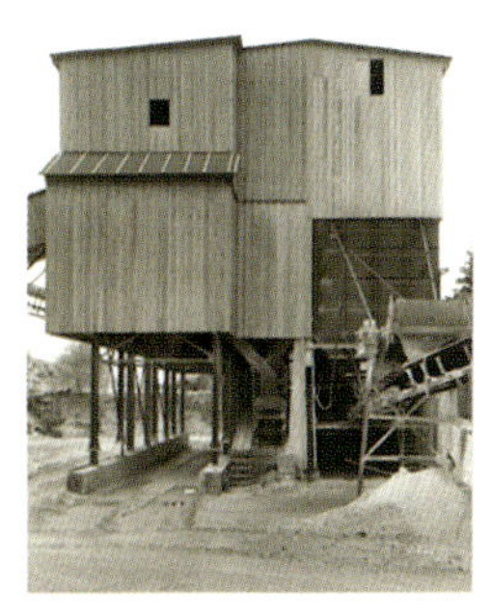
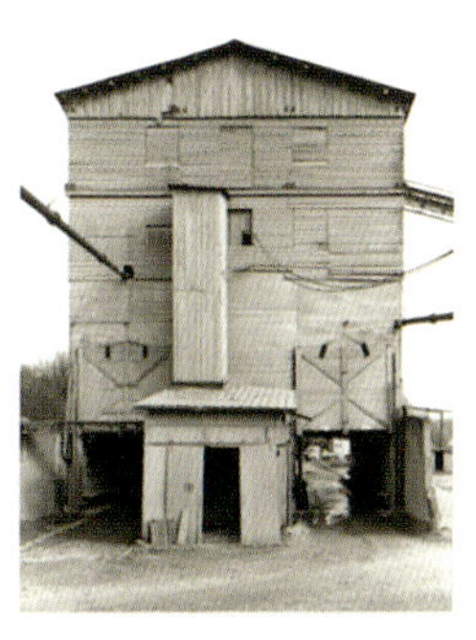
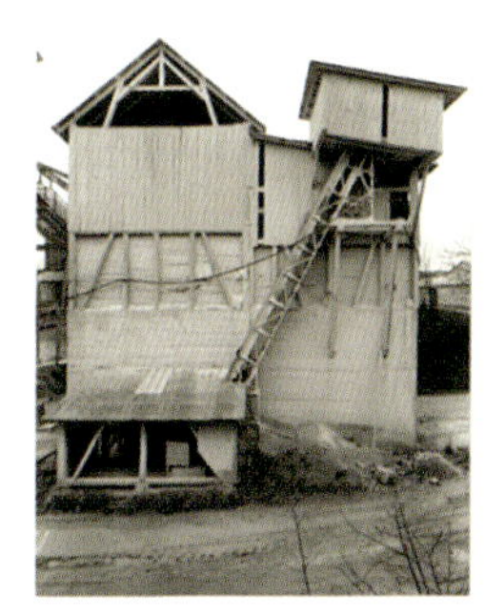
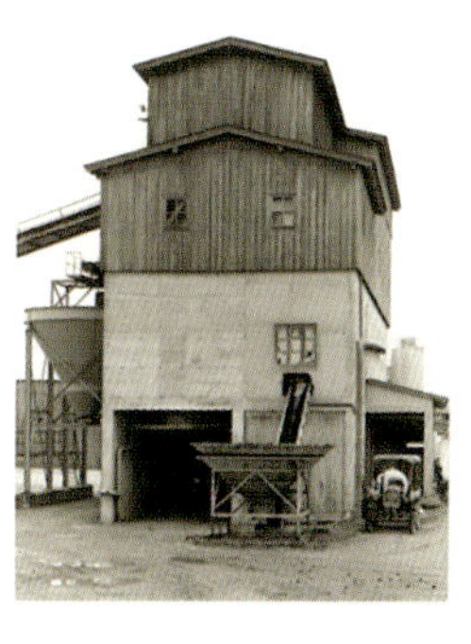
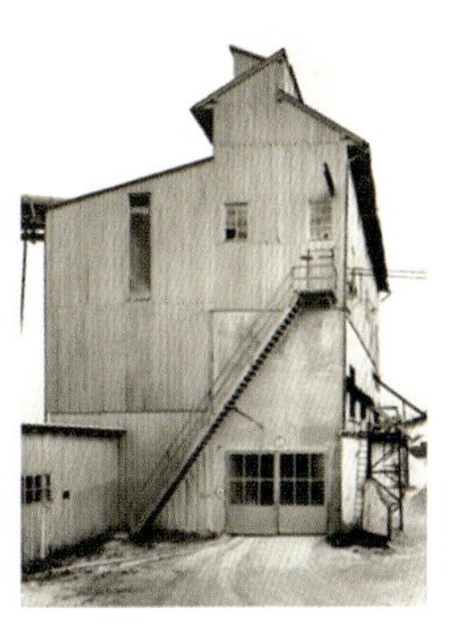
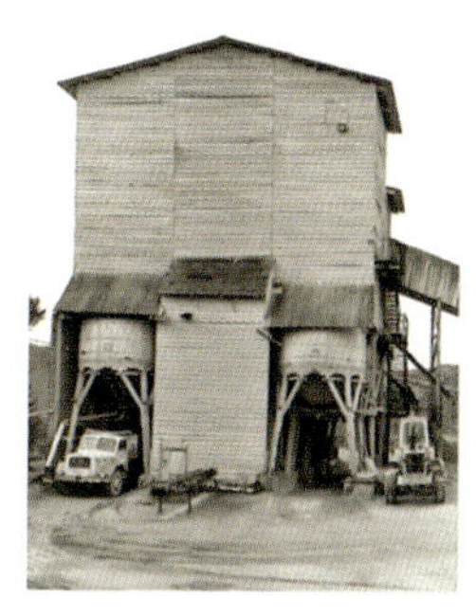
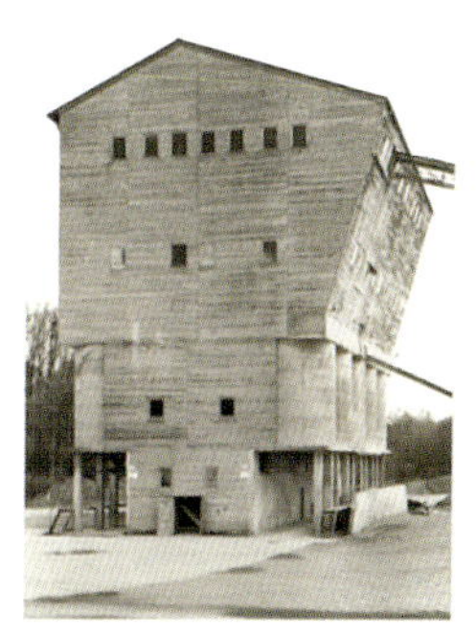

Jane and Louise Wilson

Atomgrad, Nature Abhors A Vacuum V
C-type print on aluminium
180 × 220 cm

Atomgrad, Nature Abhors A Vacuum I
C-type print on aluminium
180 × 220 cm

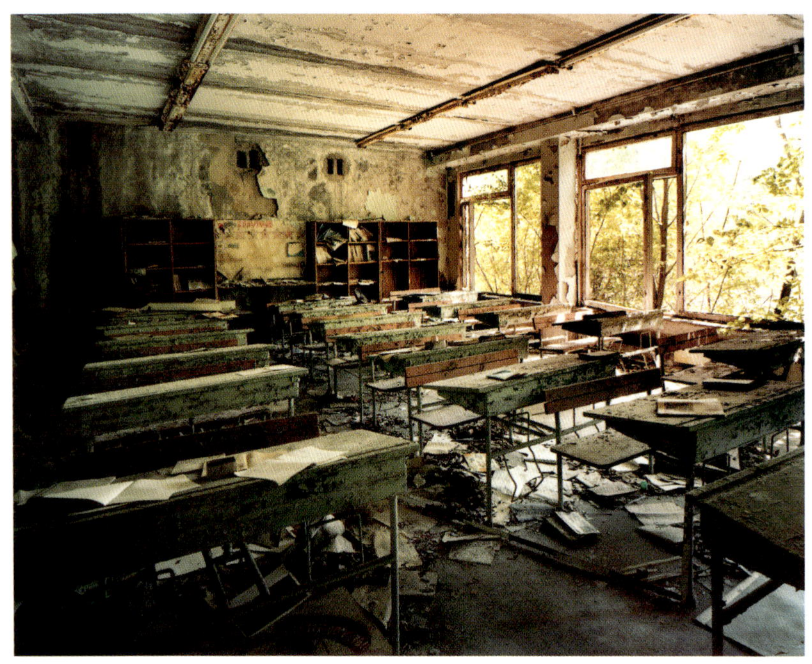

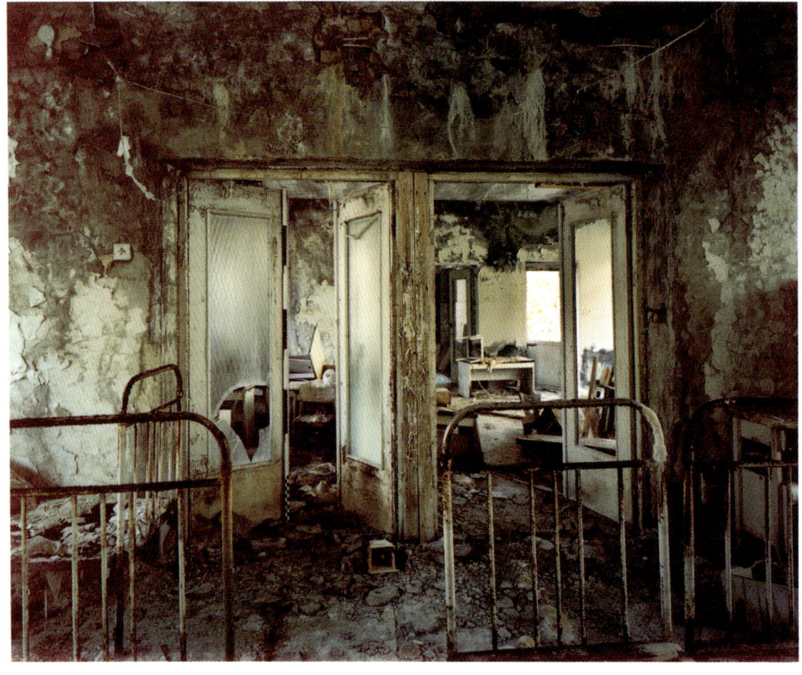

Zatorski + Zatorski
Self-portrait as Charcoal on Paper
Mixed media
242 × 150 cm

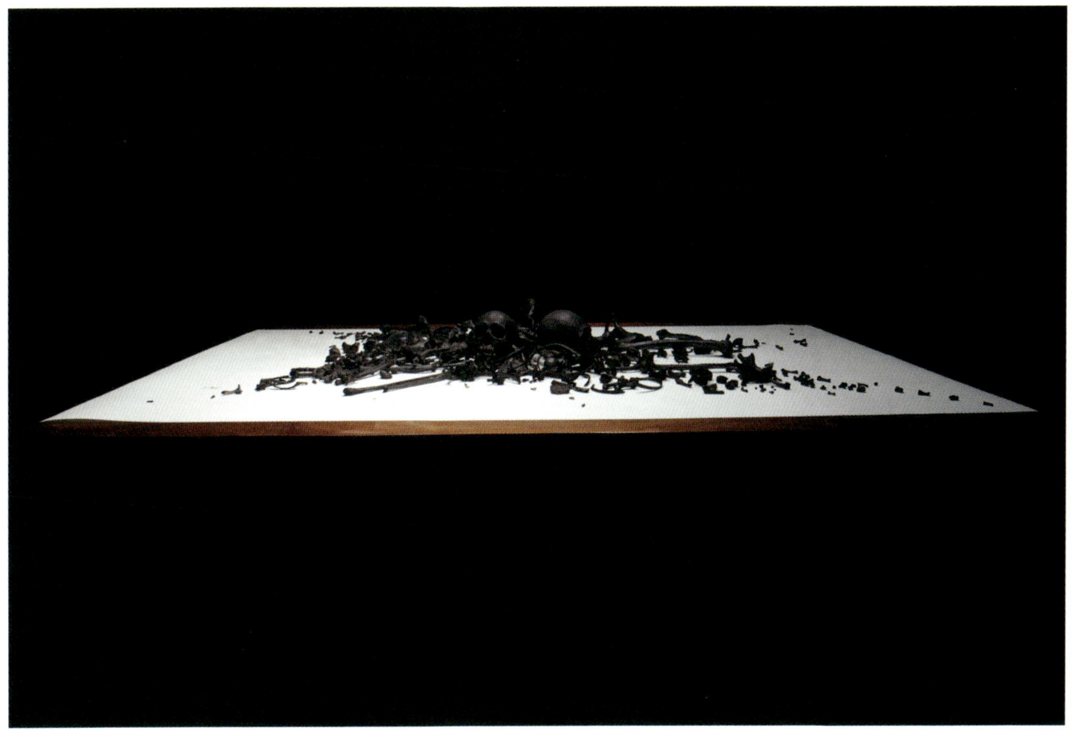

Pierre et Gilles
Marie Antoinette, The Queen's Hamlet (Model: Zahia Dehar)
Hand-painted photograph on canvas
154 × 139 cm

Tim Noble and Sue Webster
Forever (Yellow)
Enamelled aluminium, neon and LED lamps
125 × 326 cm

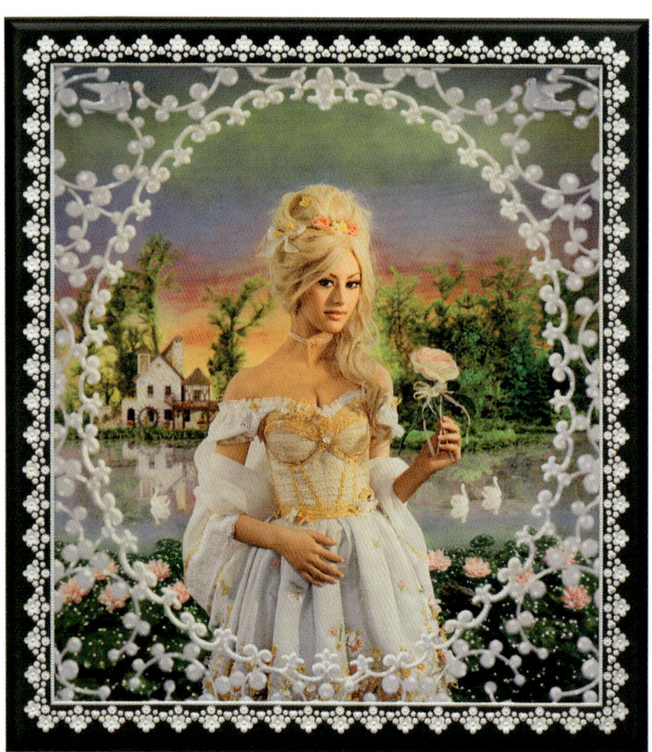

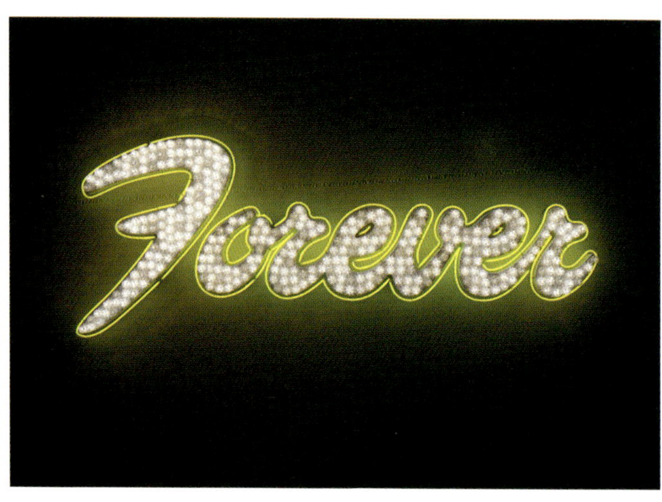

Ilya & Emilia Kabakov
Emergency Exit #4
Oil
238 × 219 cm

Gert & Uwe Tobias
Untitled
Woodcut on canvas
205 × 305 cm

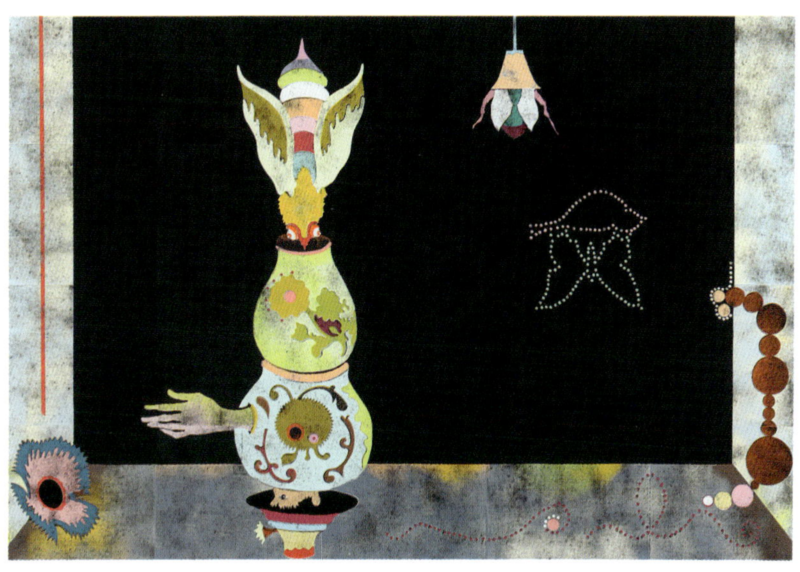

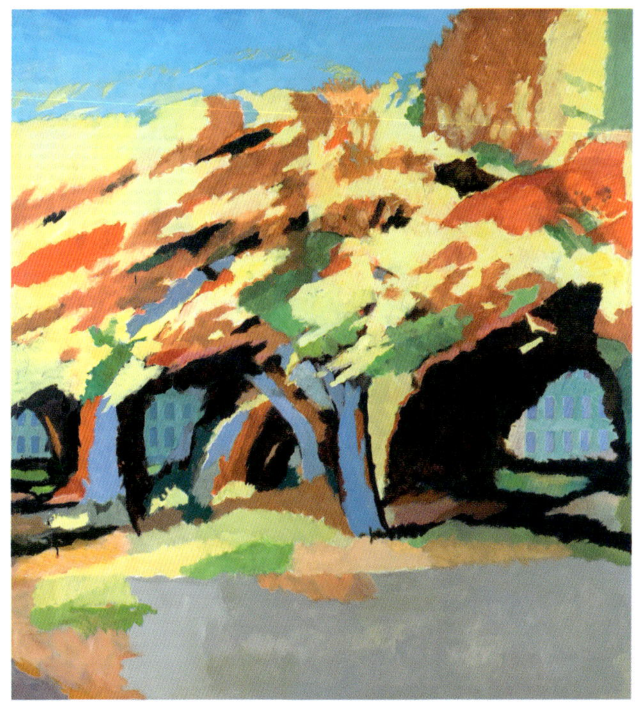

Dalziel + Scullion

Tumadh, Portal I
Film still

Tumadh, Portal II
Film still

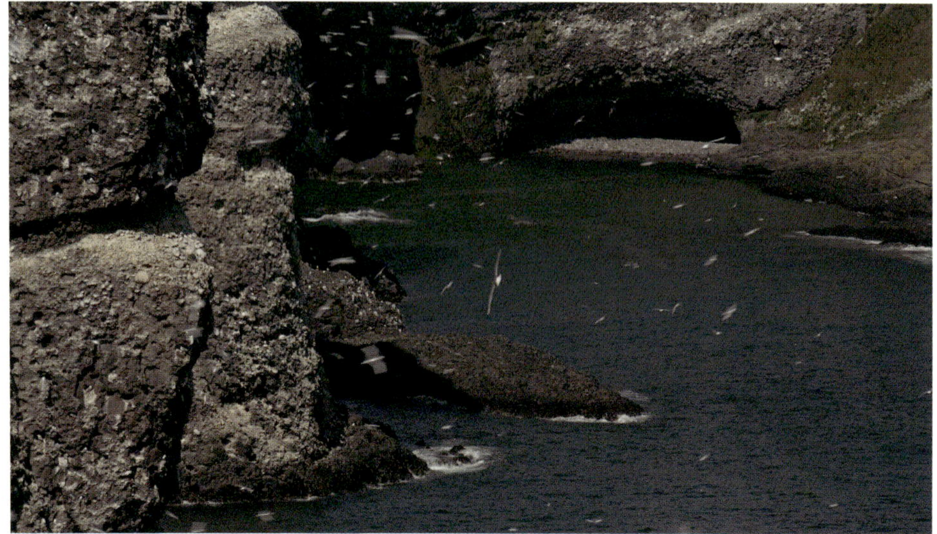

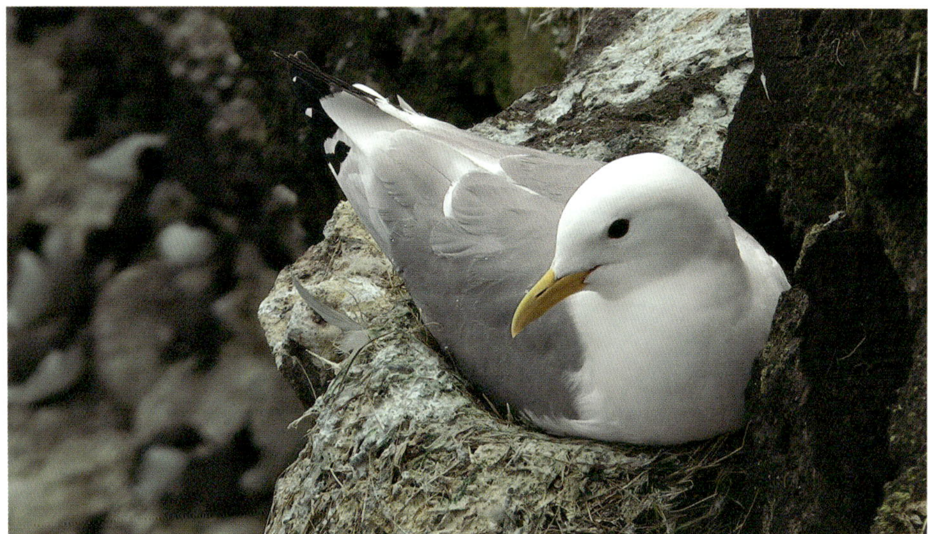

Langlands & Bell
GC-HQ
Mixed media
130 × 130 cm

Bill Woodrow RA and Richard Deacon CBE RA
Bouteille de Sorcière 5
Glass, mirror, sealing wax and Perspex
H 72 cm

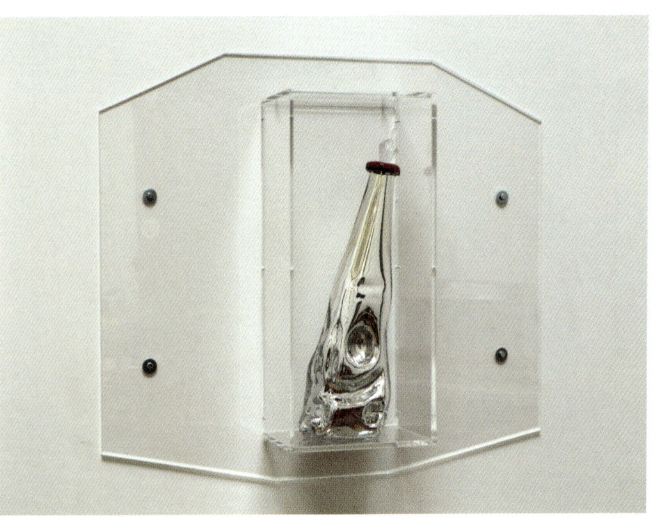

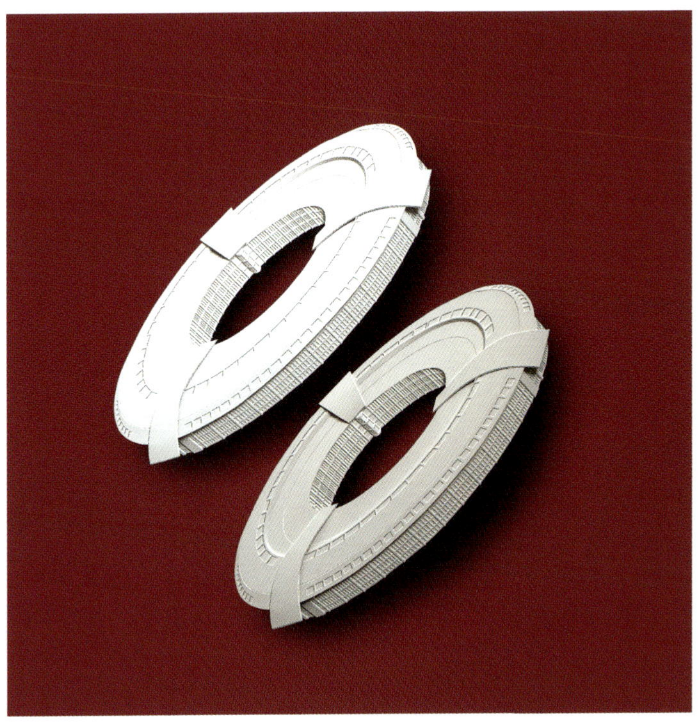

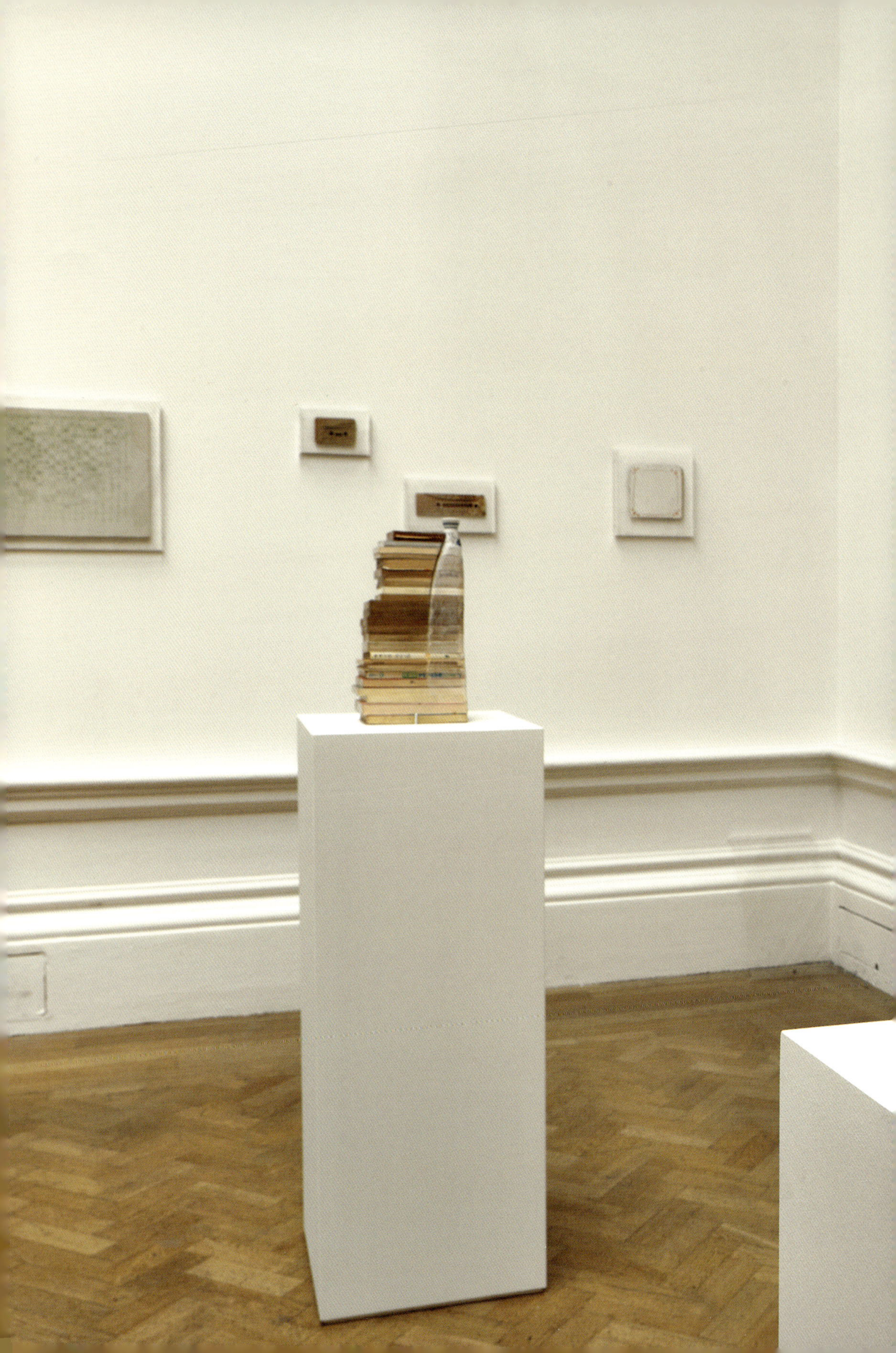

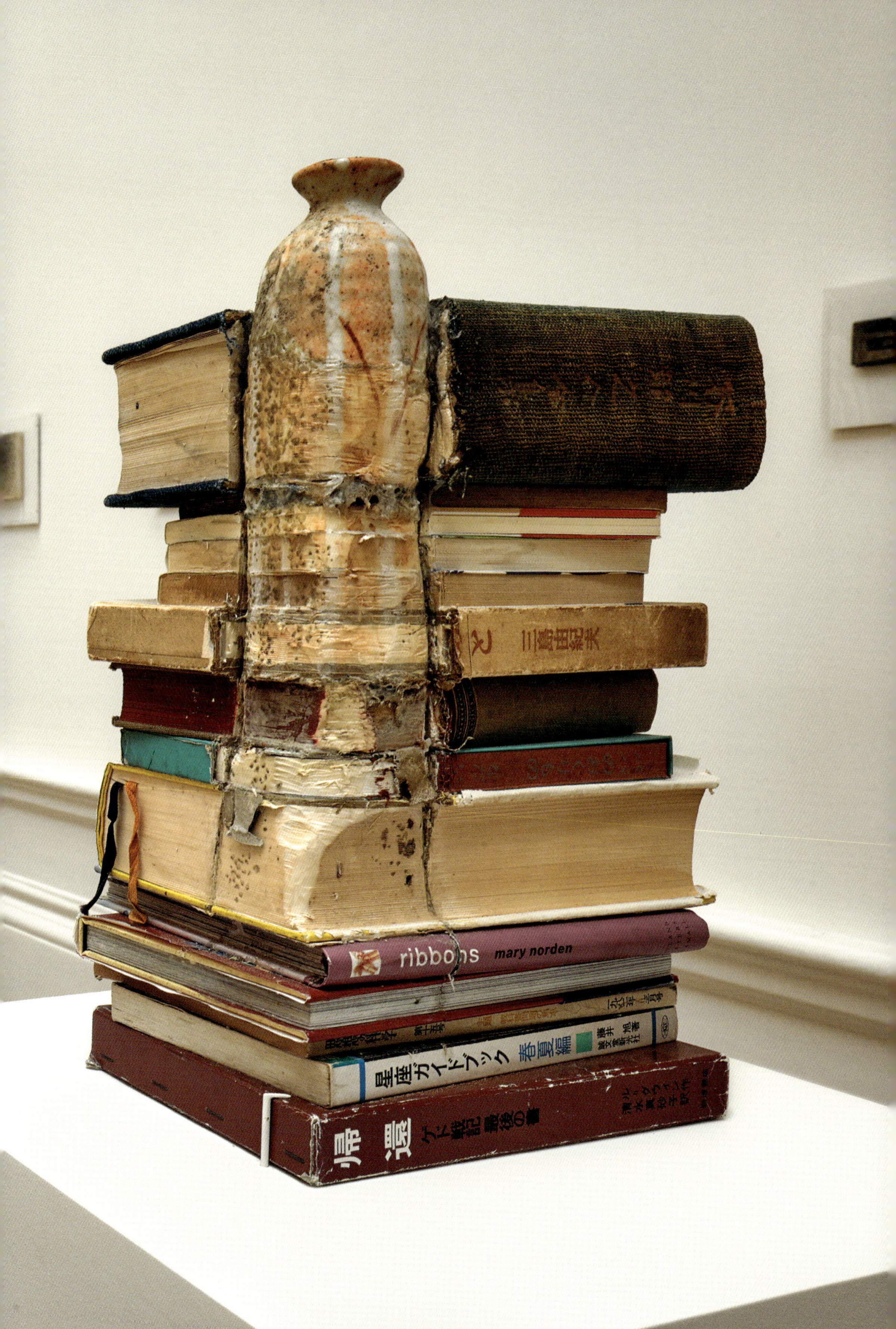
三島由紀夫
ribbons
mary norden
星座ガイドブック
春夏編
帰還
ゲド戦記 最後の書

William Kentridge Hon RA
Mantegna
Lithograph on panel and cotton
197 × 197 cm

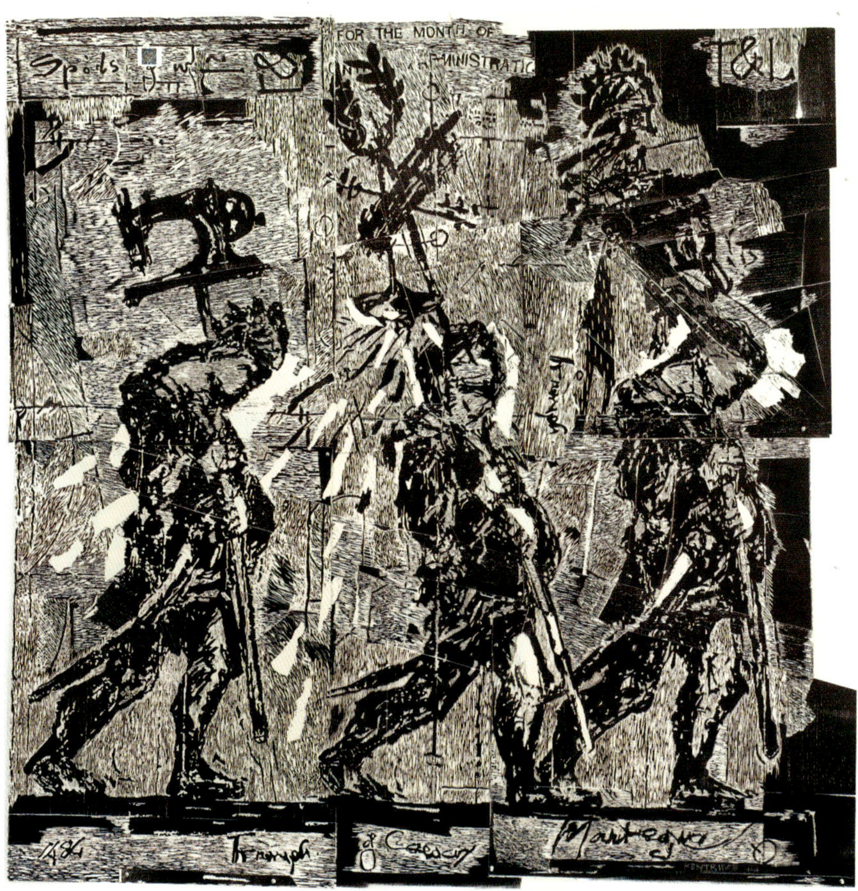

Mimmo Paladino Hon RA
Untitled
Oil and collage on wood
300 × 300 cm

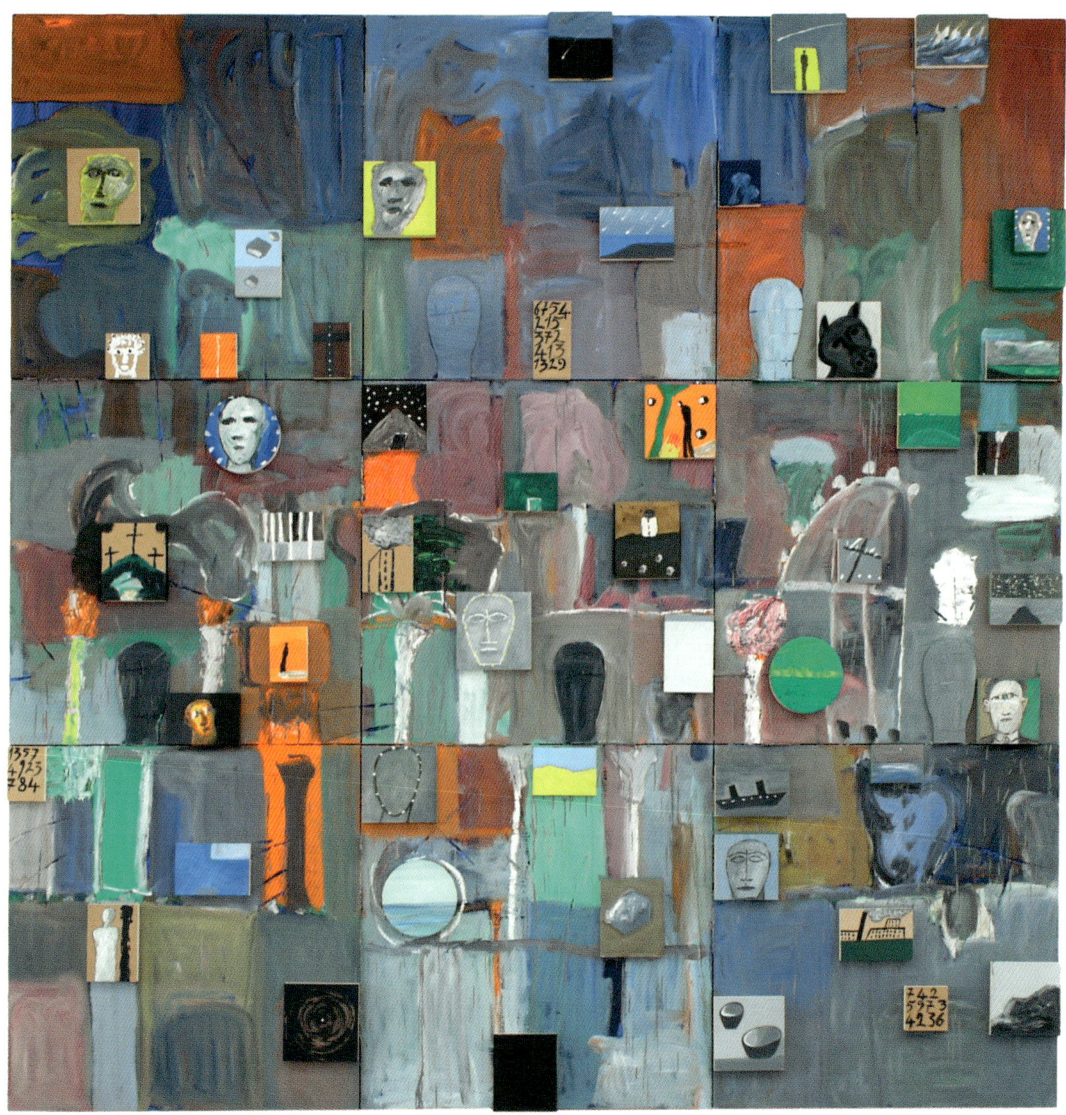

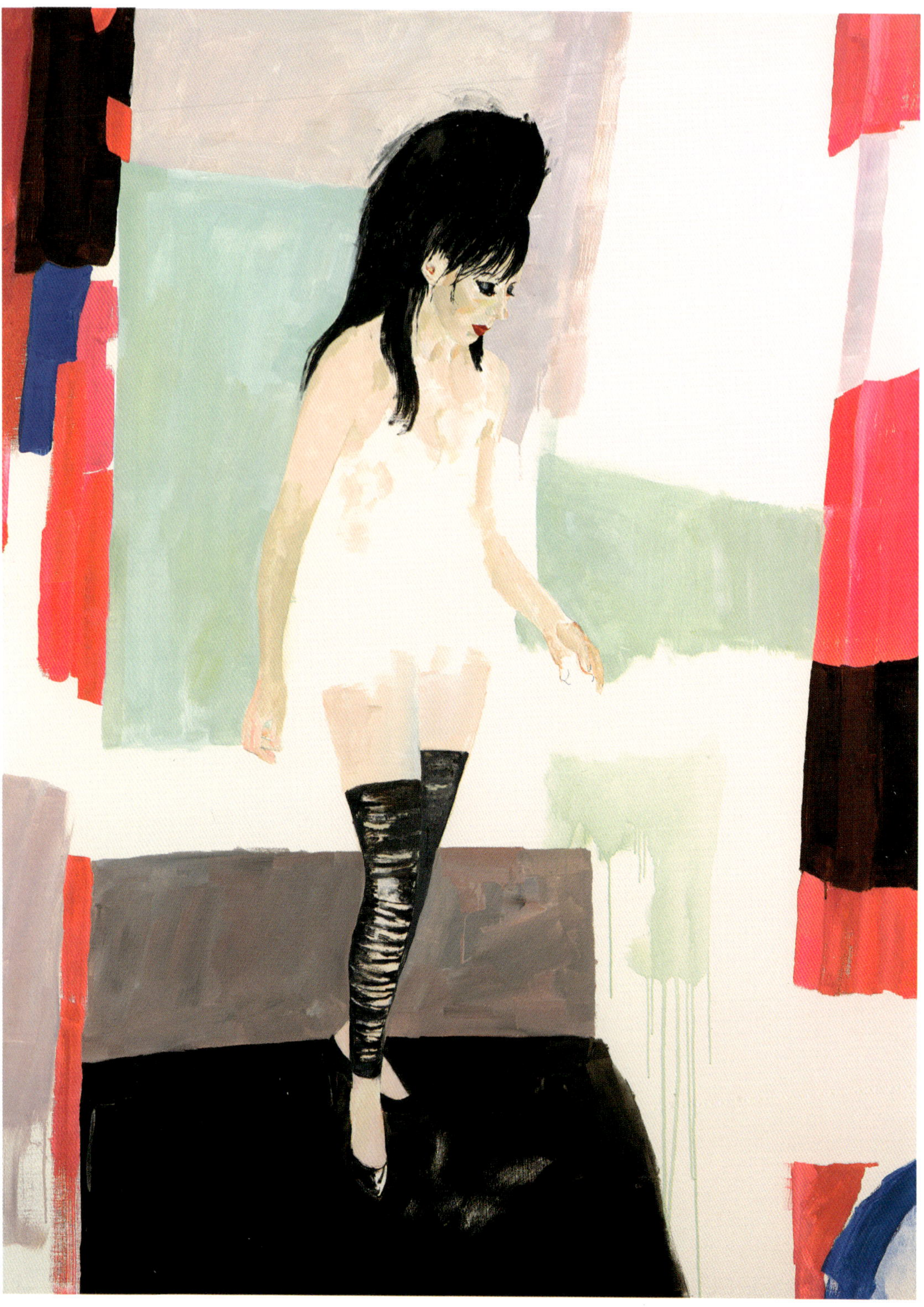

David Remfry MBE RA
It Begins Again
Oil
153 × 112 cm

James Butler MBE RA
Skipping
Bronze
H 70 cm

Joe Tilson RA
PC from Venice Anzolo Rafael
Oil
170 × 120 cm

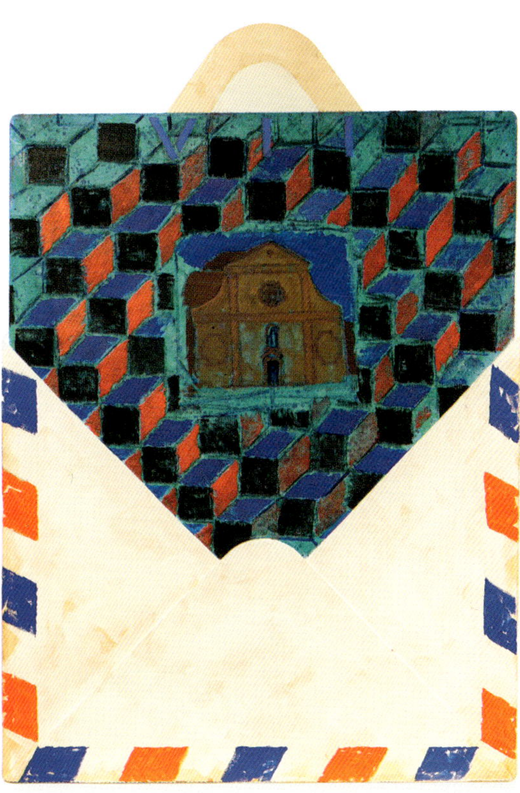

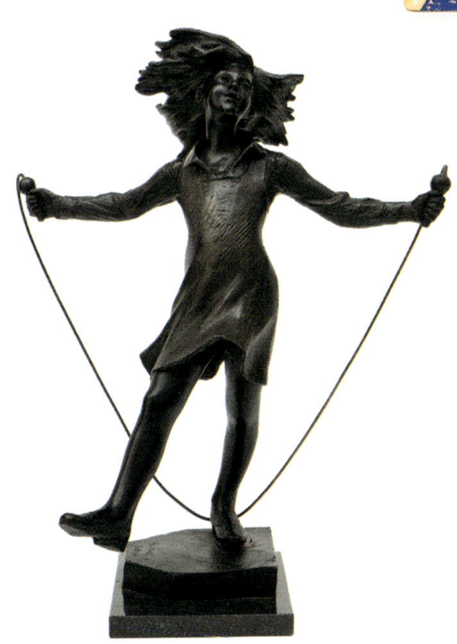

Mick Moon RA
Evening Fishing
Acrylic on canvas mounted on board
140 × 122 cm

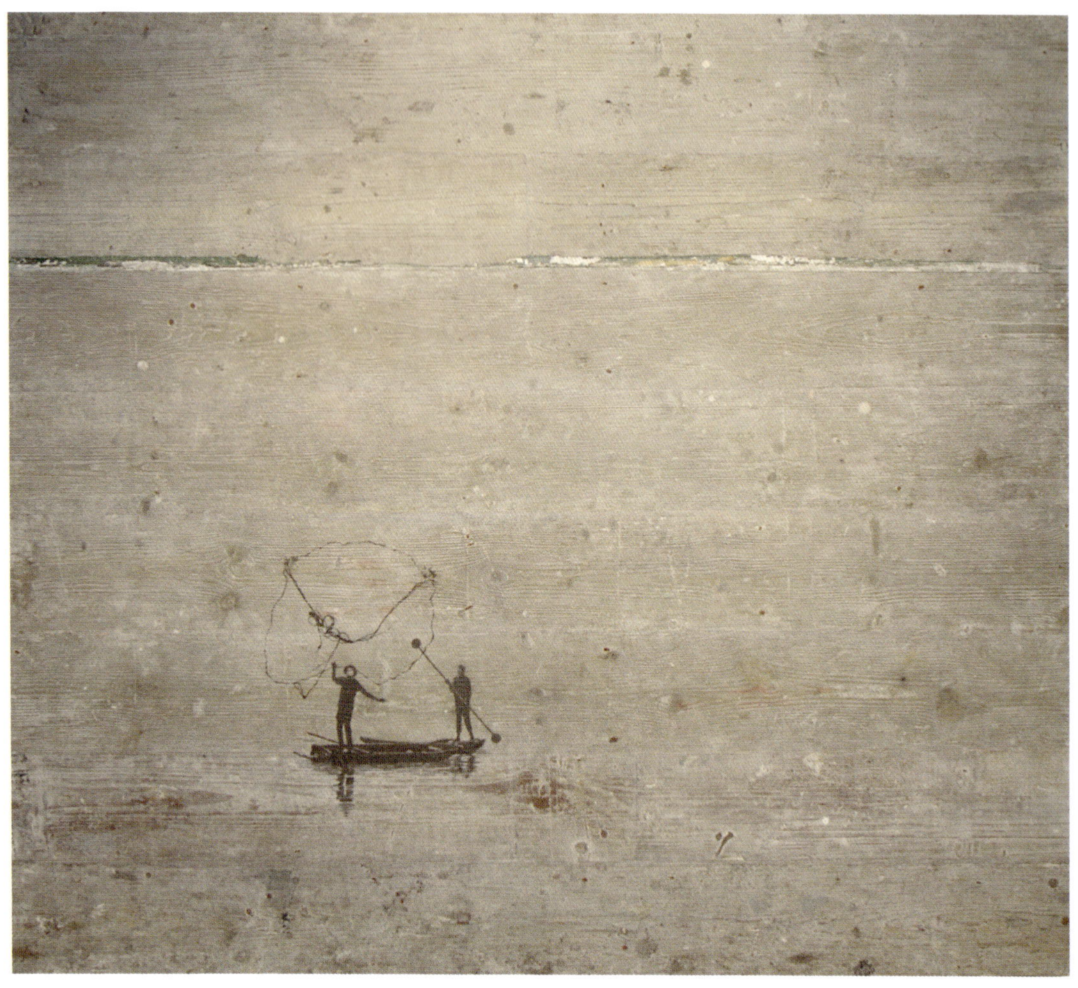

Terry Setch RA
Excavation
Encaustic wax, pigment and beach detritus on board
92 × 61 cm

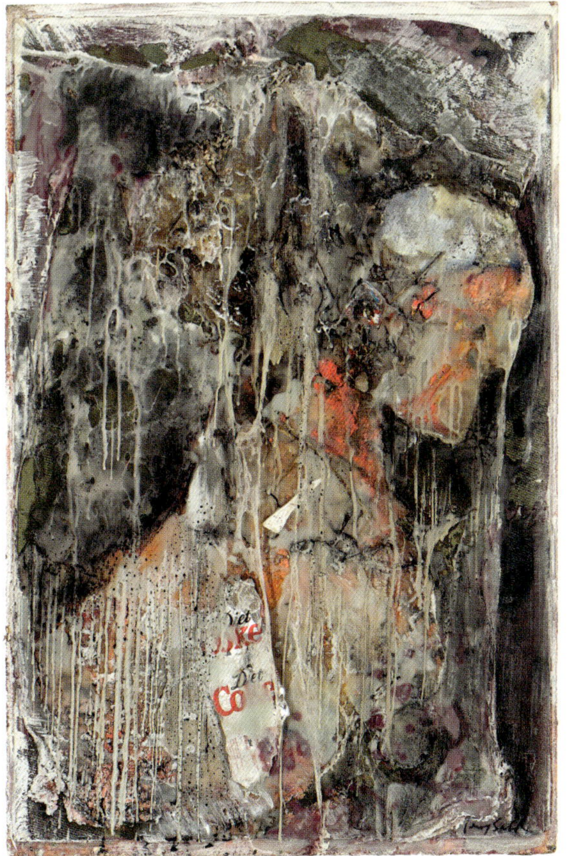

Emma Stibbon RA
Stromboli Smoke
Intaglio and woodcut
59 × 38 cm

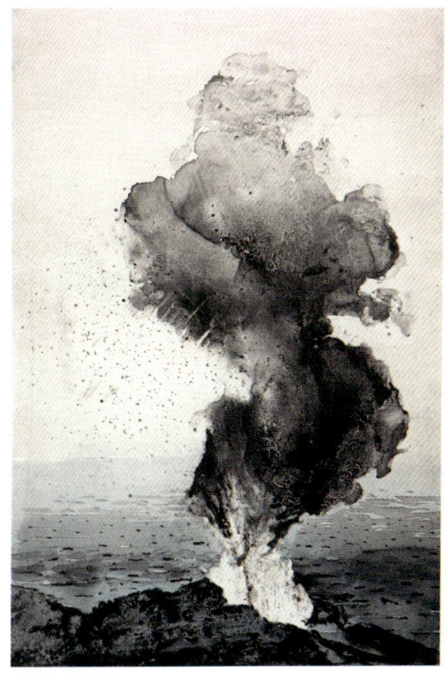

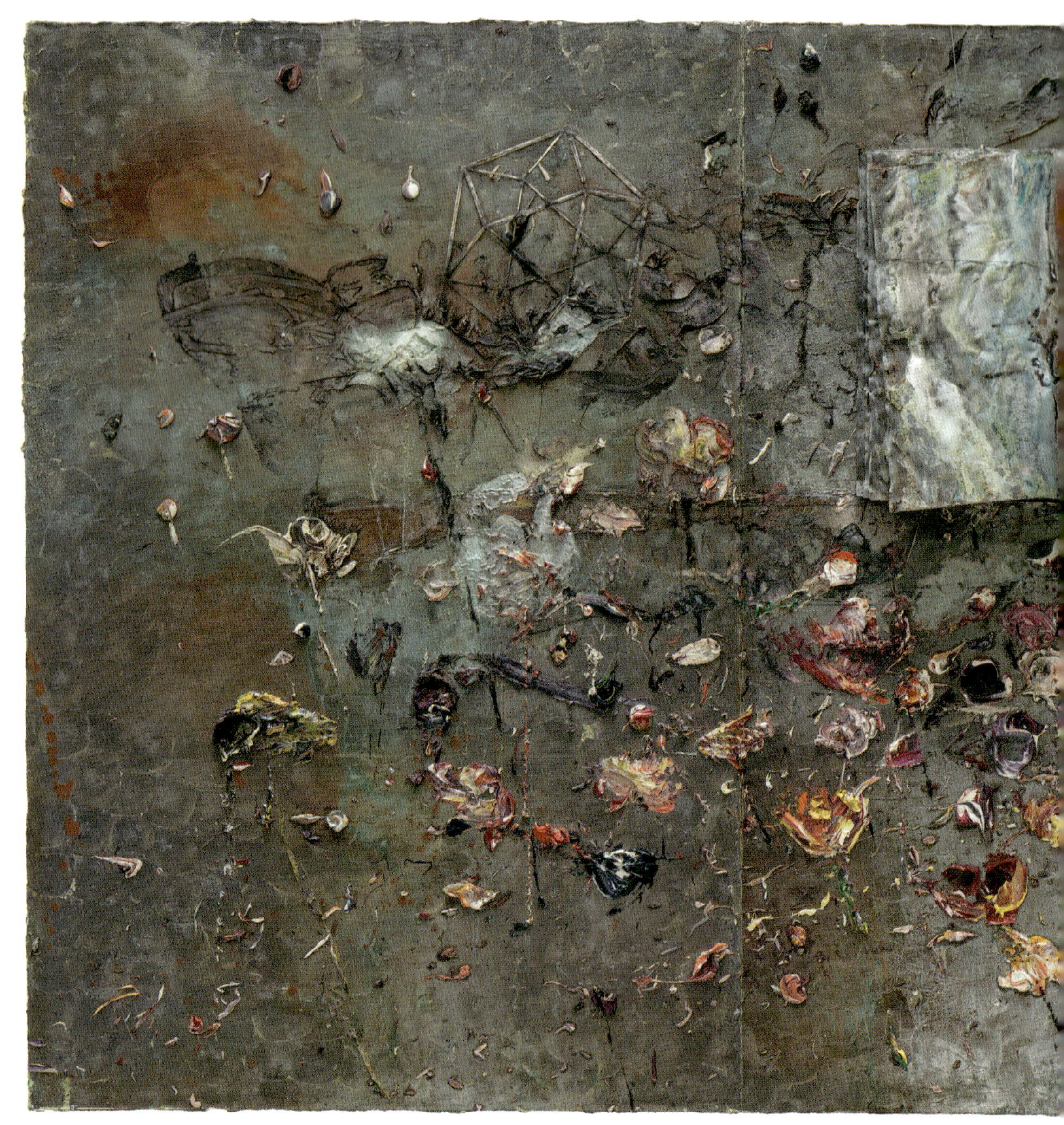

Anselm Kiefer Hon RA
Böse Blumen
Oil, emulsion, acrylic, shellac, lead and sediment of electrolysis on lead sheet on canvas
280 × 570 cm

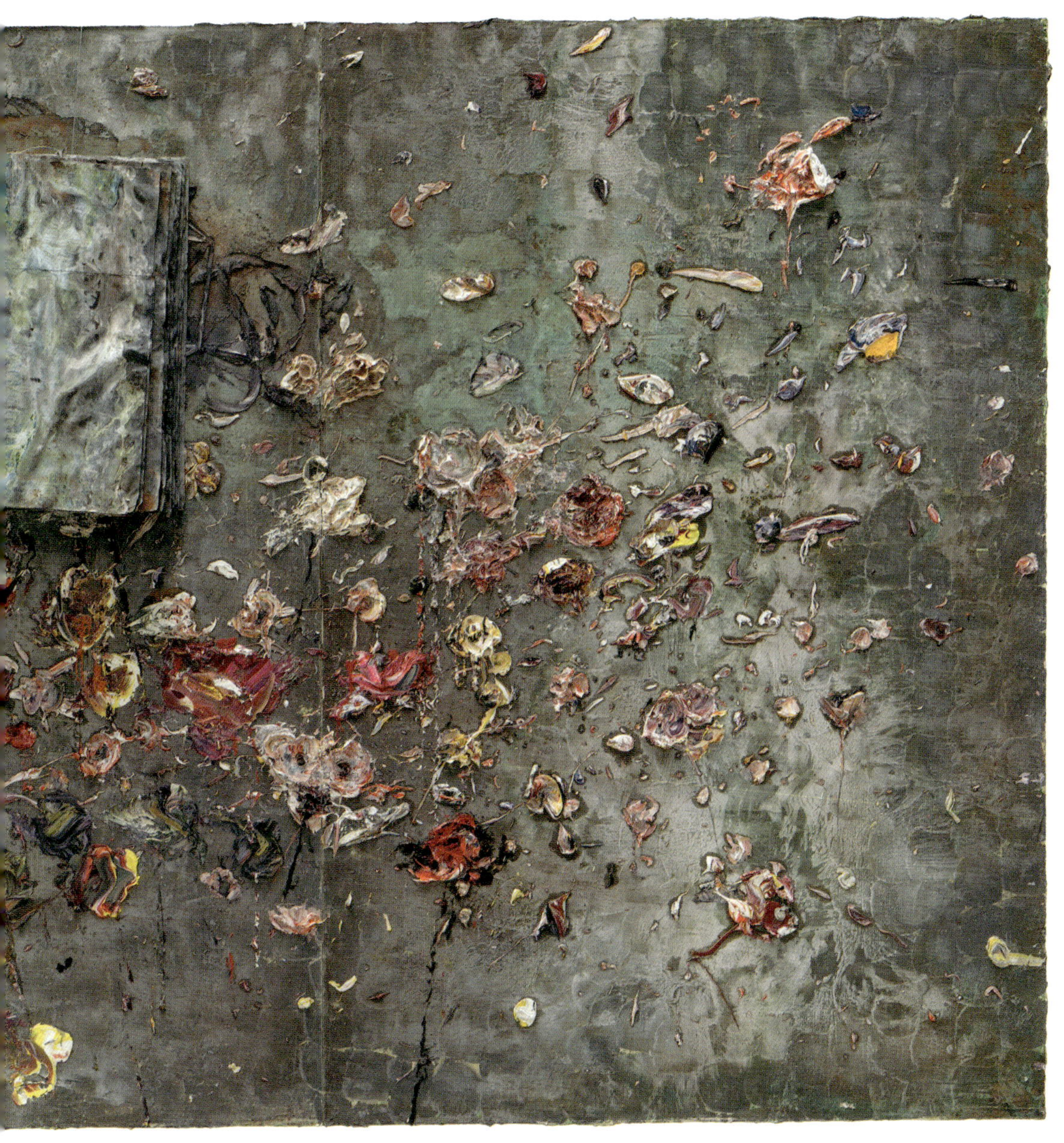

Rose Wylie RA
Party Clothes (RW and Cat)
Oil
183 × 169 cm

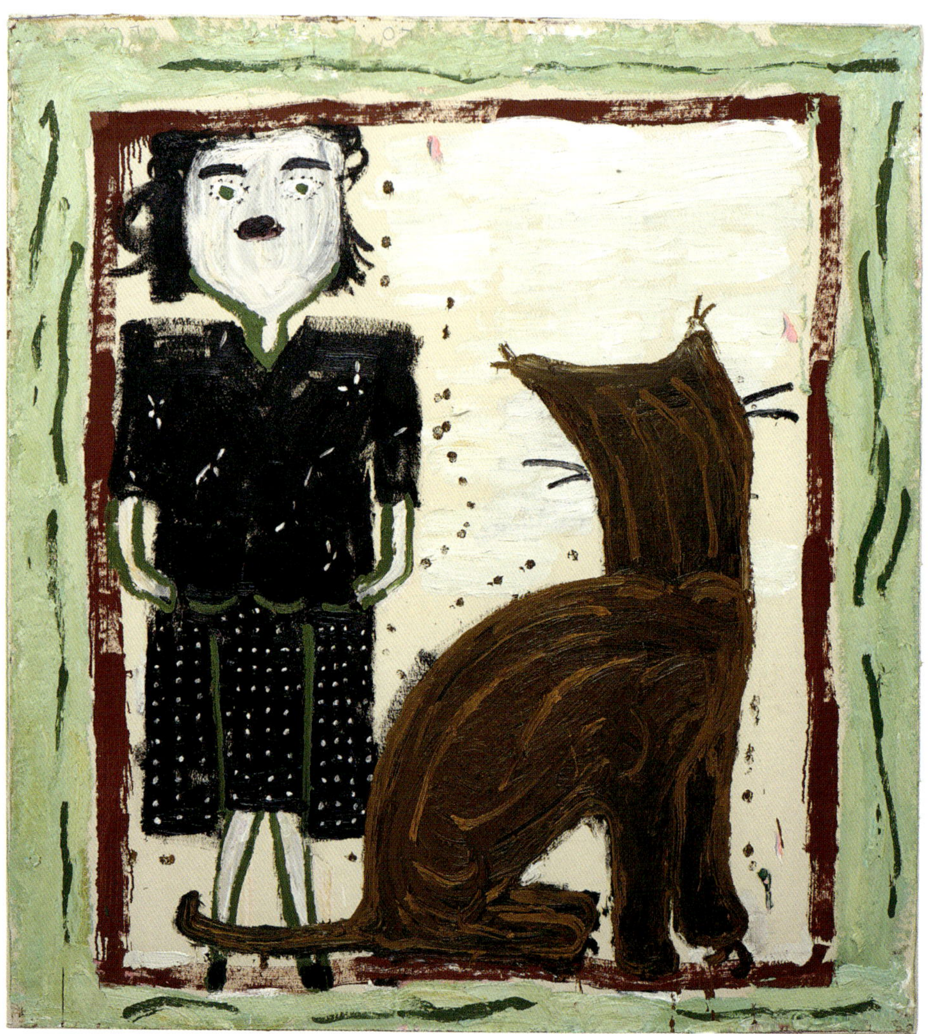

Tracey Emin CBE RA
Grand Hotel I
Polymer gravure
45 × 53 cm

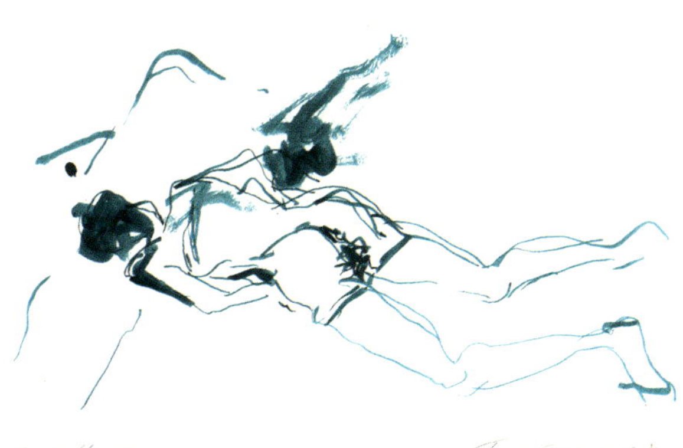

Sarah Lucas
Blue Bunny
C-type print
87 × 84 cm

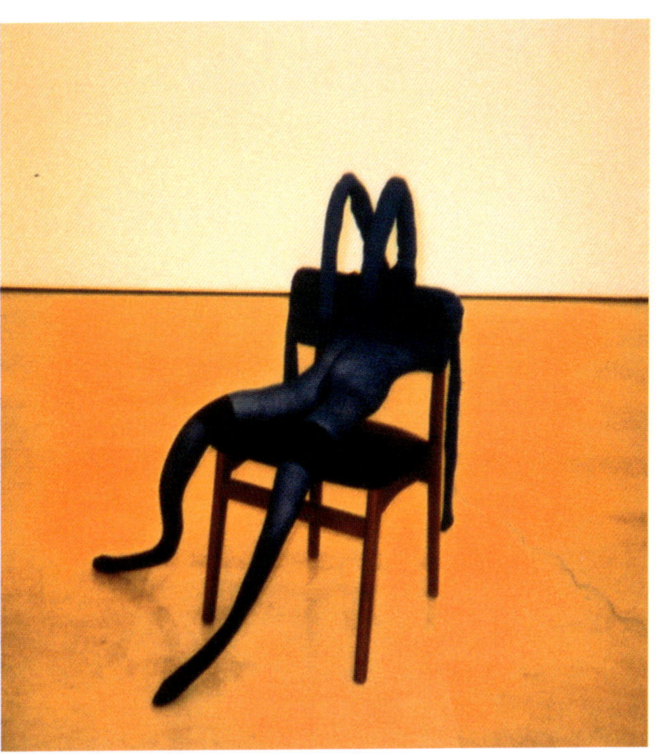

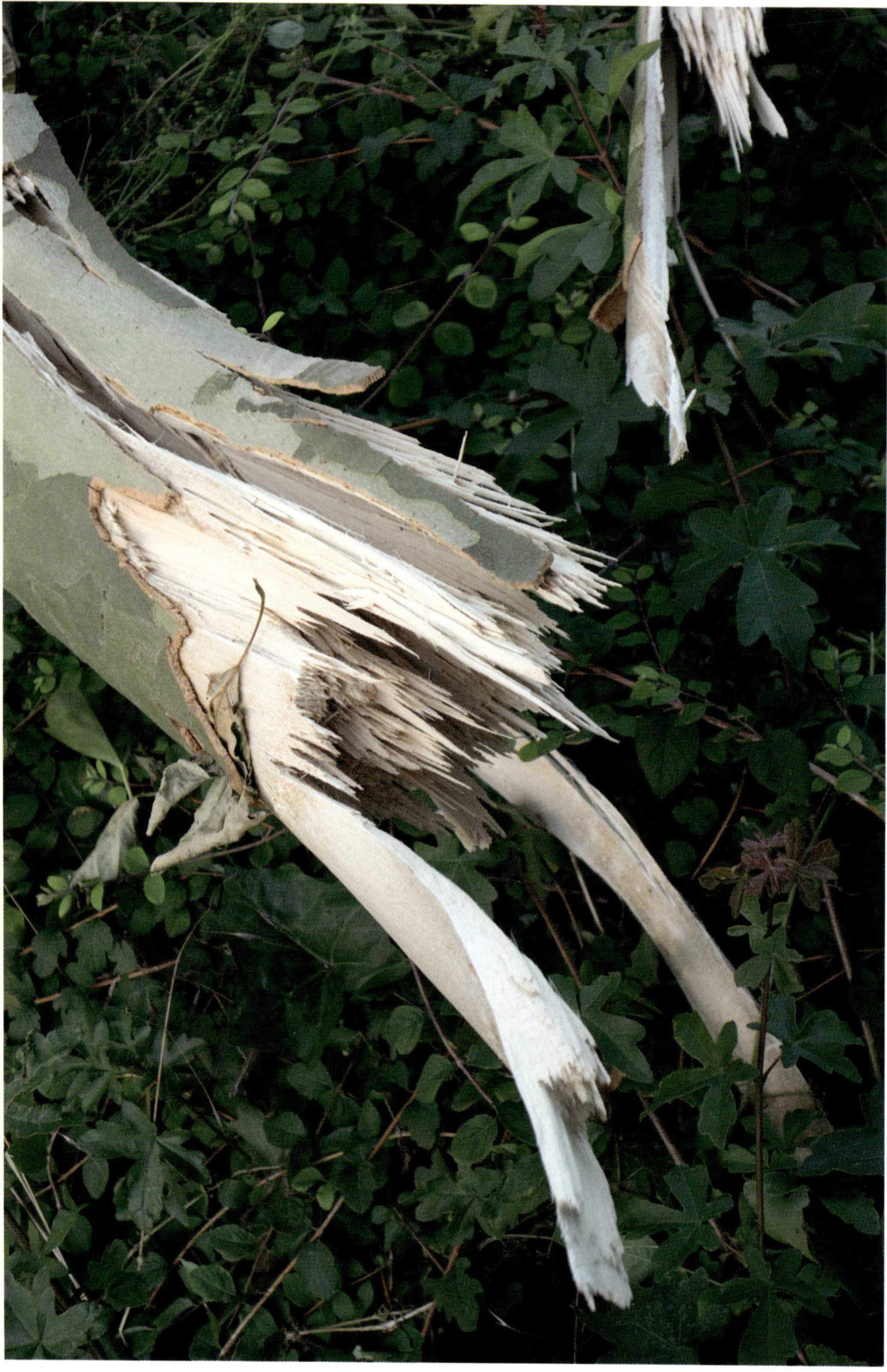

Wolfgang Tillmans RA
Lignin Duress (D)
Inkjet print on aluminium
91 × 74 cm

Gordon Cheung
Ej Eelkema II (Small New Order)
Archival inkjet print
82 × 61 cm

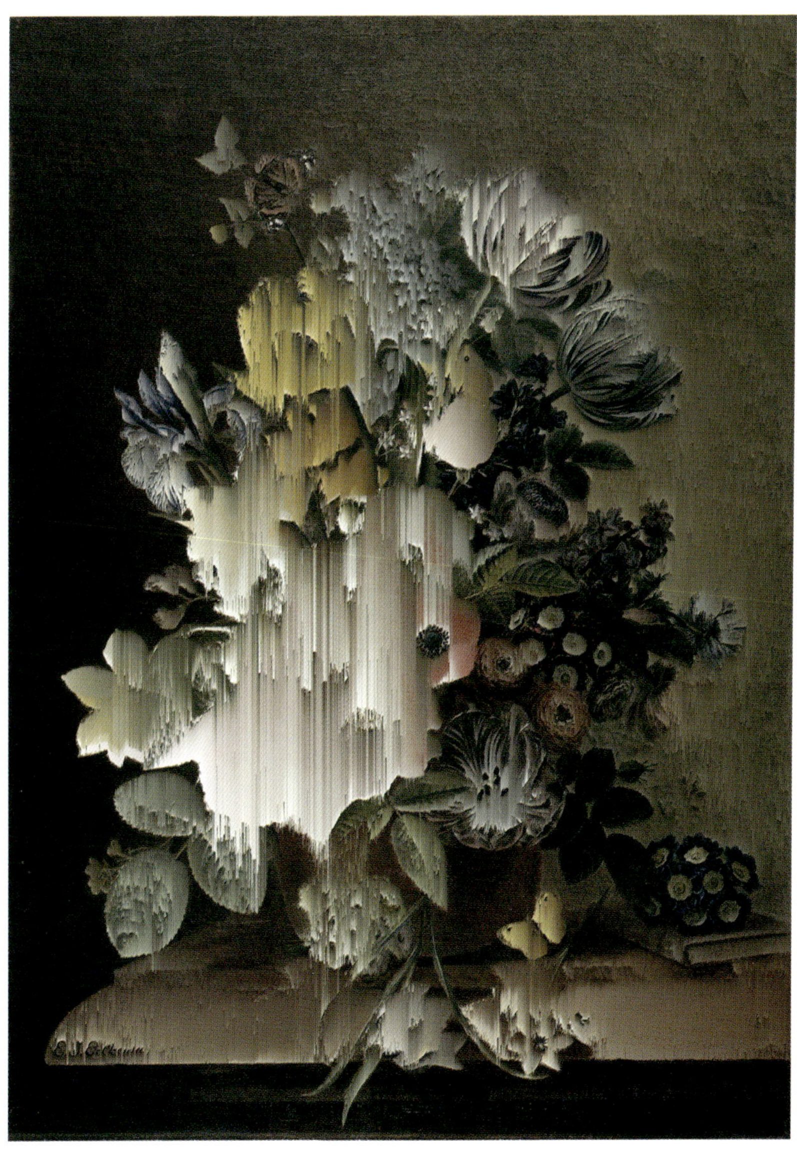

Tom Phillips CBE RA
In Memoriam Yogi Berra
Oil
198 × 137 cm

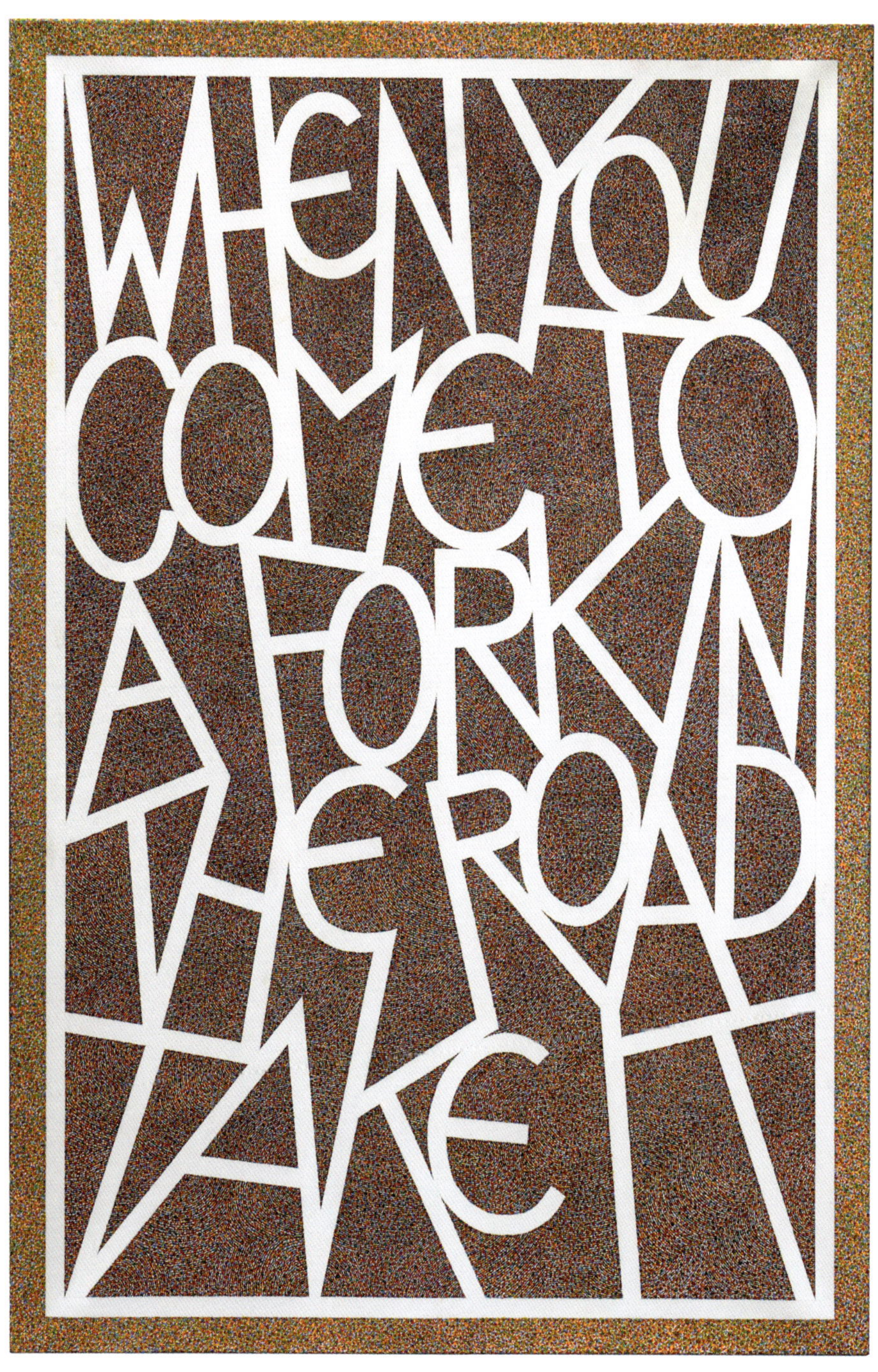

Jonathan Baldock
Form with Limbs II
Felt, silk thread, wood, polymer and terracotta
H 52 cm

Colin Allen
The Painting Becomes Itself (Balloon Bear)
Polyurethane, hessian and acrylic
H 280 cm

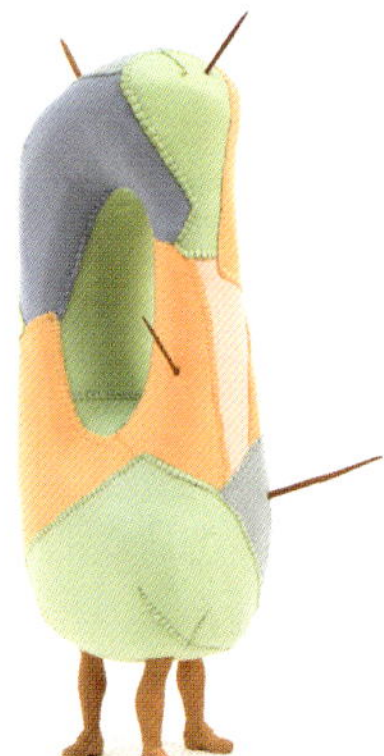

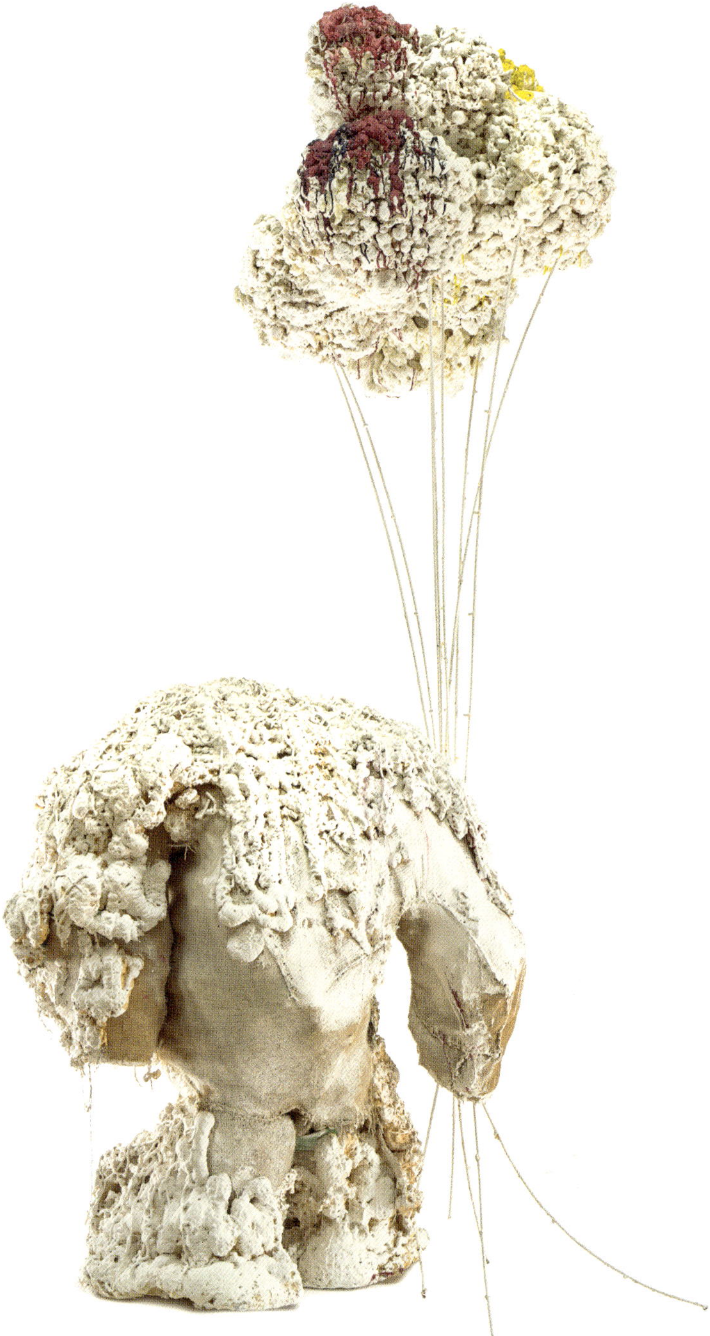

Frank Bowling OBE RA
Oriental Couple Robed under Tree
Acrylic
186 × 92 cm

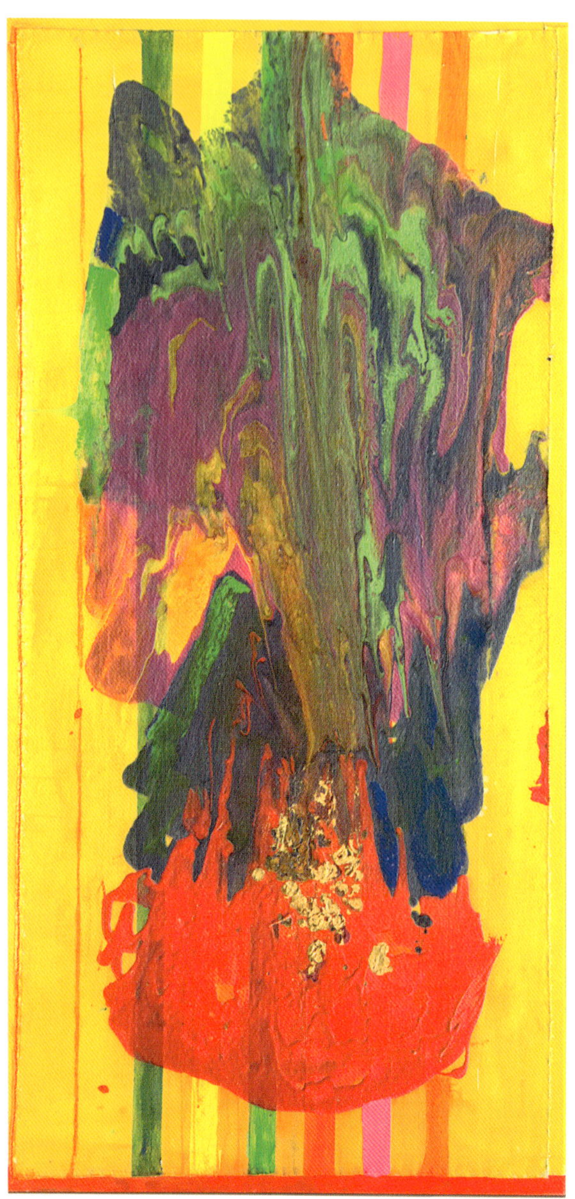

Stephen Cox RA
Louis Khan: Silva Kali: Grey
Oil stick
155 × 155 cm

Gillian Ayres CBE RA
The Making of the Wild Sky
Oil
153 × 184 cm

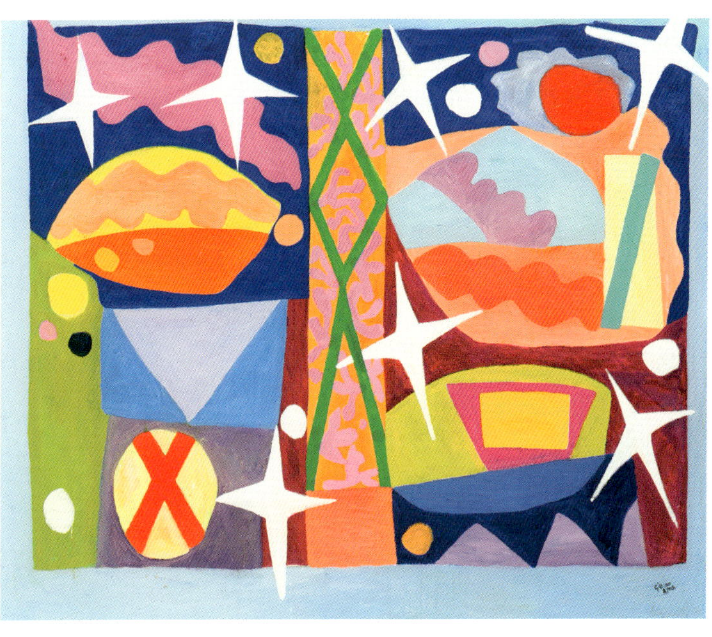

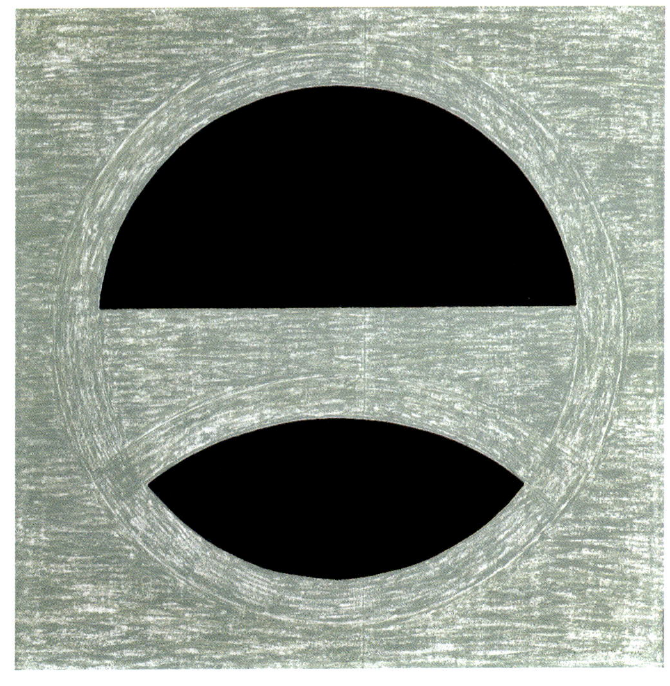

Sean Scully RA
Landline Darkness
Oil on linen
216 × 191 cm

Fiona Rae RA
Figure 1g
Oil and acrylic
183 × 130 cm

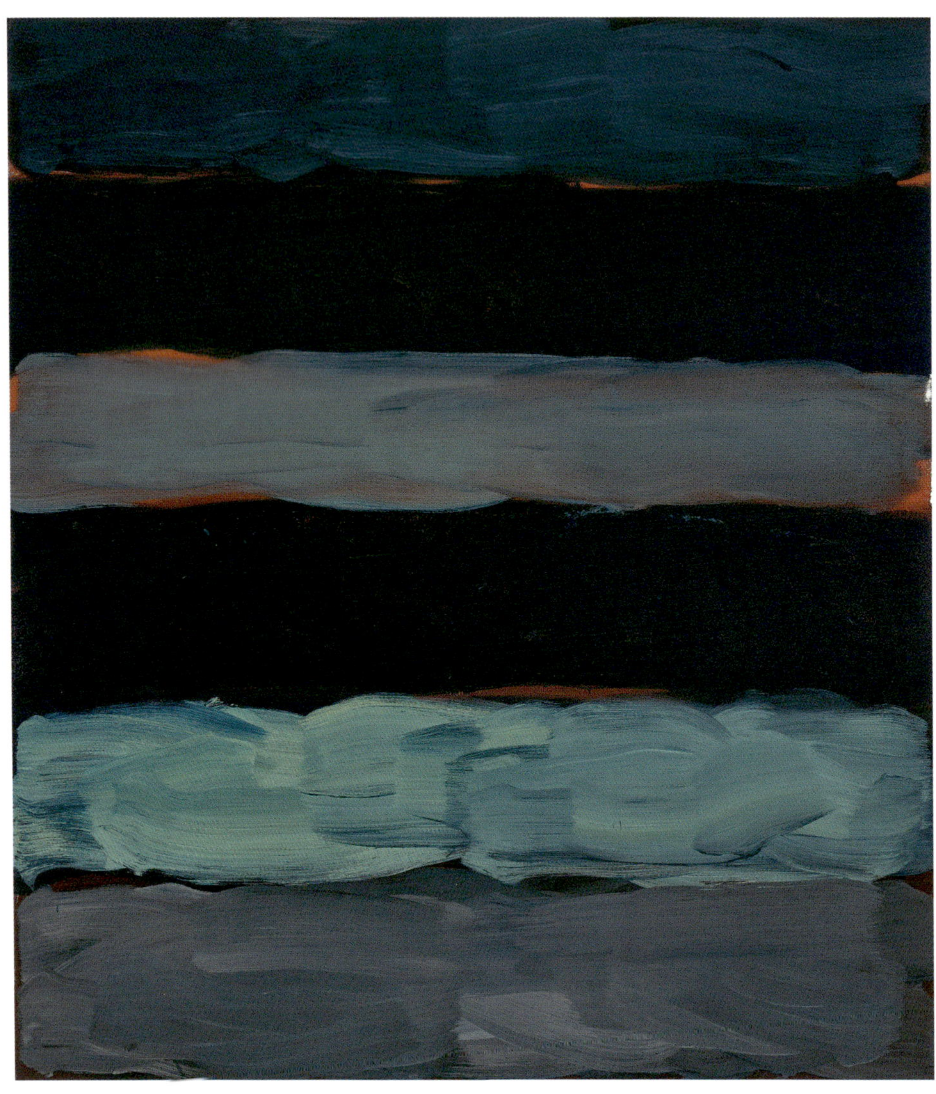

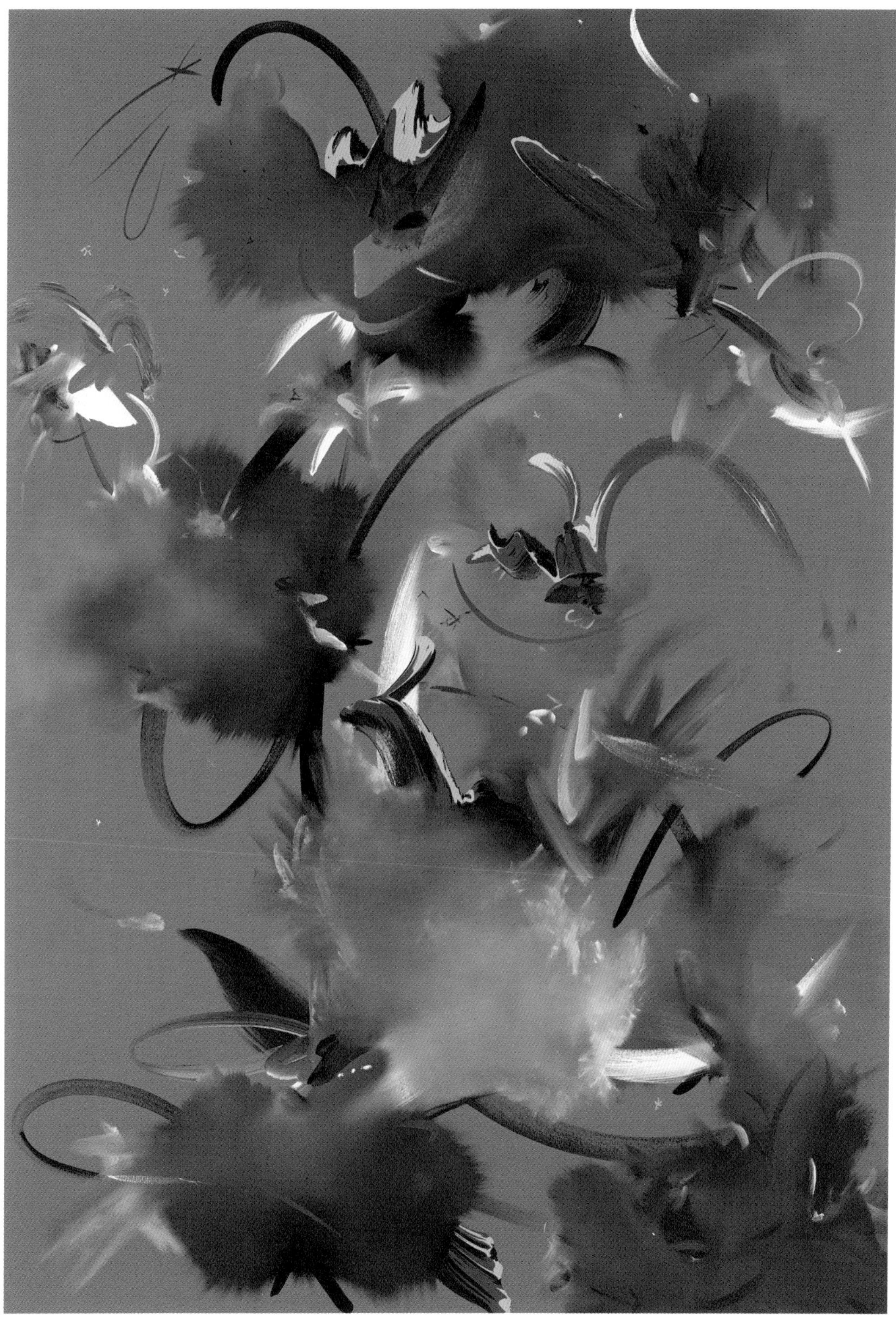

Basil Beattie RA
Ladder II
Oil, wax and acrylic spray
152 × 122 cm

Prof Phillip King CBE PPRA
Caliban
Mixed media on paper
75 × 65 cm

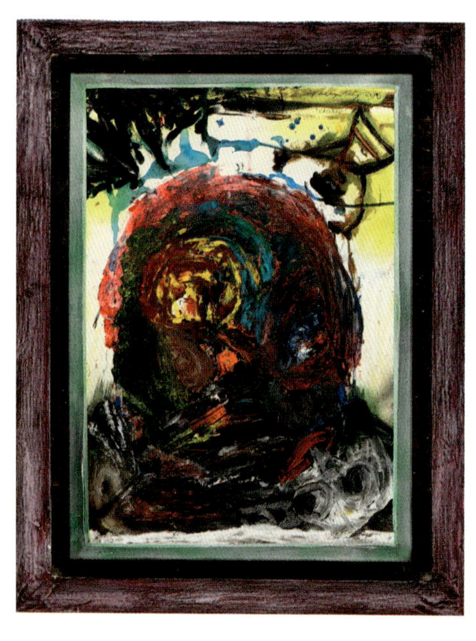

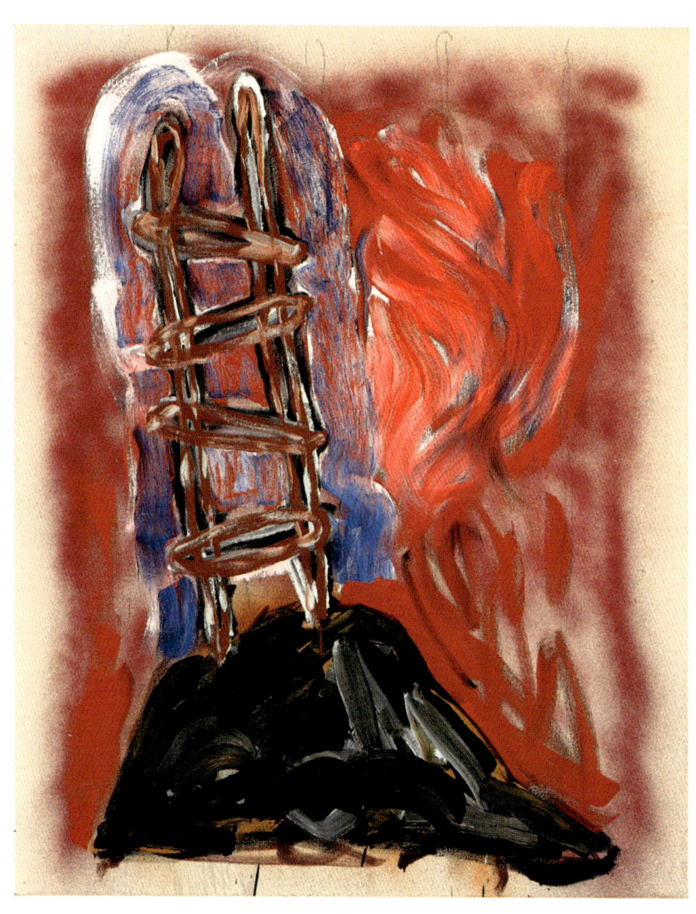

John Carter RA
Identical Shapes: 16 Orientations
Screenprint
70 × 50 cm

The late Albert Irvin OBE RA
Trinity I
Screenprint and woodblock
124 × 154 cm

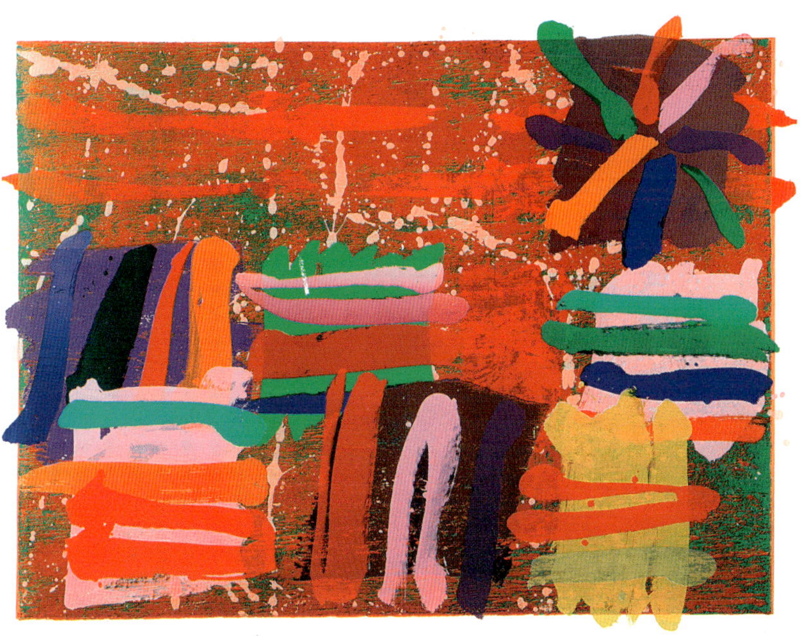

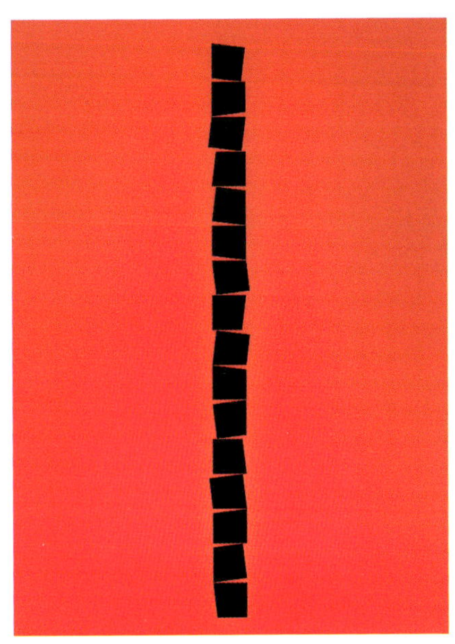

Prof Paul Huxley RA
A Square and a Circle 4
Acrylic
127 × 127 cm

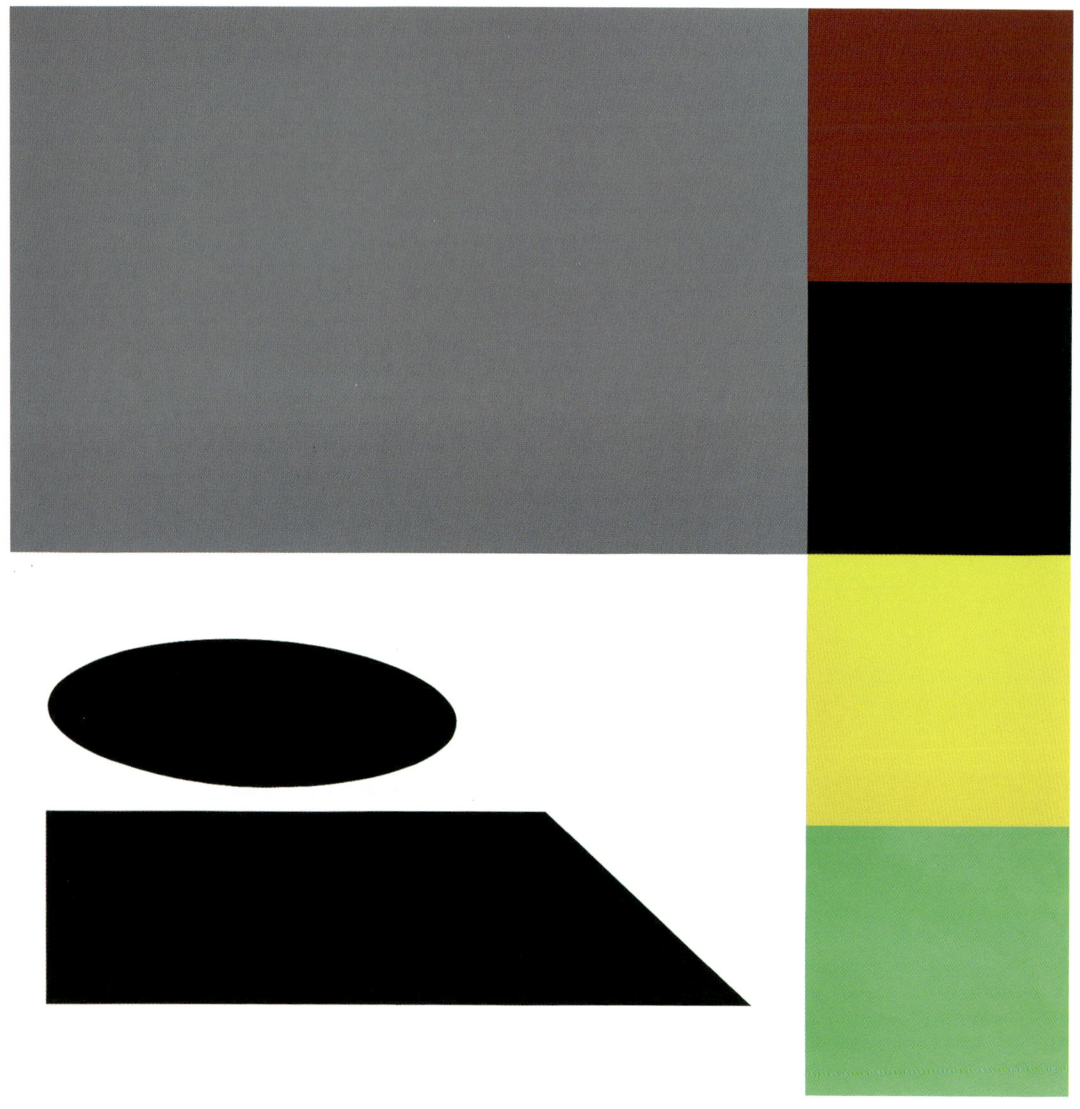

Prof Stephen Farthing RA
El Chapo Guzman's Shower
Acrylic
207 × 173 cm

Mali Morris RA
Primrose and Purl
Acrylic on paper
59 × 76 cm

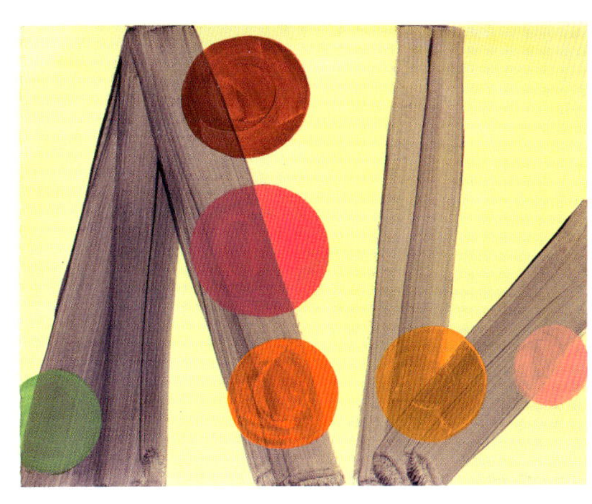

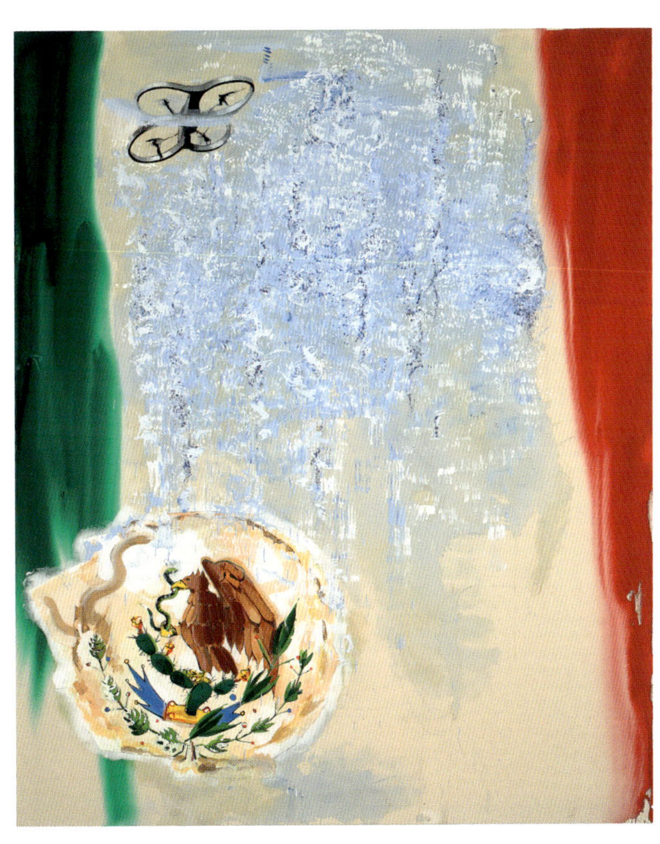

The late Ellsworth Kelly Hon RA
Leucothoe
Pencil on paper
76 × 56 cm

Georg Baselitz Hon RA
Oggi come domani
Oil on canvas
162 × 114 cm

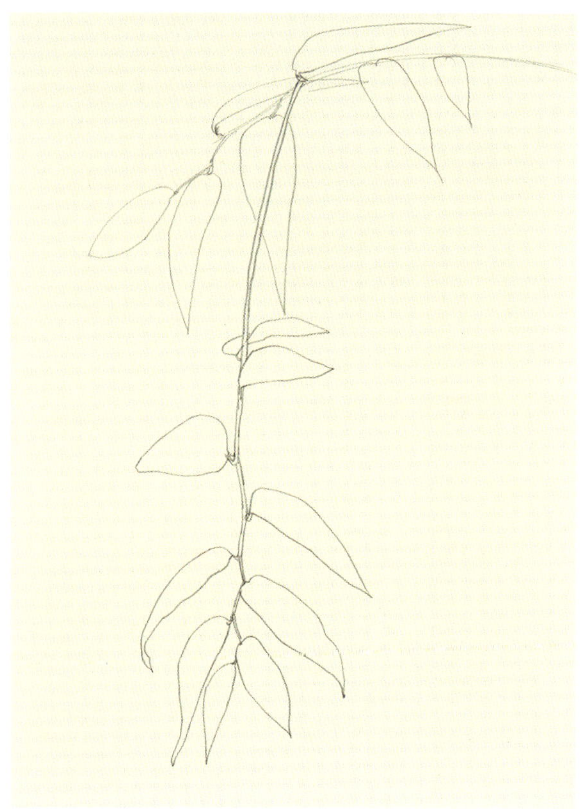

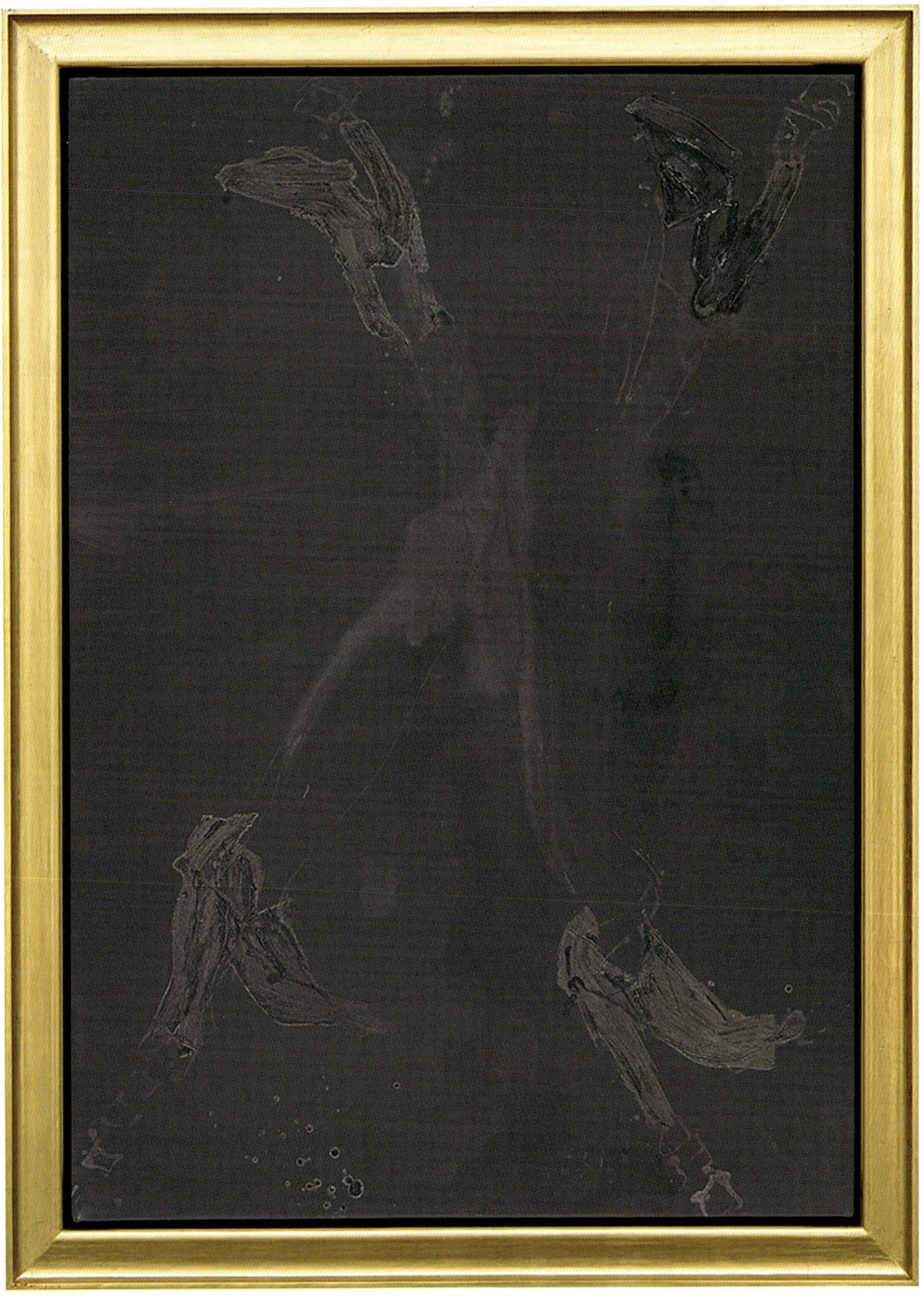

Dr Jennifer Dickson RA
Crystalline Spring: Two (Petworth Park)
Archival inkjet and watercolour print
50 × 60 cm

Miriam de Burca
Deconstructing the North VI: Rushes
Ink on paper vellum
56 × 42 cm

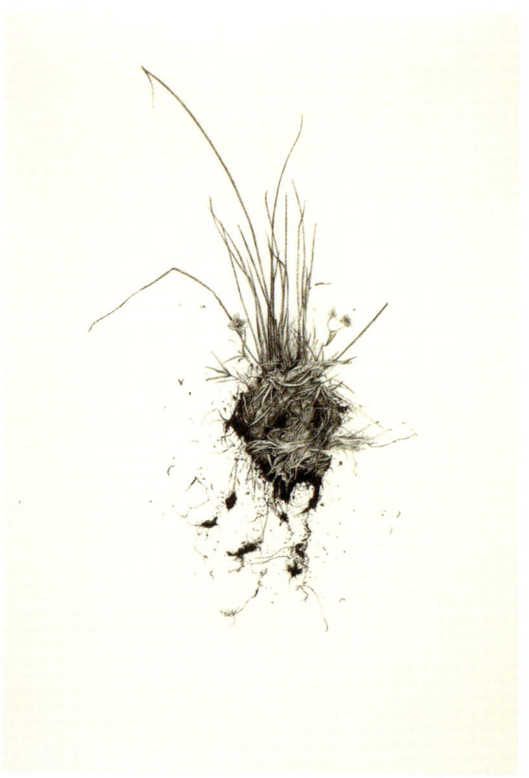

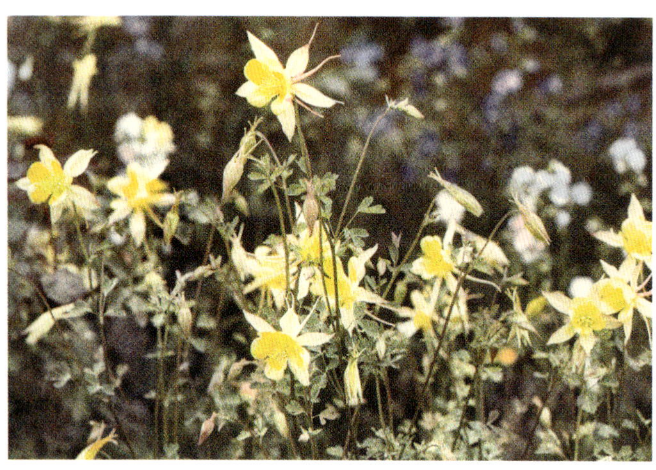

Dame Elizabeth Blackadder DBE RA
Four Fish
Screenprint
40 × 30 cm

Anne Desmet RA
Roman Labyrinth
Linocut collage on paper under convex glass
D 50 cm

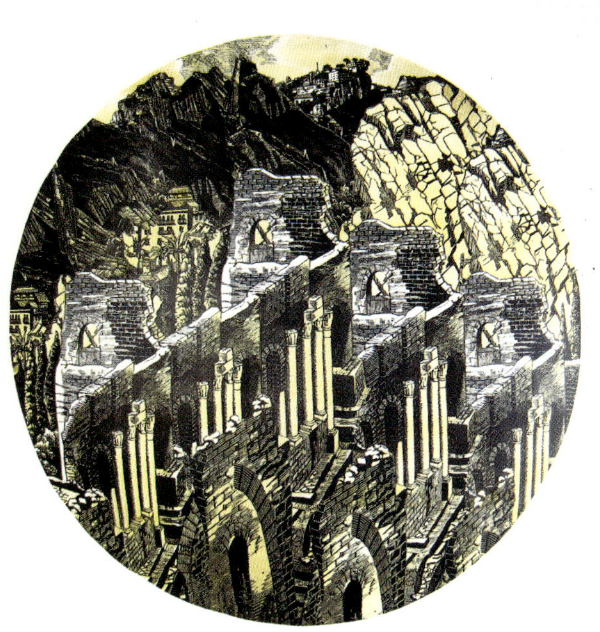

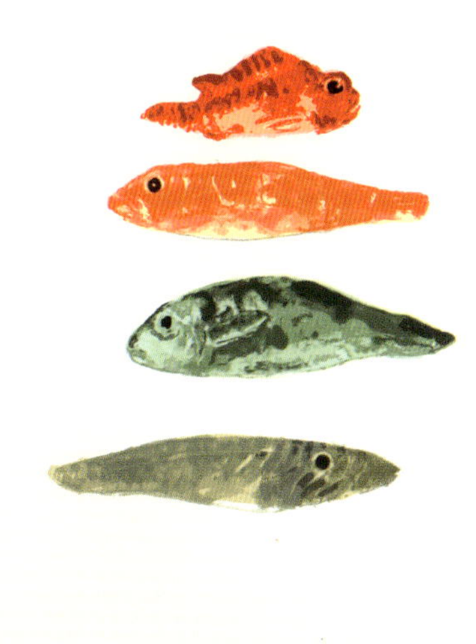

Yinka Shonibare MBE RA
Bunch of Migrants
Screenprint and gold leaf
108 × 103 cm

Michael Craig-Martin CBE RA
Chips from: Drawings
Letterpress print
48 × 48 cm

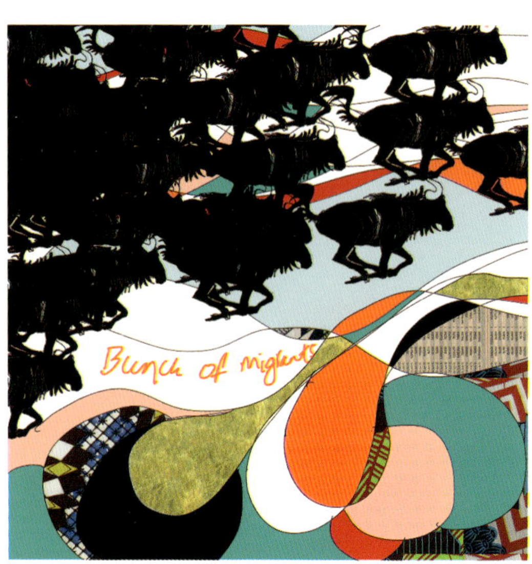

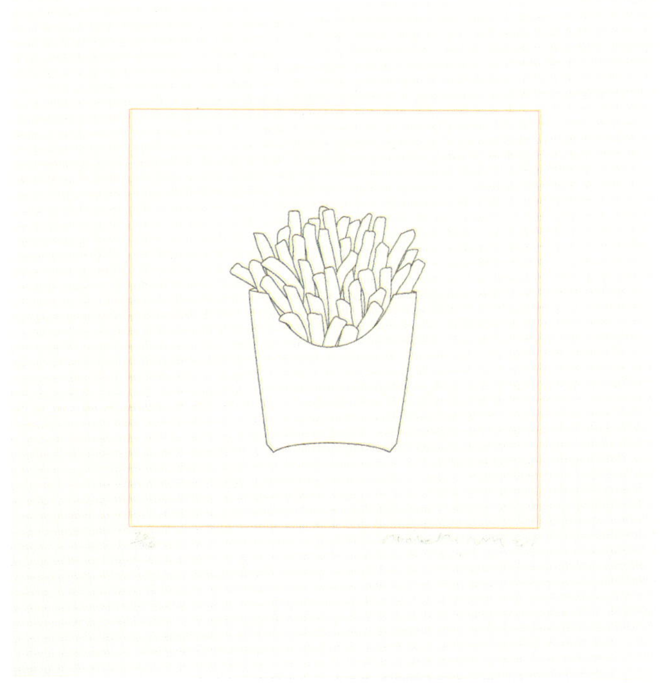

Prof Humphrey Ocean RA
Roadsign
Enamel on steel
60 × 60 cm

Cornelia Parker OBE RA
The End From: One Day this Glass will Break
Polymer photogravure etching
56 × 80 cm

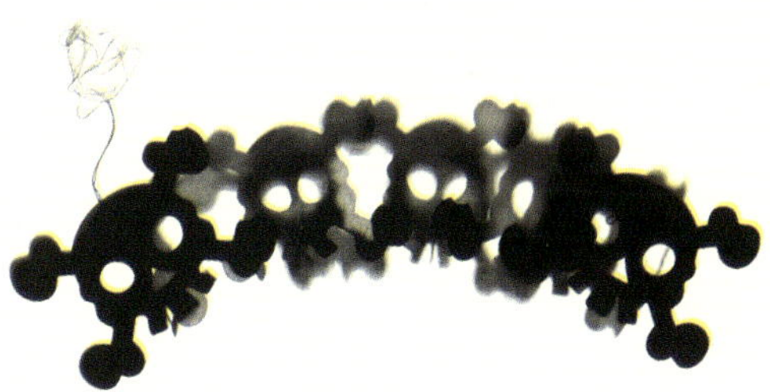

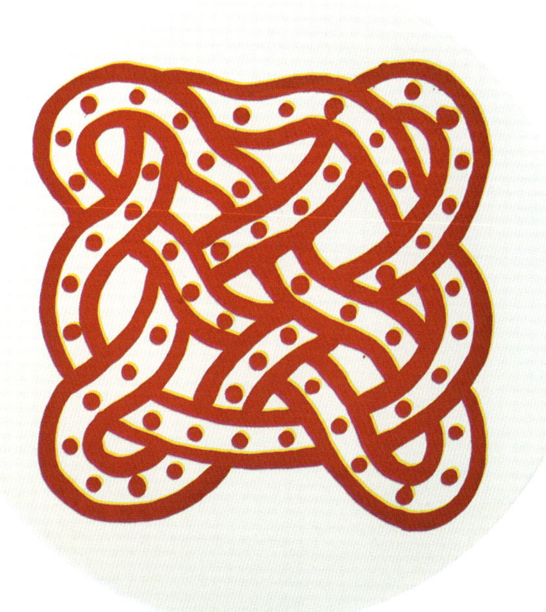

Paula Rego
Death of the Blind Sister
Acrylic and conté pencil
137 × 102 cm

Peter Freeth RA
Mr Parkinson and the Wild West Wind
Aquatint
53 × 30 cm

Prof Chris Orr MBE RA
Mountaineering
Screenprint
113 × 90 cm

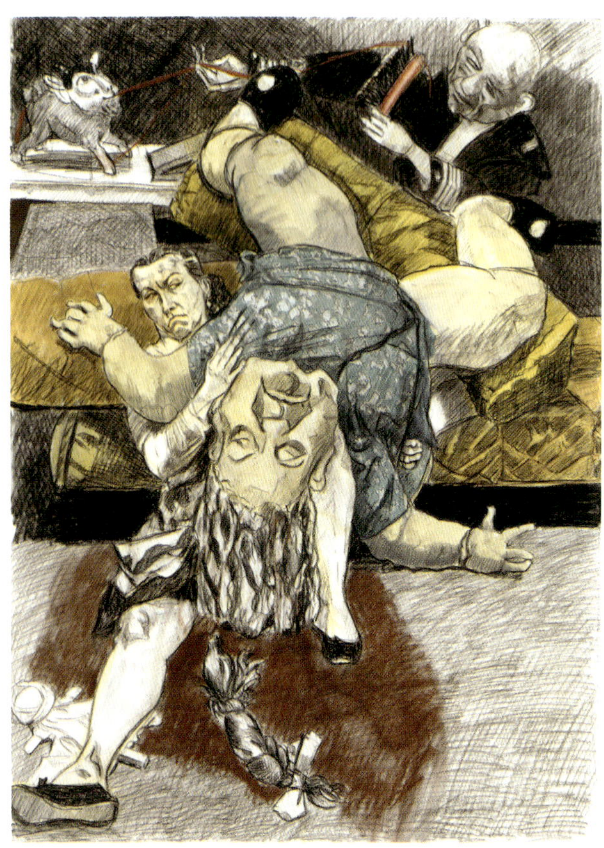

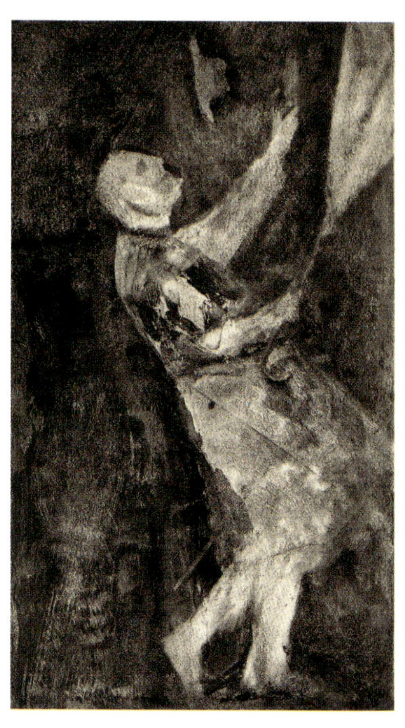

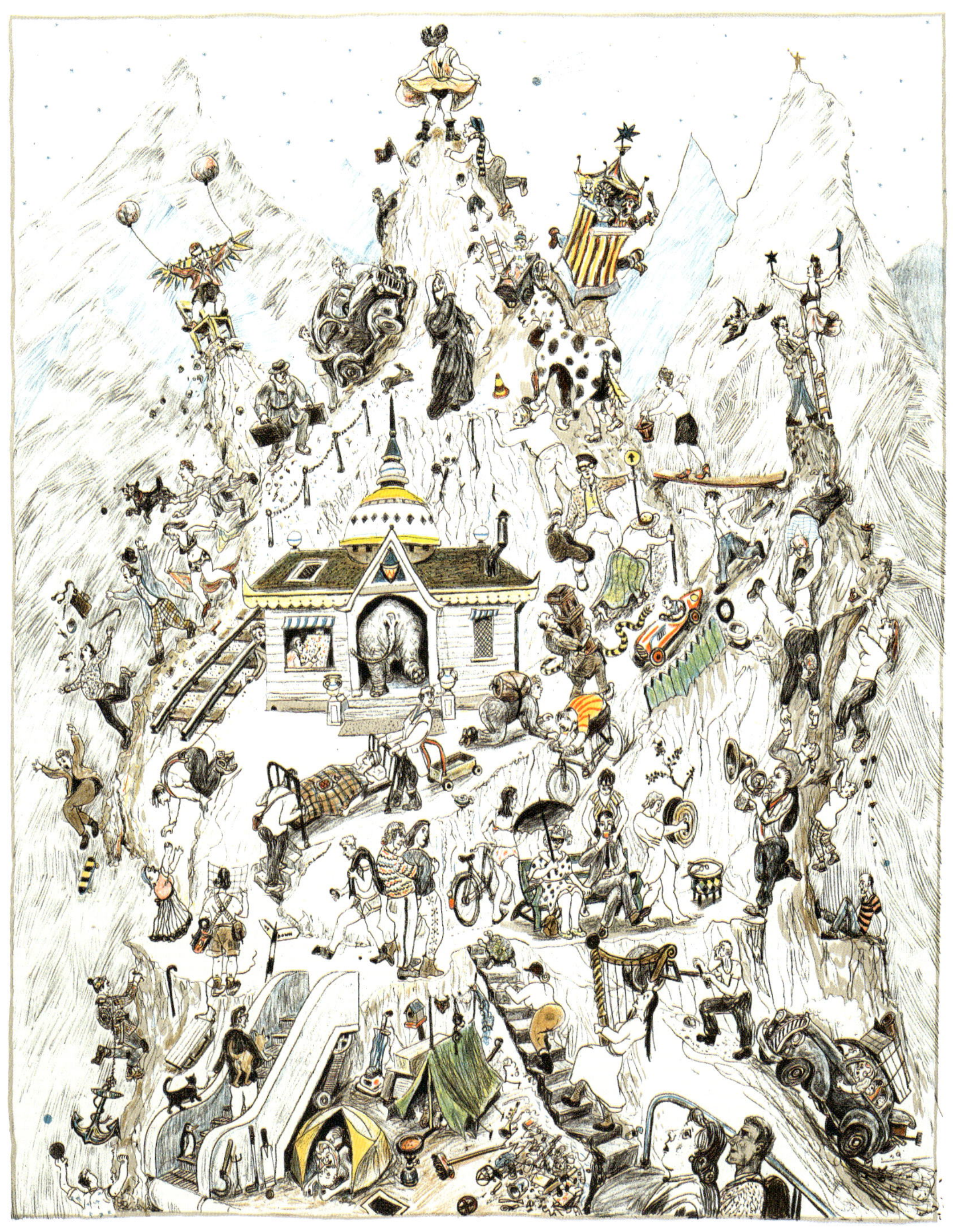

Ian Davenport
Duplex Etching: Purple, Green
Etching and chine-collé
116 × 113 cm

Christiane Baumgartner
Eldridge Street 2.0
Woodcut on Misumi paper
60 × 78 cm

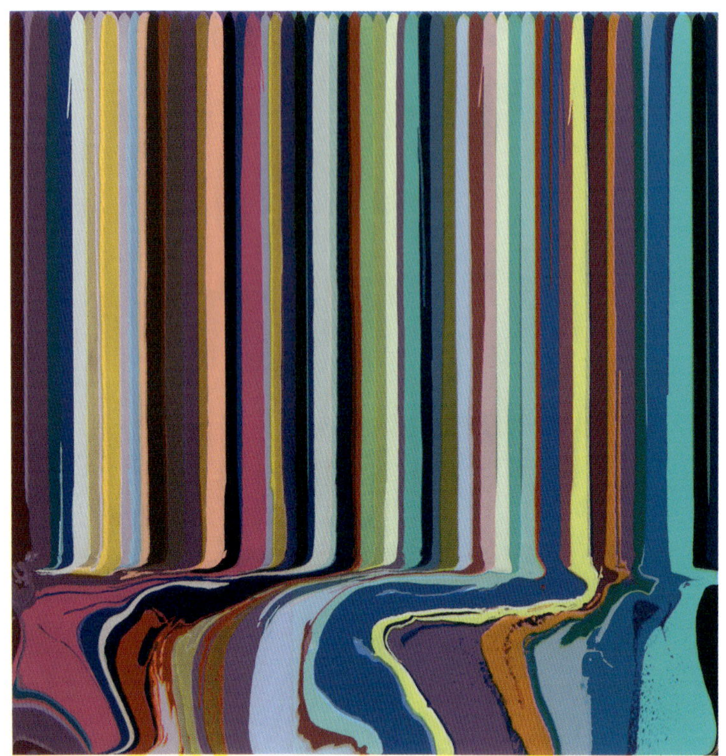

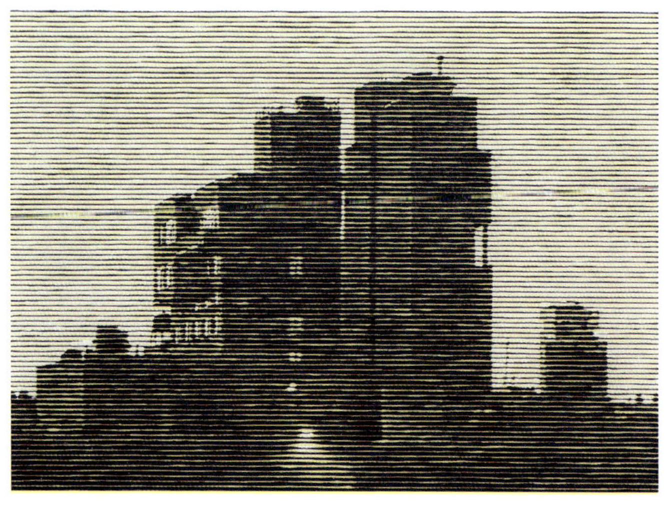

Jim Dine Hon RA
20 Second Dream of Africa
Hand-painted relief etching
170 × 125 cm

Julian Opie
Minnows. From: Nature 2
Print
62 × 62 cm

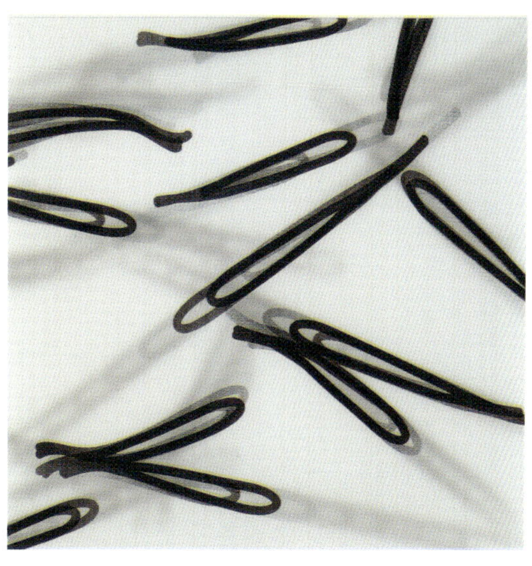

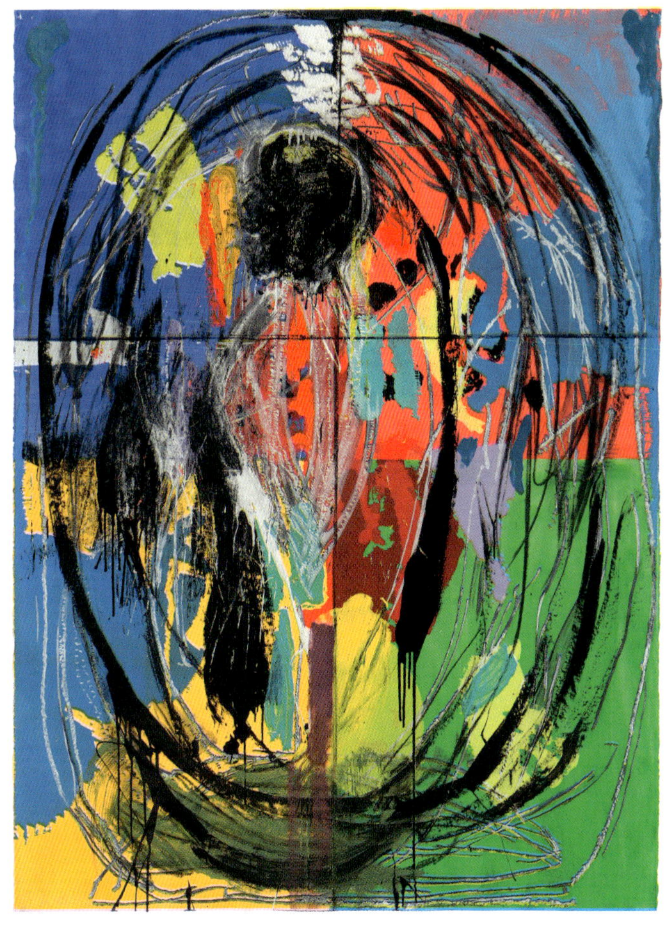

Tony Bevan RA
Tree
Charcoal and acrylic
86 × 122 cm

Prof Ian McKeever RA
Eagduru 3
Photopolymer gravure
41 × 53 cm

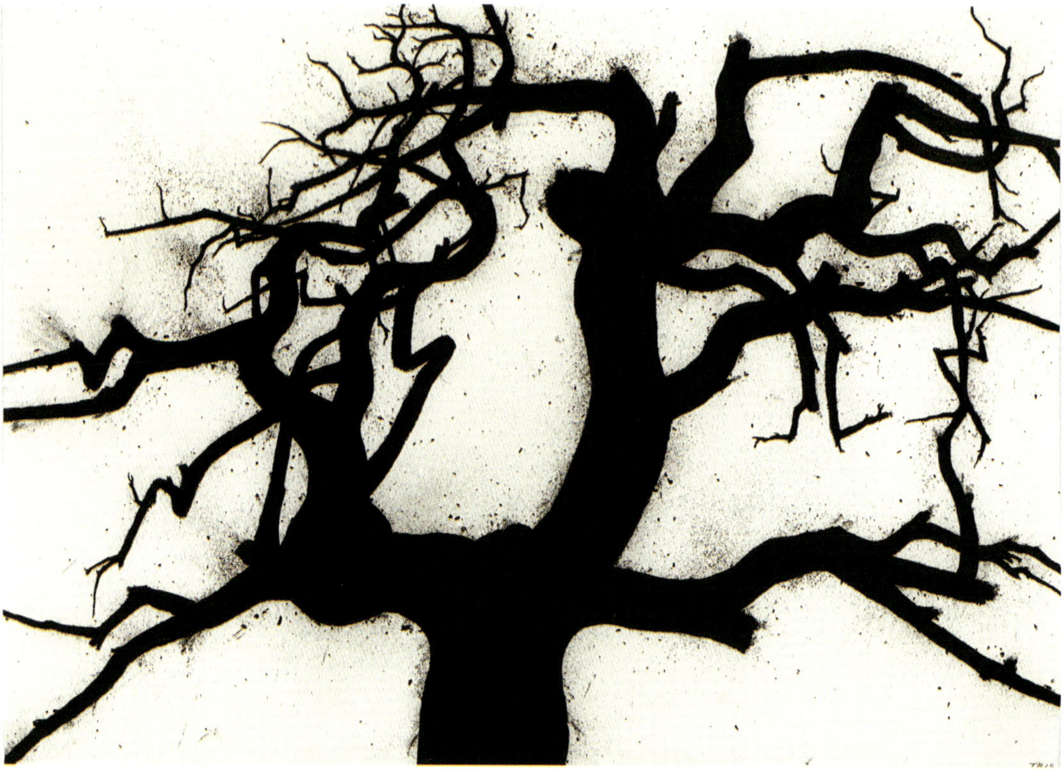

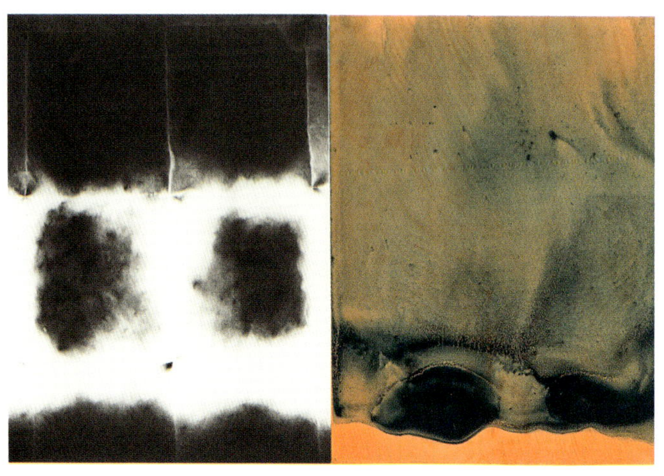

Anthony Whishaw RA
Window View
Acrylic collage on canvas
49 × 120 cm

Jennifer Durrant RA
From a Series 'Ghirlanda III': Due Blu
Acrylic
24 × 29 cm

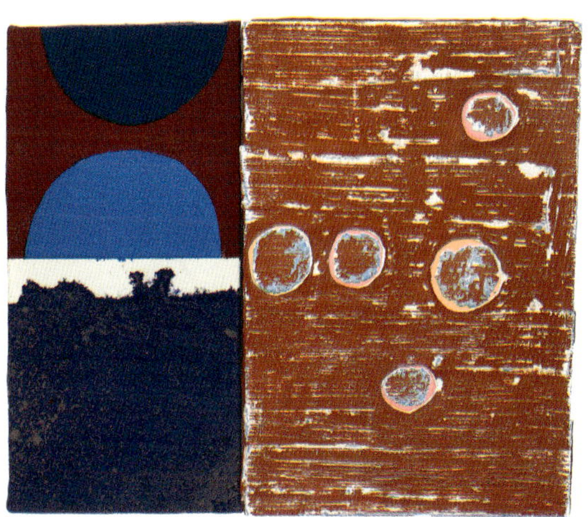

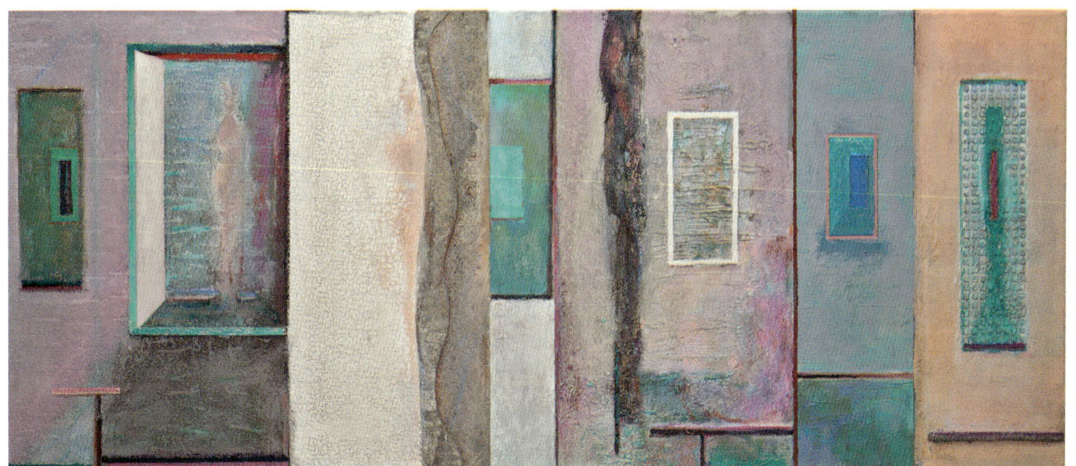

Rebecca Salter RA
Tessella 1 and 2
Japanese woodblock
78 × 45 cm

Tess Jaray RA
Nine Thorns
Screenprint
59 × 55 cm

Eva Rothschild RA
MMXIV
Resin, wool and steel
H 91 cm

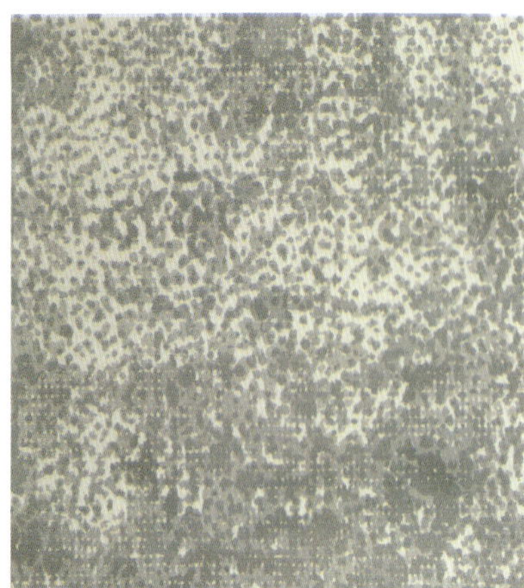

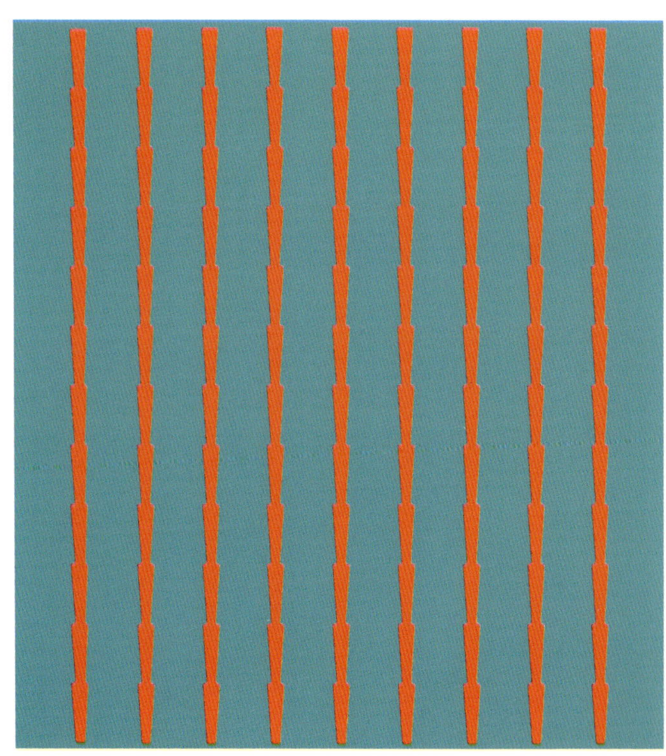

Dr Barbara Rae CBE RA
Sanctuary – Spring
Etching and collagraph
98 × 90 cm

Hughie O'Donoghue RA
Morning Afloat
Carborundum print
40 × 54 cm

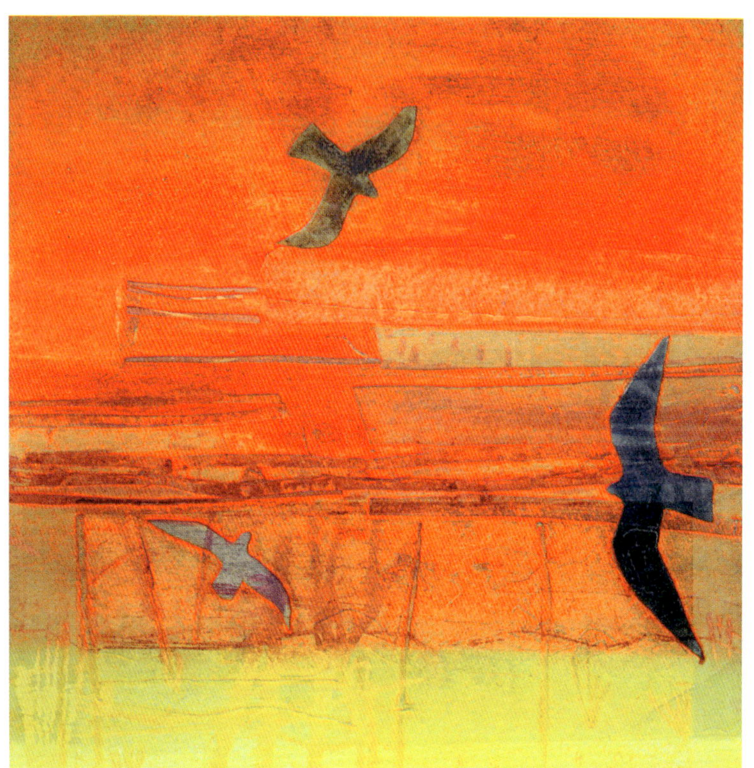

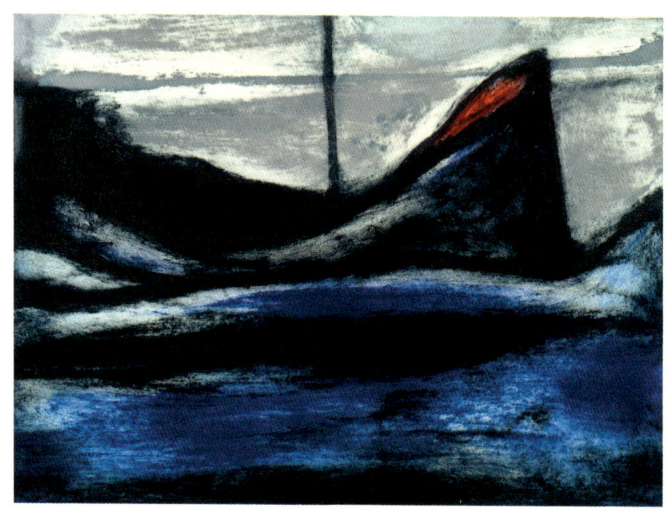

Idris Khan
London Eye, London
Platinum-palladium print
62 × 77 cm

Prof Norman Ackroyd CBE RA
A Wiltshire Skyline
Etching
22 × 20 cm

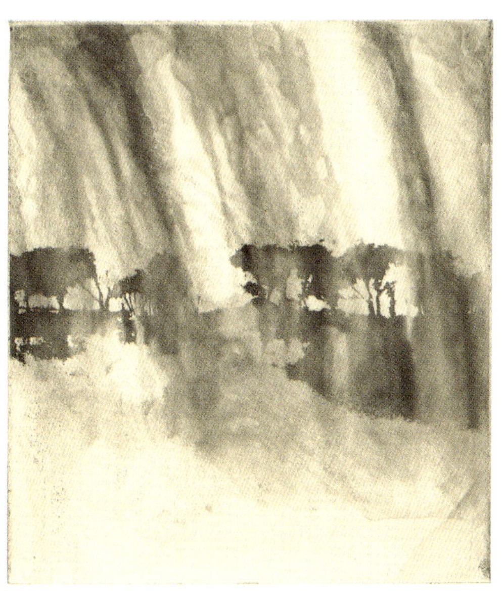

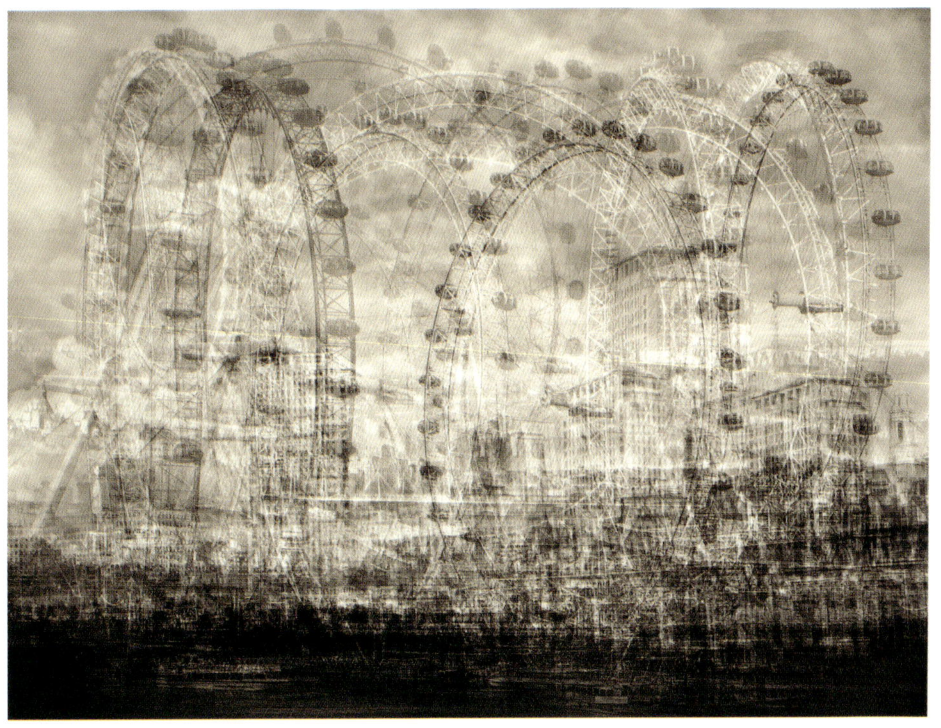

Prof Sir Peter Cook RA
Waterside Workplace (Print)
Print
59 × 84 cm

The late Dame Zaha Hadid DBE RA
Cardiff Bay Opera House – Aerial View
Acrylic on black cartridge
145 × 199 cm

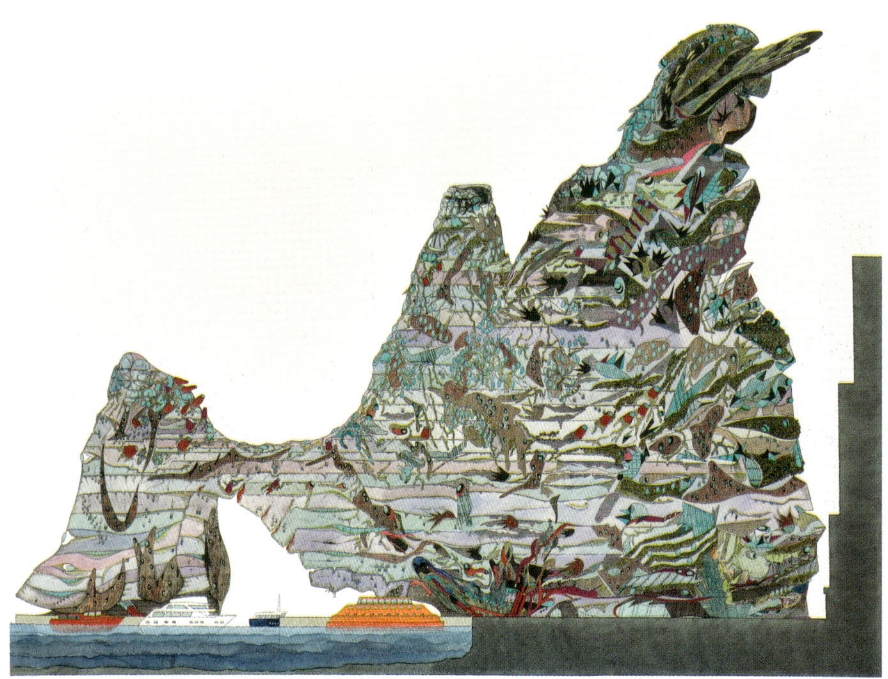

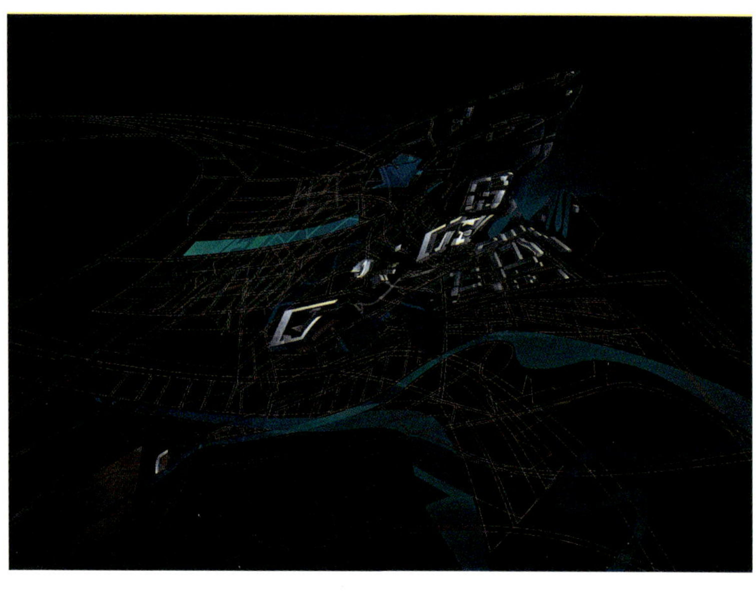

Chris Wilkinson OBE RA
Tintagel Castle: Bridge Competition
Acrylic, stainless steel and cherry veneer
24 × 68 cm

Lord Rogers of Riverside CH RA
Rogers Weekend House, presentation model, scale 1:50
Acrylic, styrene and metal etchings
H 30 cm

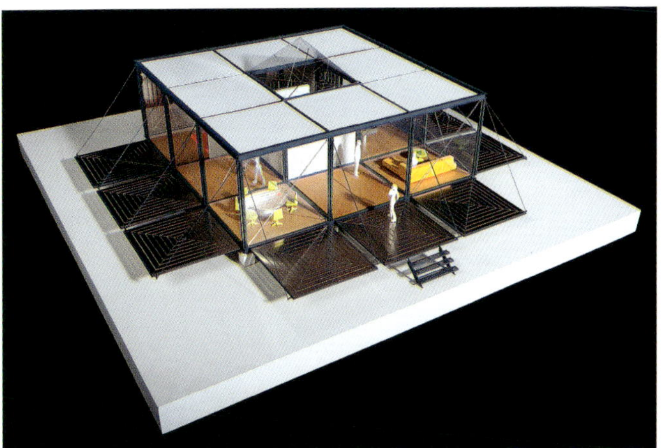

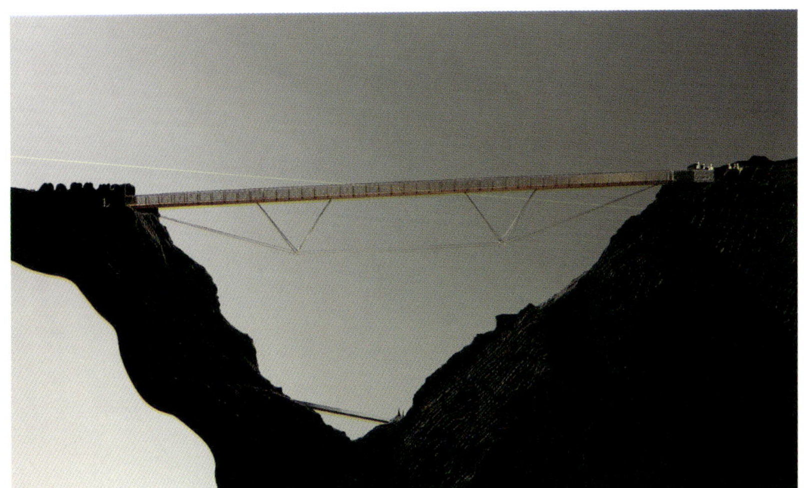

Prof Gordon Benson OBE RA
Dysfunctional Paradise Lost
Mixed media
80 × 60 cm

Eva Jiricna CBE RA
Revolucni Building, Mixed Use Redevelopment, Prague, Czech Republic
Inkjet print
60 × 85 cm

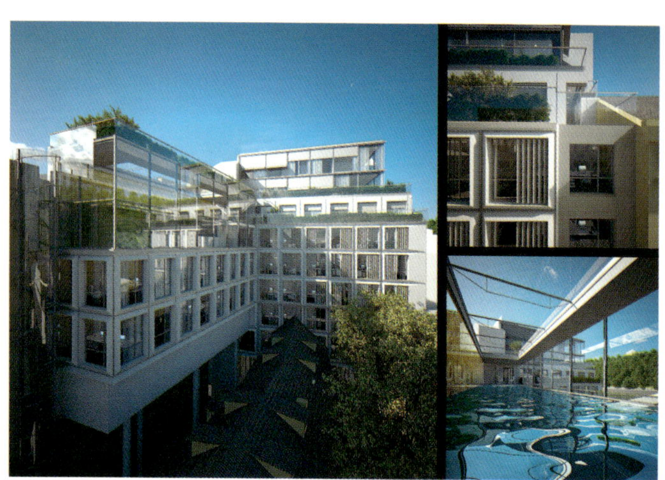

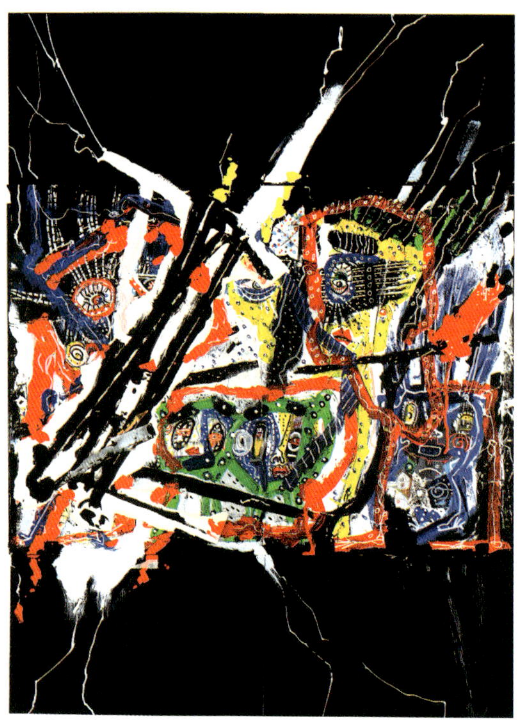

Prof Will Alsop OBE RA
Drawing Wall
Acrylic
100 × 120 cm

Sir David Chipperfield CBE RA
Competition Entry for Queen Elizabeth Olympic Park, scale 1:1000
Jesmonite
H 15 cm

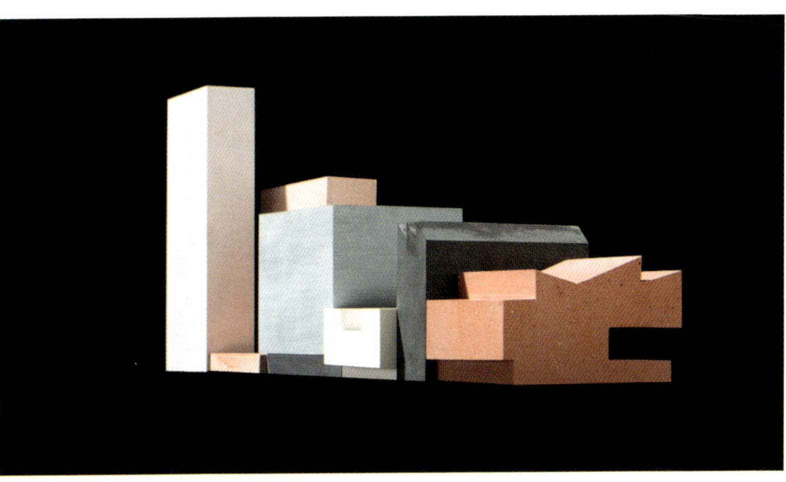

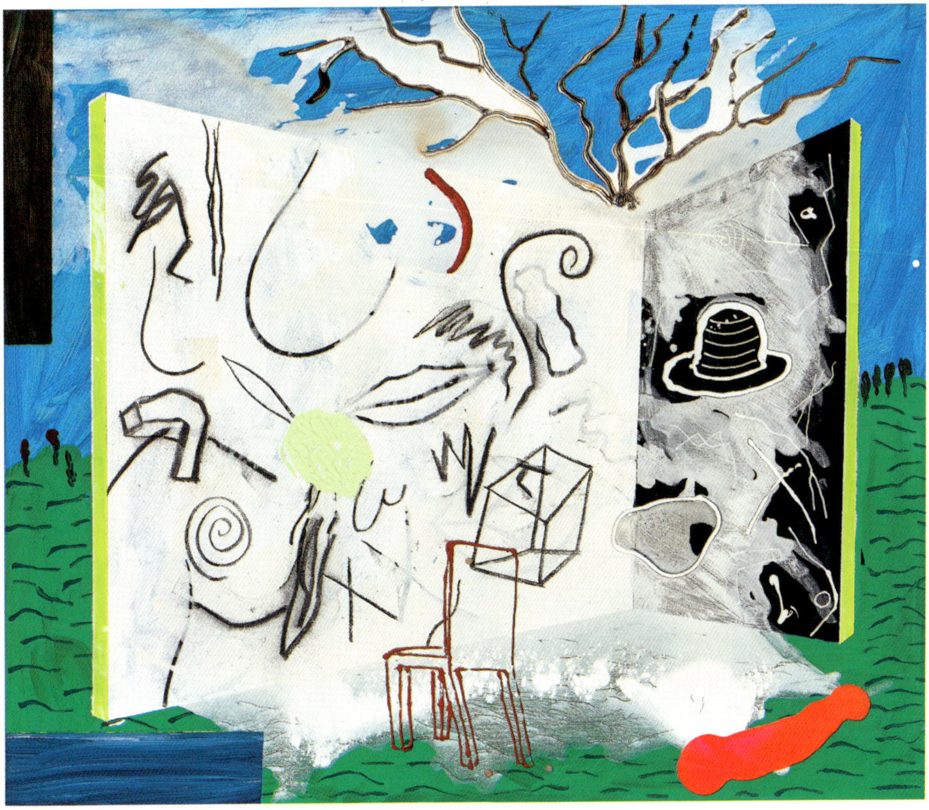

Sir Michael Hopkins CBE RA
Kyoto City Archive
Perspex and wood
88 × 122 cm

Prof Tadao Ando Hon RA
Nakanoshima Project II (Urban Egg) (detail)
Mixed media
55 × 237 cm

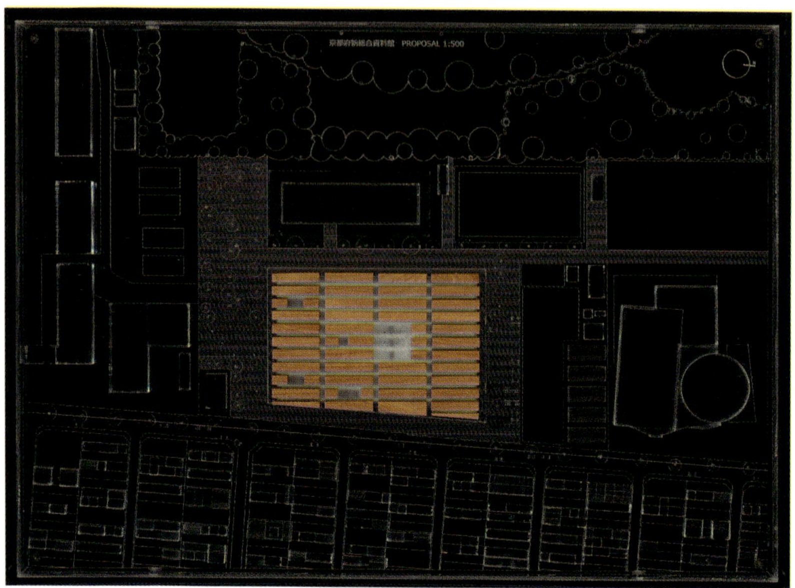

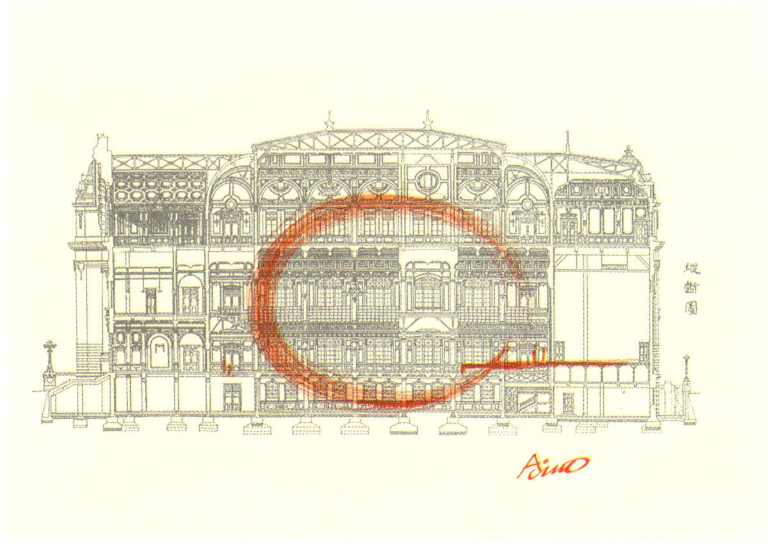

Thomas Heatherwick CBE RA
Coal Drops Yard
Mixed media
H 33 cm

Spencer de Grey CBE RA
Ferring Pharmaceuticals HQ, Copenhagen Study Models
Mixed media
28 × 132 cm

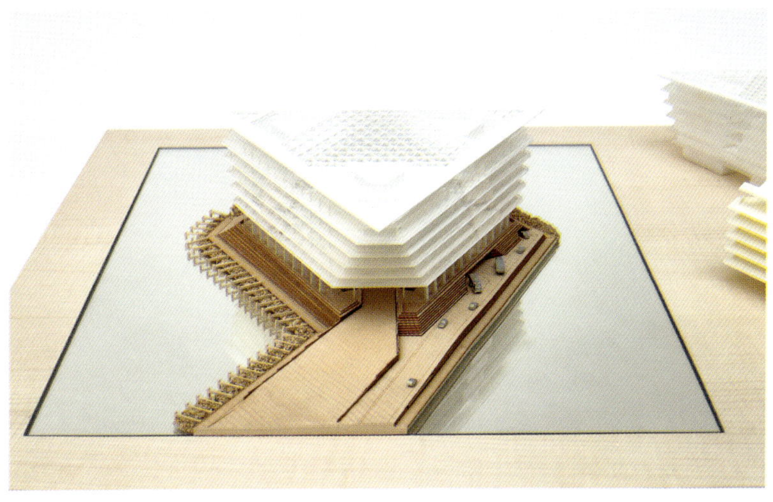

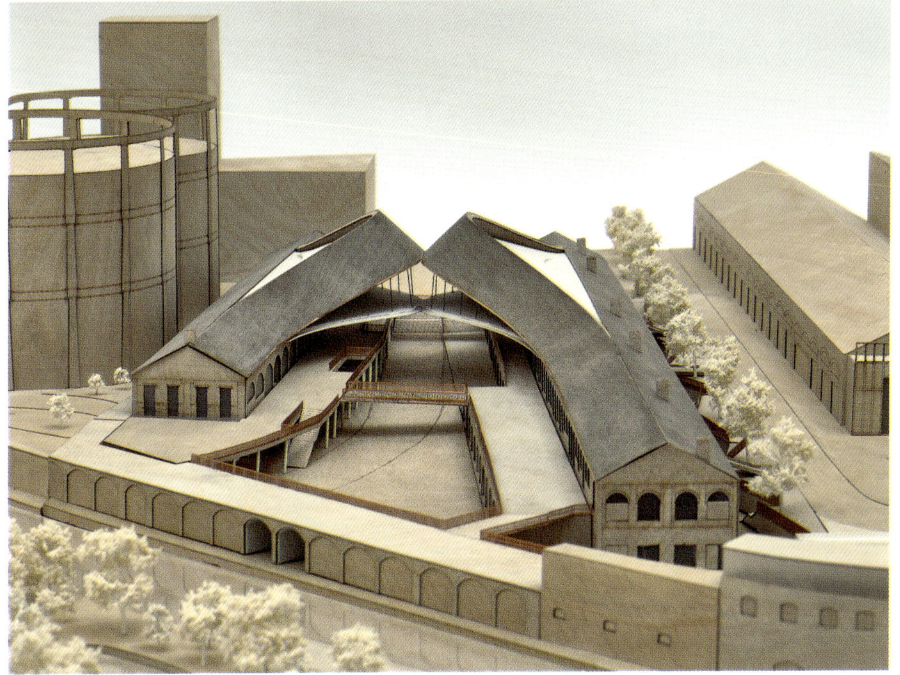

Sir Nicholas Grimshaw CBE PPRA
Studies for Dulwich College Laboratory Facades (in collaboration with Peter Randall-Page RA)
Watercolour
30 × 30 cm

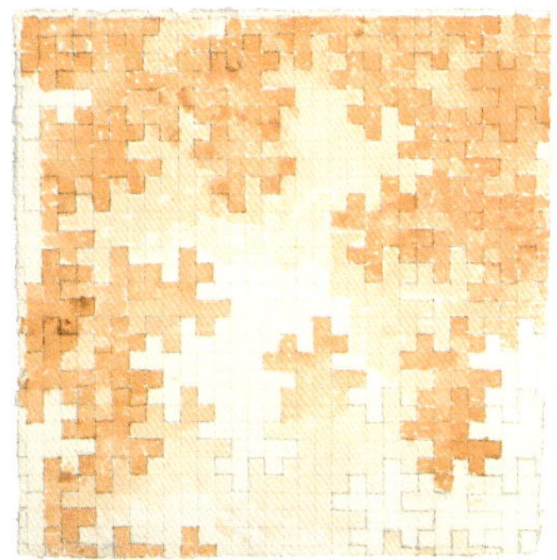

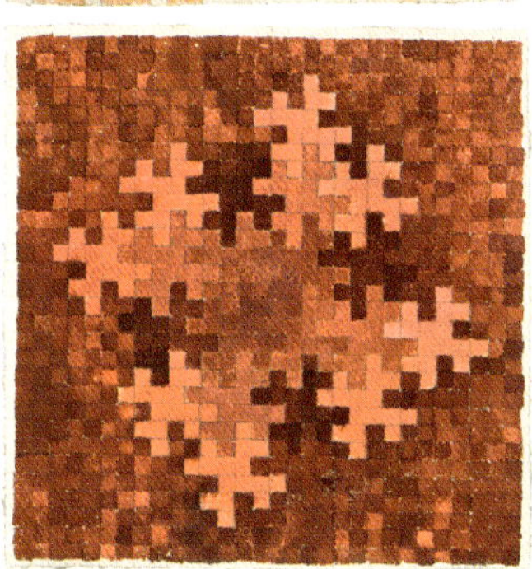

Lord Foster of Thames Bank OM RA
Droneport Sketches (detail)
Pencil
60 × 40 cm

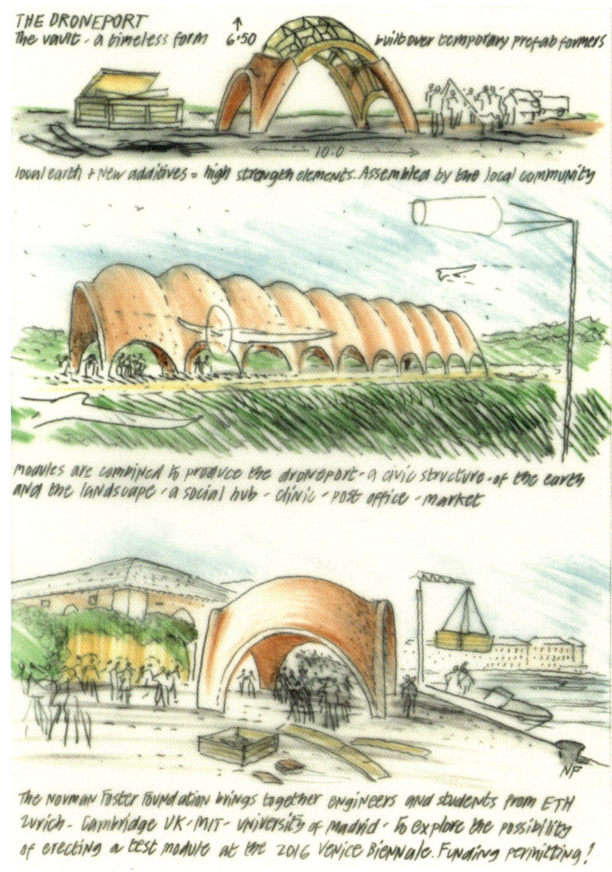

Prof Trevor Dannatt OBE RA
Scaffold, Home and Abroad (detail)
Pencil
30 × 43 cm

Michael Manser CBE RA PPRIBA
Unbuilt
Photograph
65 × 65 cm

Paul Koralek CBE RA
Leaf Forms 2
Pencil
41 × 31 cm

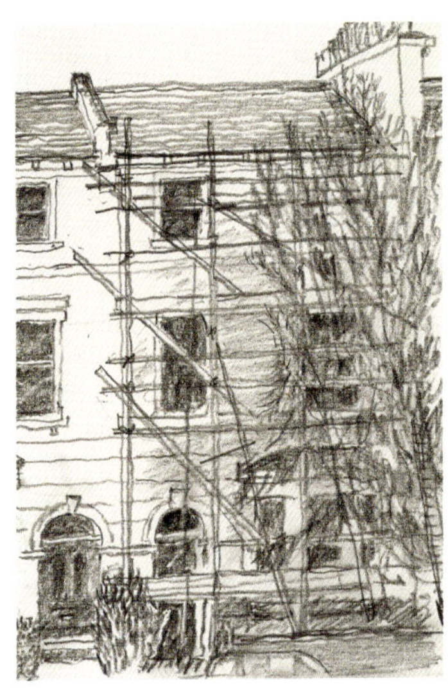

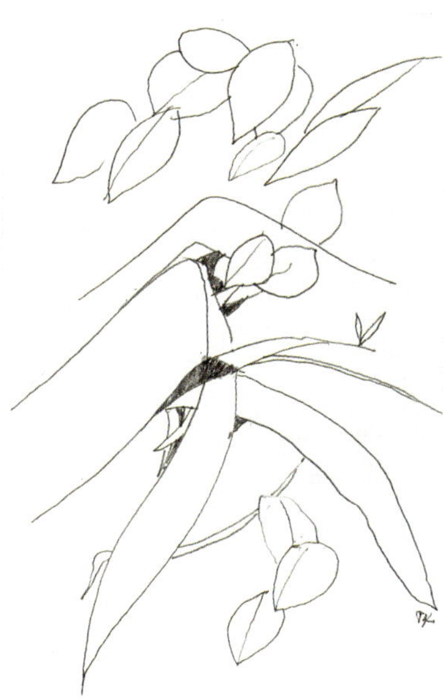

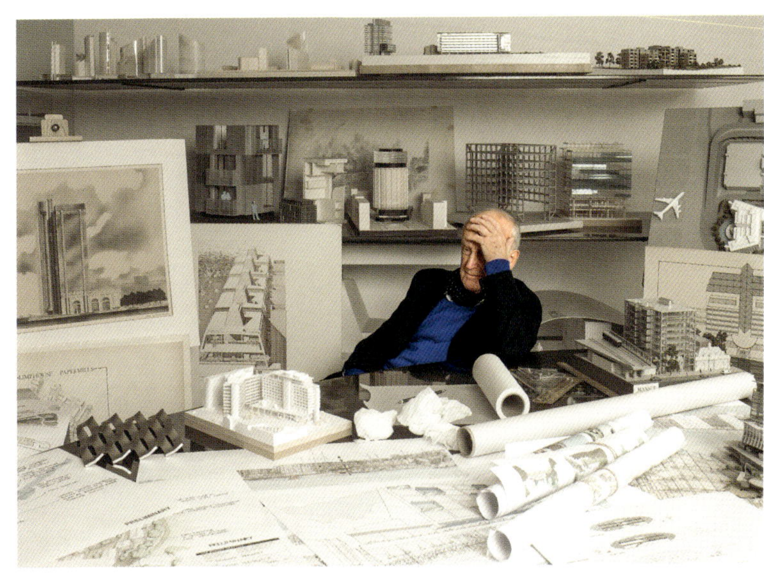

Stanton Williams
Intangible
Jesmonite
H 150 cm

Farshid Moussavi RA
EC3M 5DJ
Digital print on aluminium
100 × 80 cm

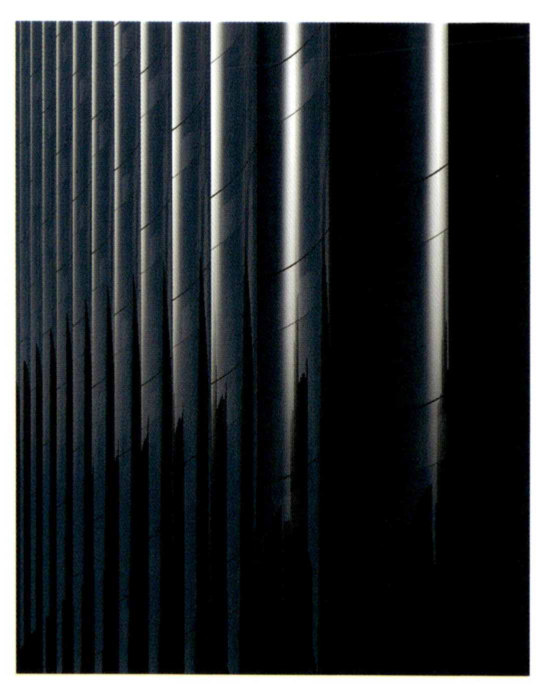

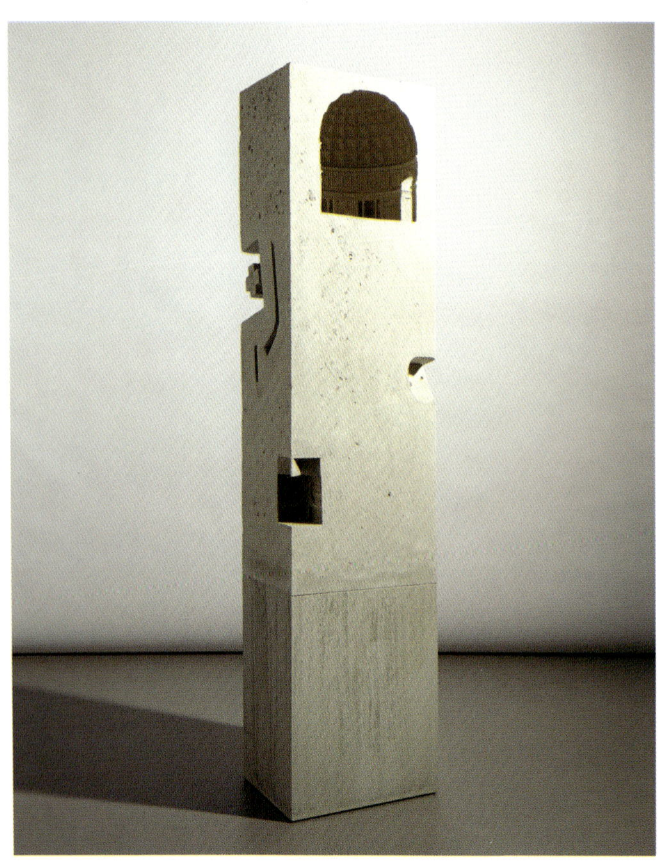

Louisa Hutton OBE RA
Homage to the City
Digital print
120 × 120 cm

Prof Ian Ritchie CBE RA
Triangle de la Folie, La Défense, Paris
Etching
27 × 35 cm

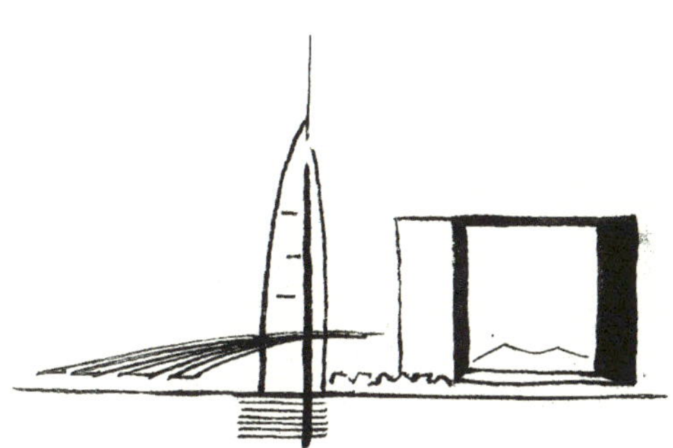

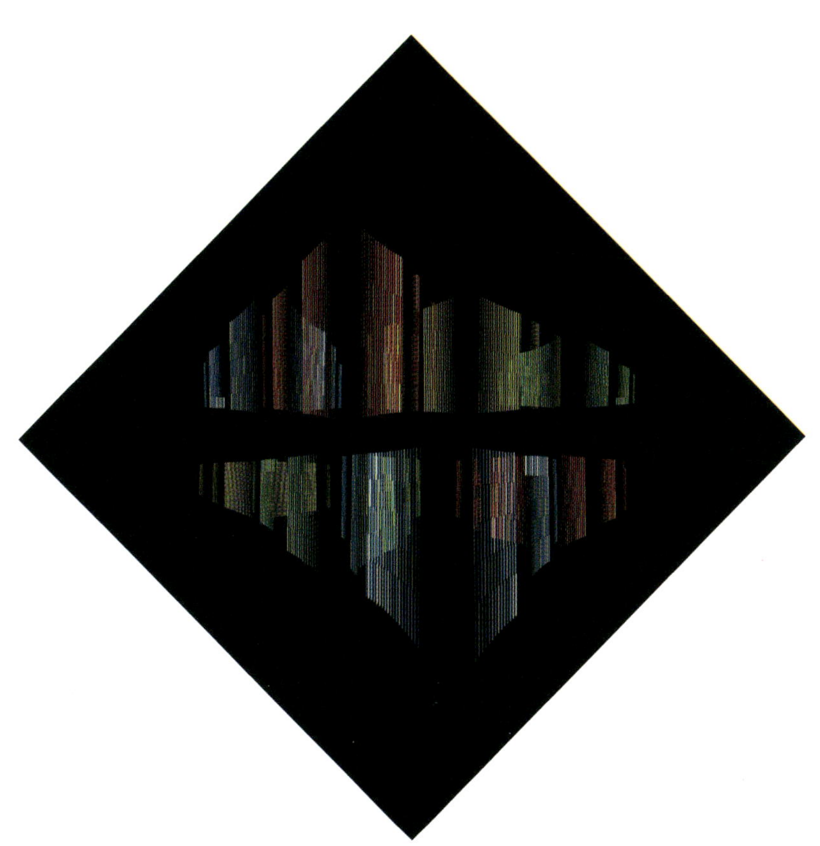

Prof Michael Sandle RA
Vanitas
Mixed media
188 × 122 cm

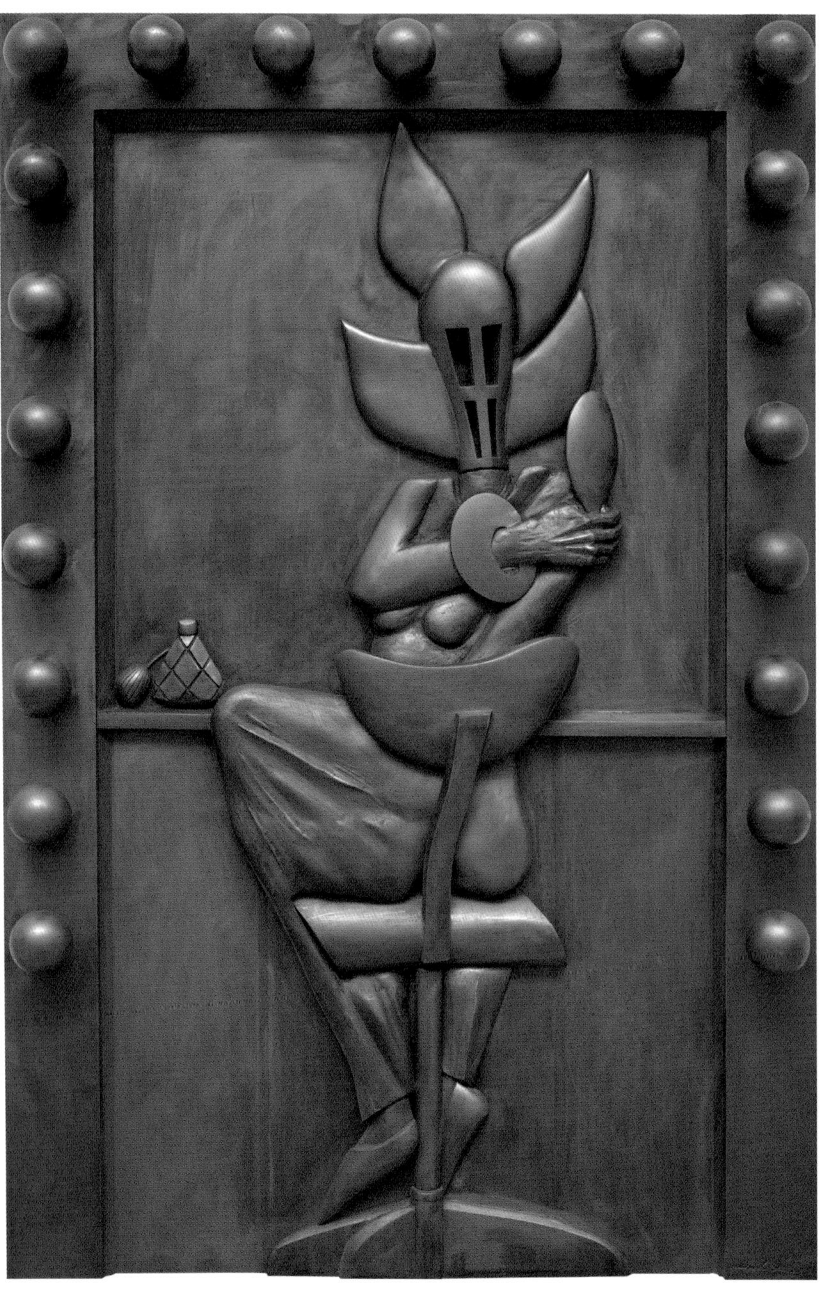

Tim Shaw RA
Eric
Old clothes, fabric and steel
H 180 cm

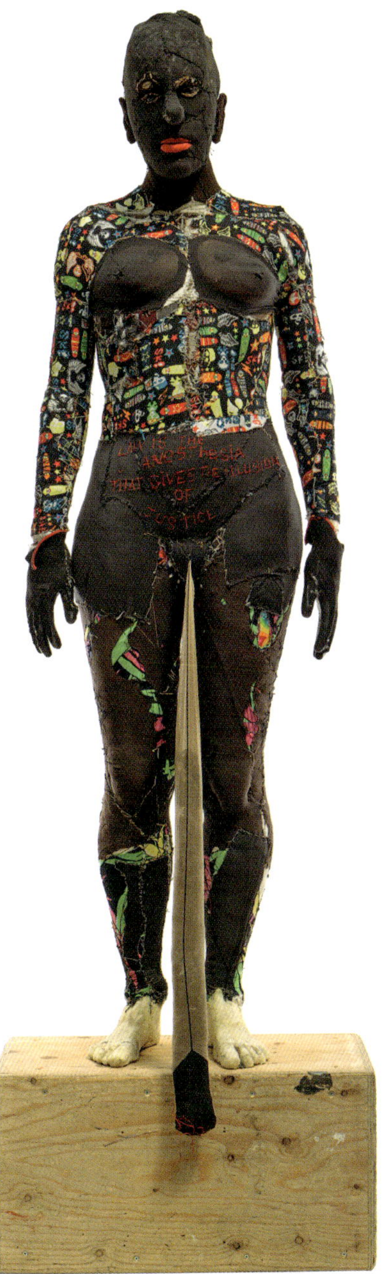

Stephen Haines
Iggy
Bronze
H 172 cm

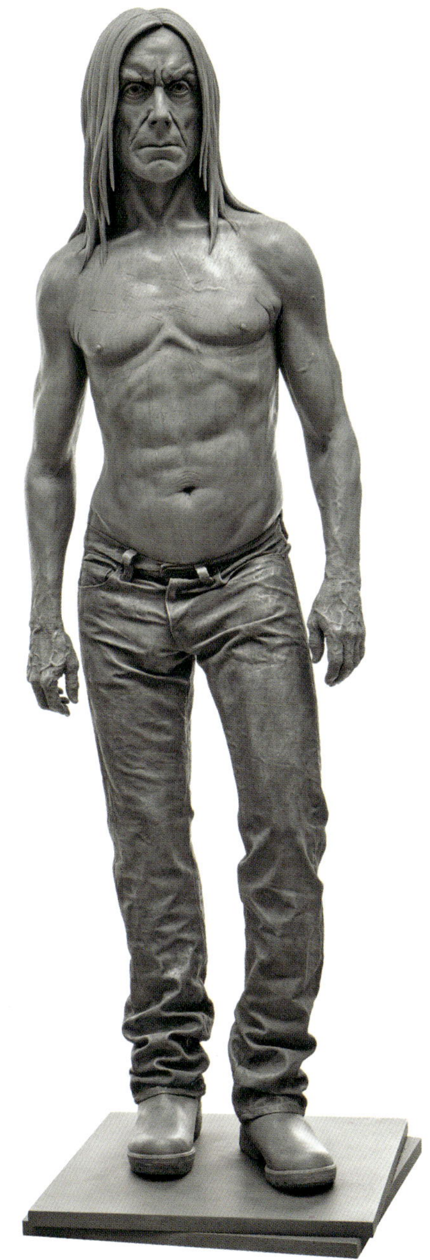

John Maine RA
Echo
Conté
96 × 130 cm

Madi Acharya-Baskerville
The Bride
Wood and found objects
H 35 cm

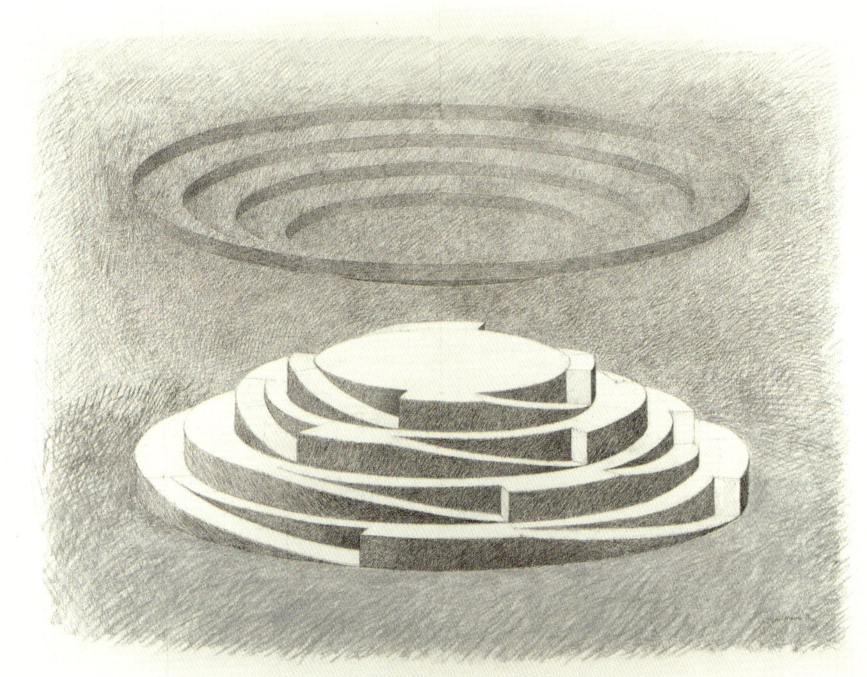

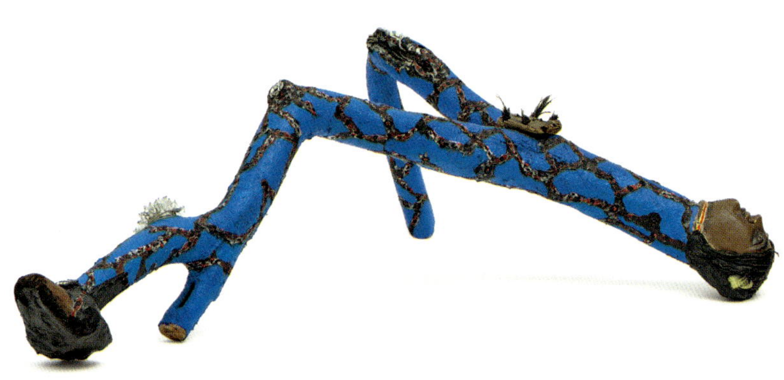

Conrad Shawcross RA
Plosion 3 (Blue)
Aluminium and glass
H 119 cm

Richard Woods
Bad Bricks 7
Wood
H 89 cm

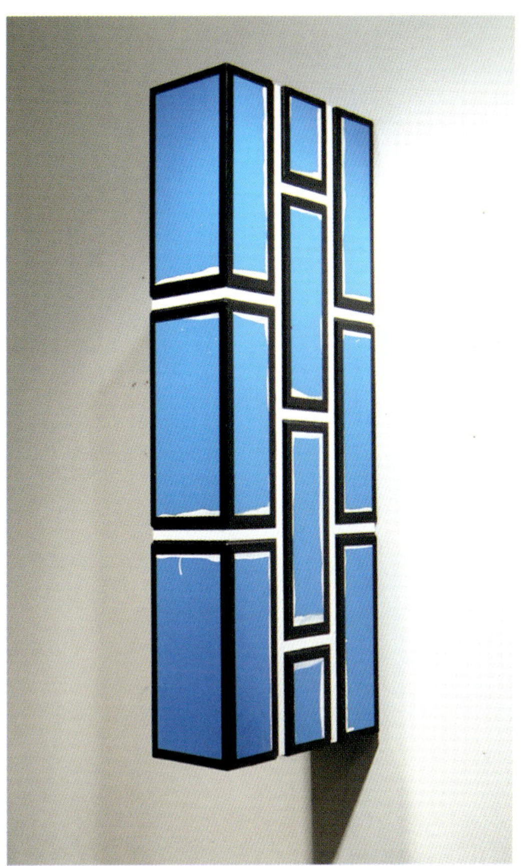

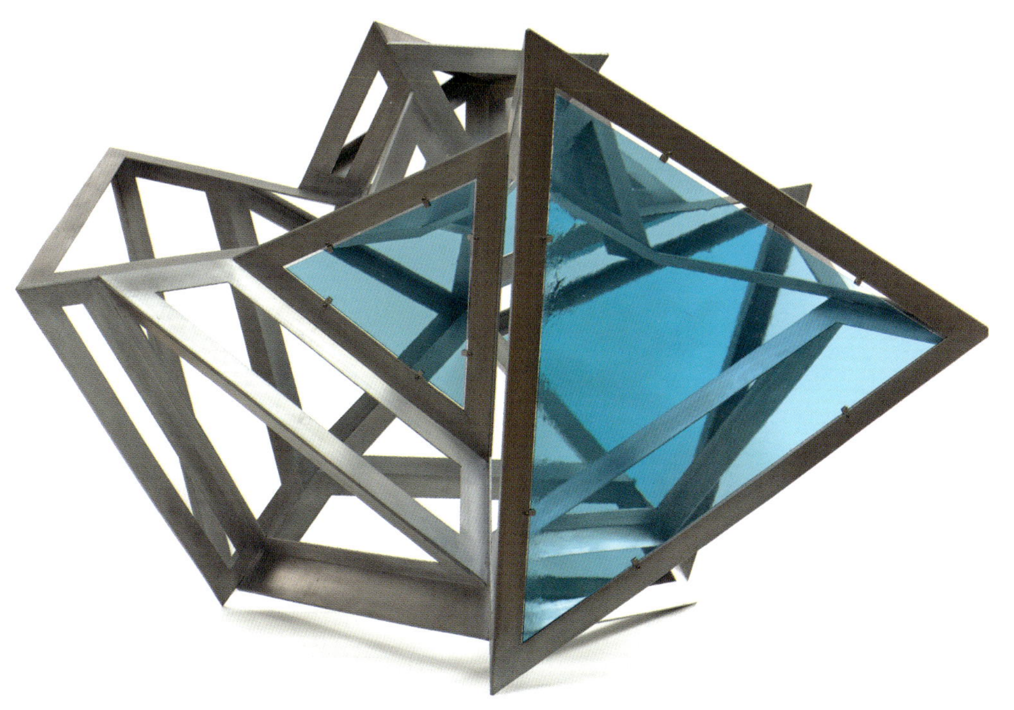

Lisa Milroy RA
Outfit
Lithograph and chine-collé
73 × 58 cm

William Tucker RA
Study for Odalisque
Bronze
H 71 cm

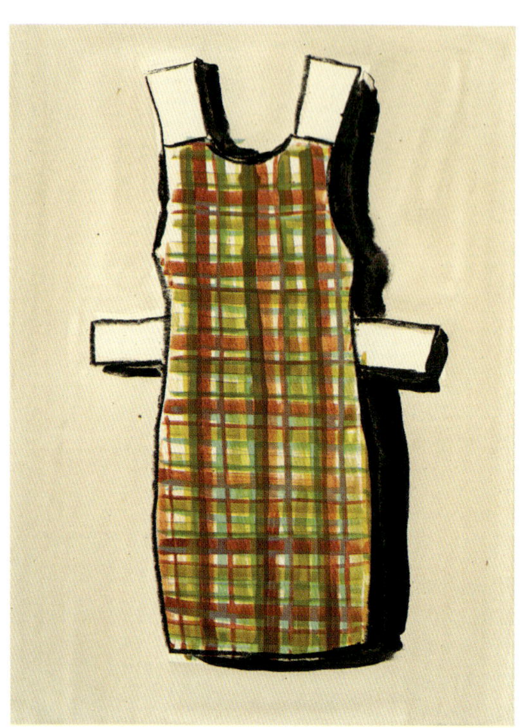

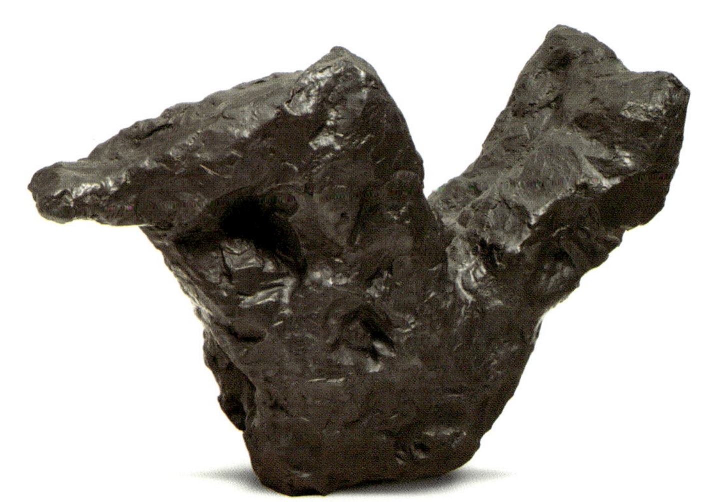

Allen Jones RA
Action Painting
Painted fibreglass, stainless steel and paint pot
H 205 cm

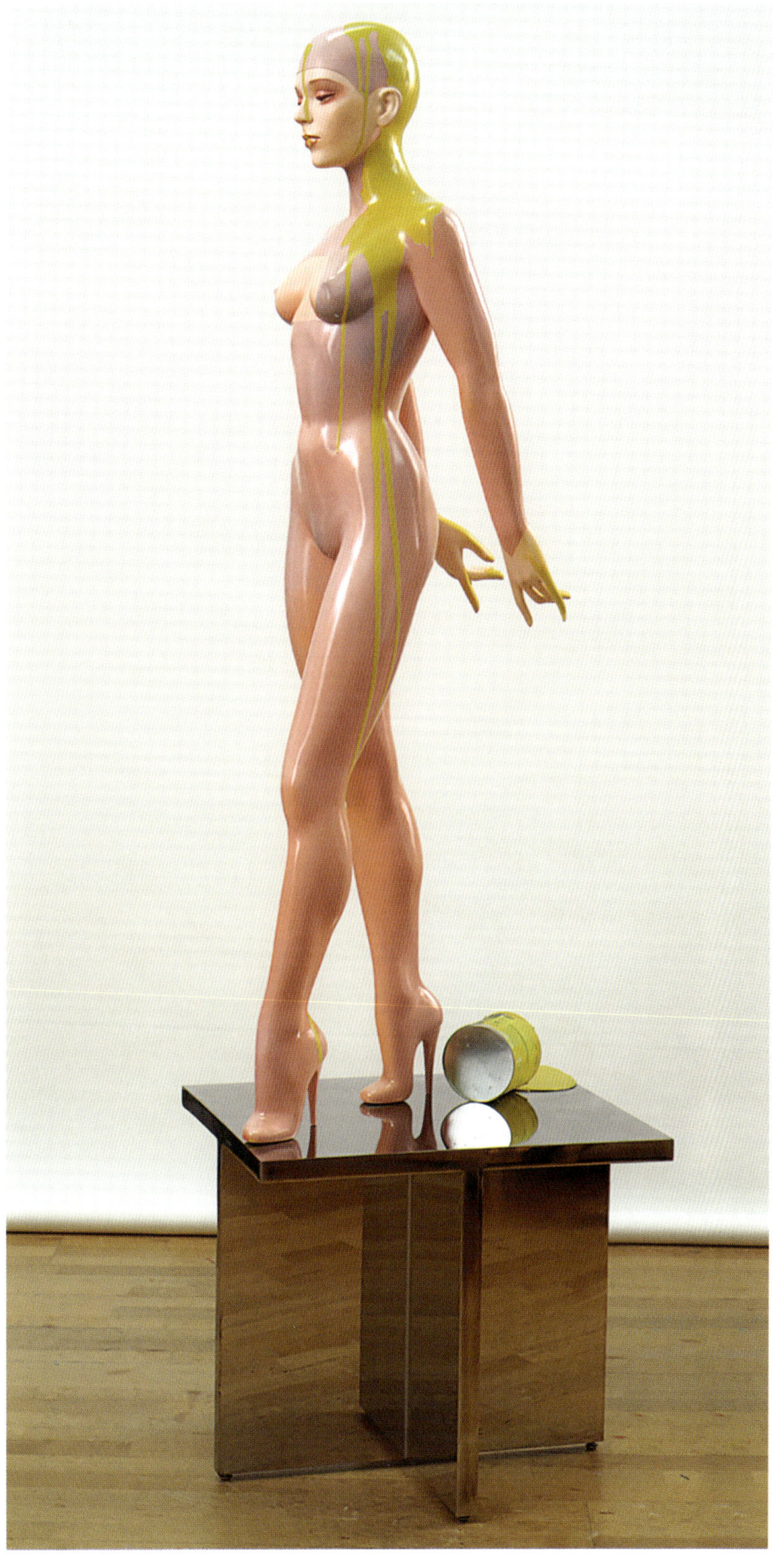

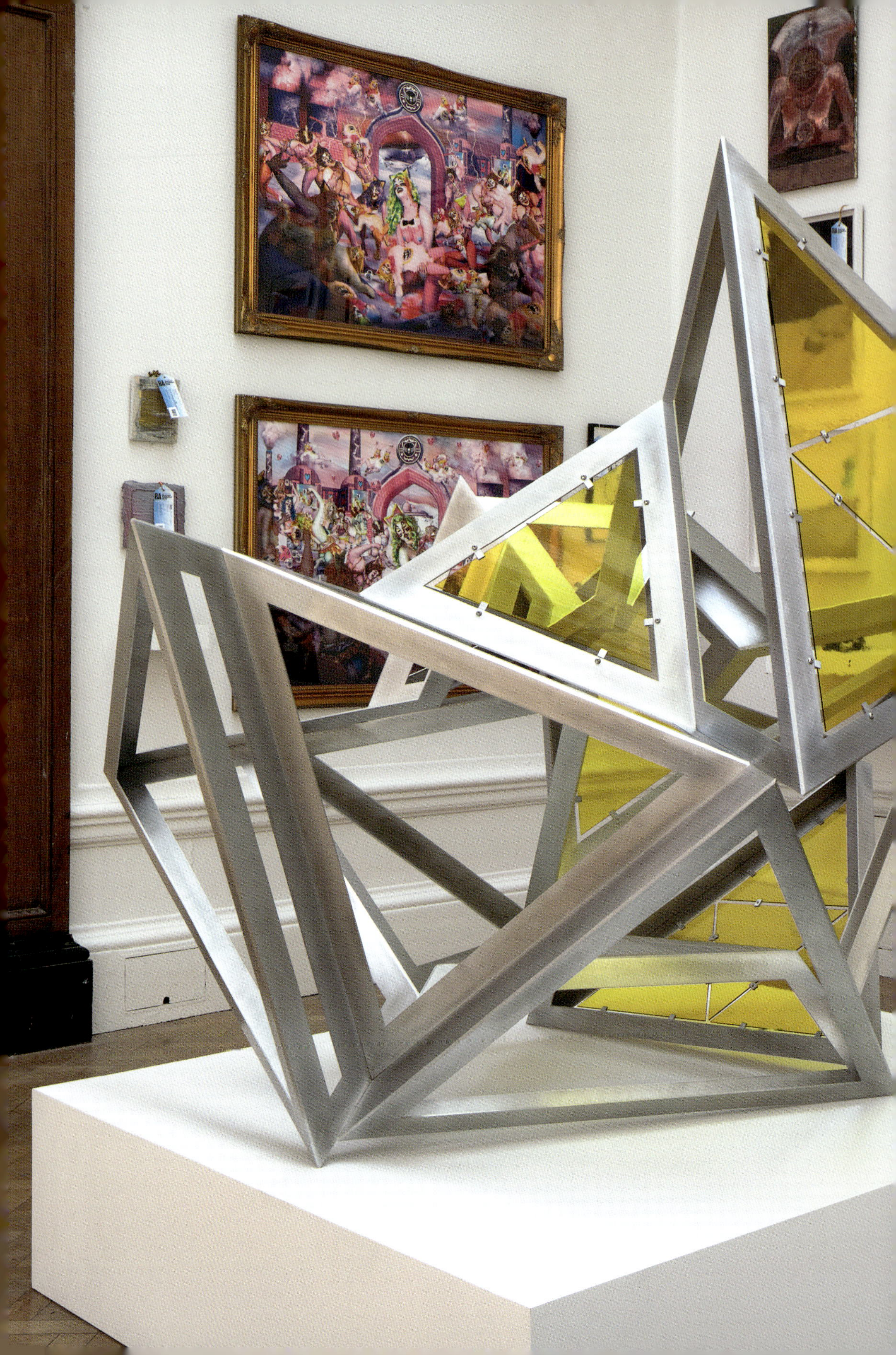

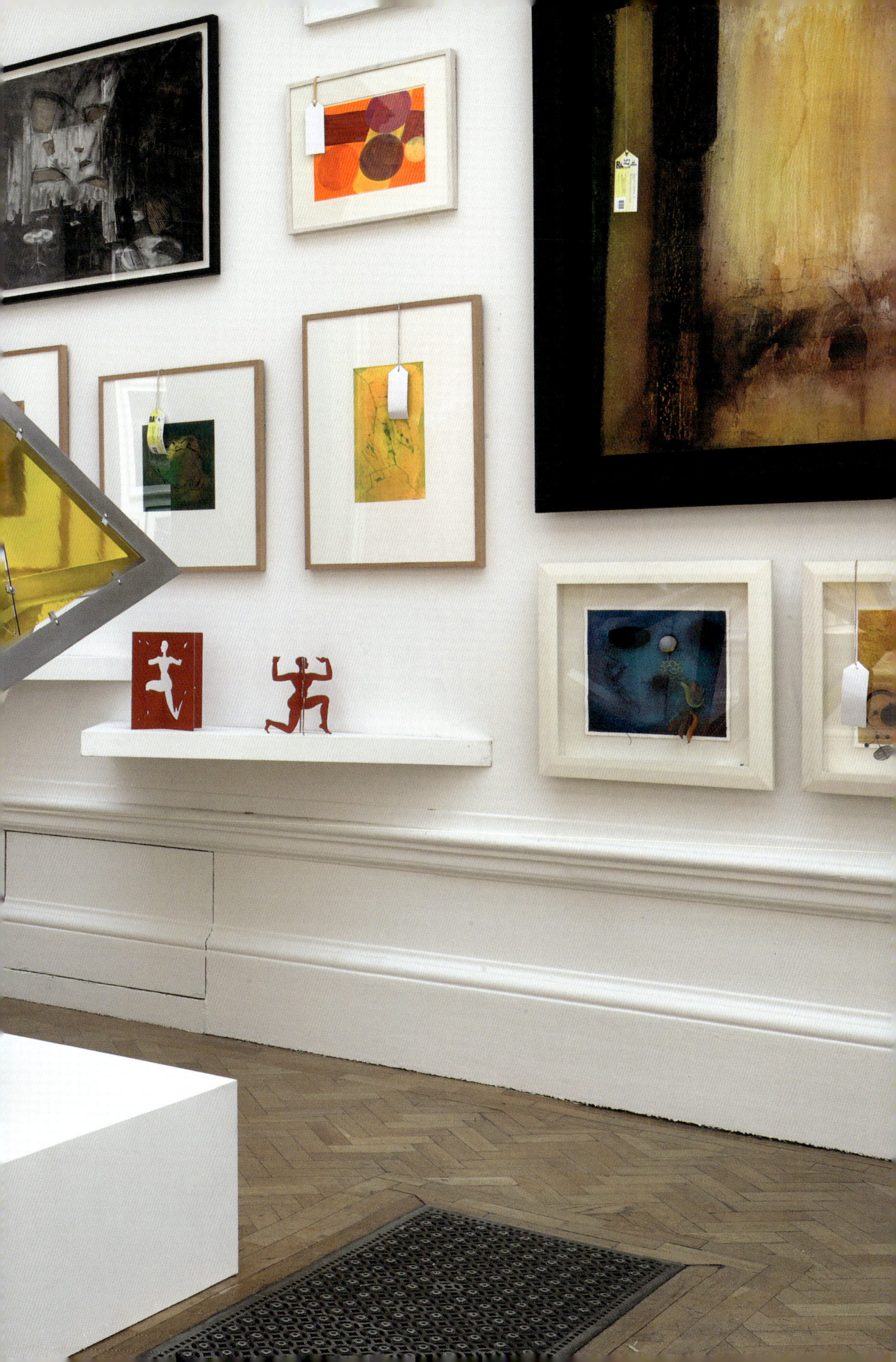

Prof Brian Catling RA
Flea Bowl 2 (After Blake)
Mixed media
H 130 cm

Beatrice Haines
Allochthonous Body
3D print and carbon
H 25 cm

David Nash OBE RA
Big Black
Charred redwood
H 380 cm

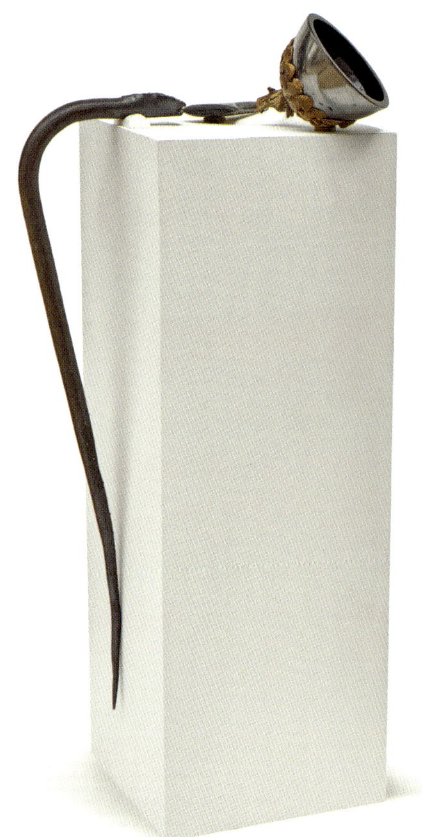

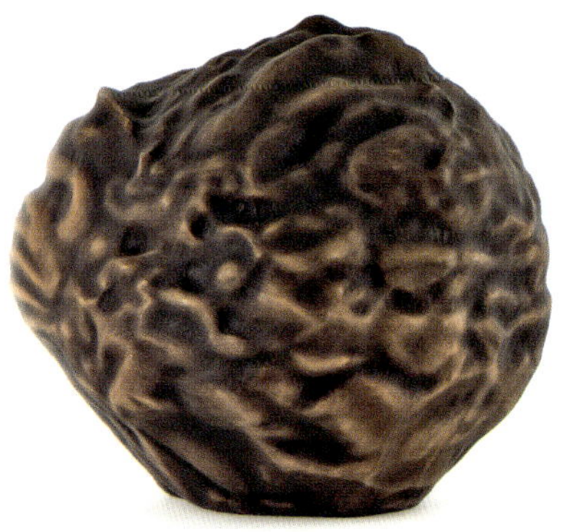

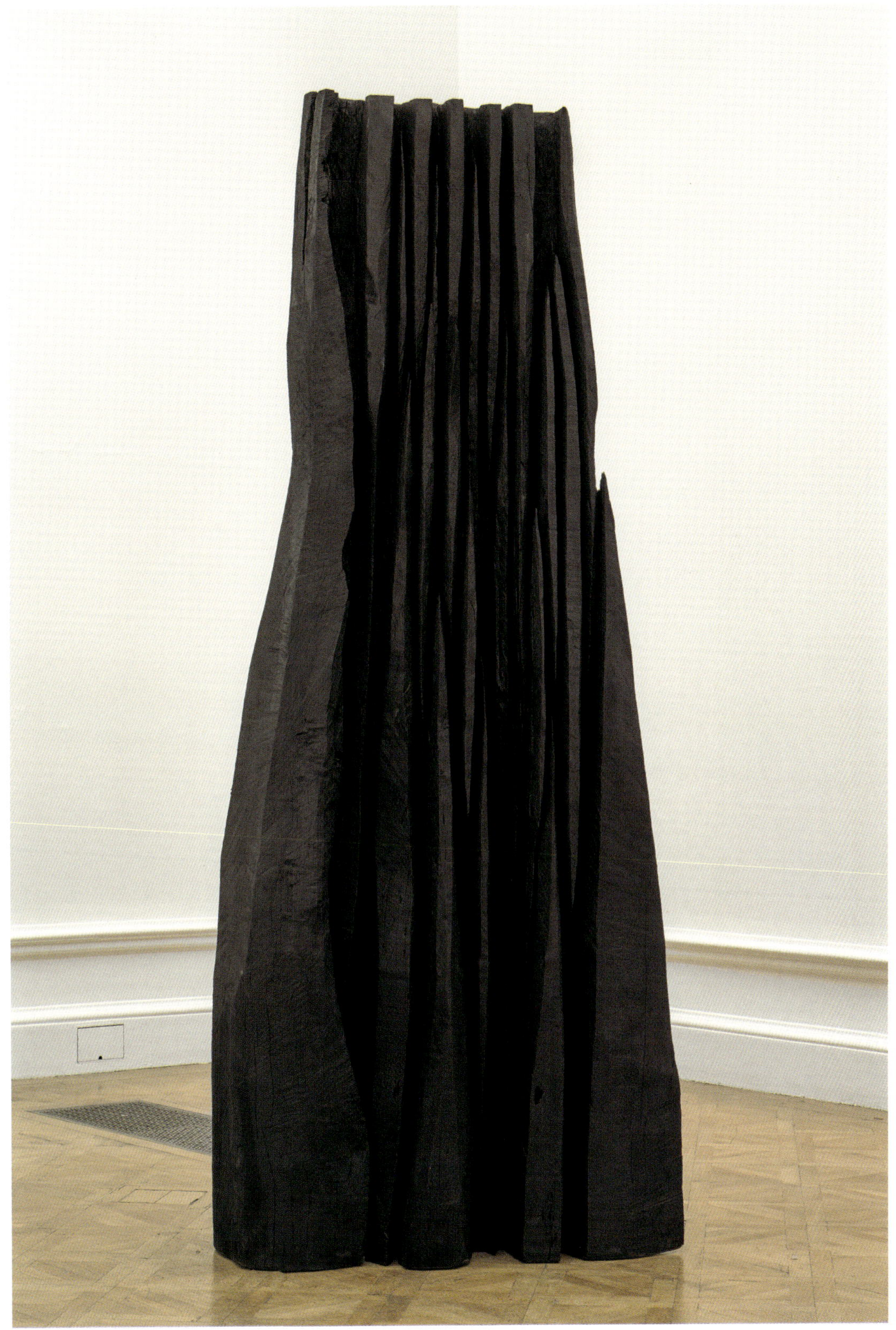

Cathy de Monchaux
Migration
Mixed media
70 × 200 cm

Michael Burton + Michiko Nitta
The Abandoned Biobot Type 3
Mixed media
H 106 cm

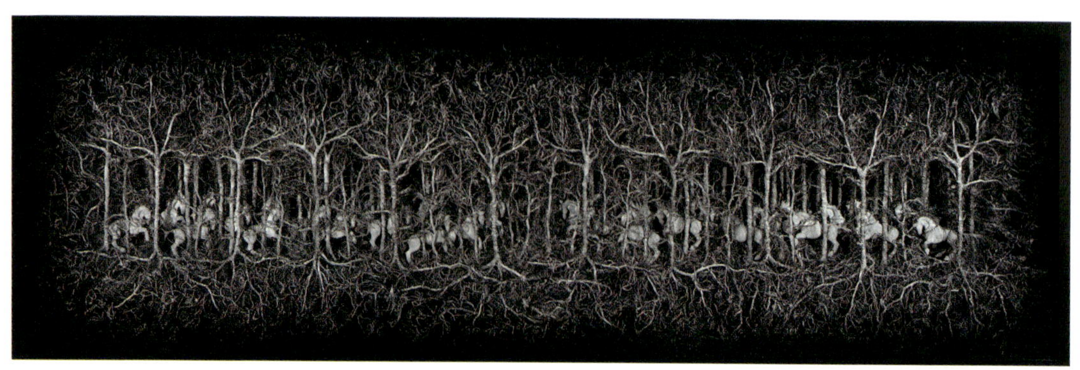

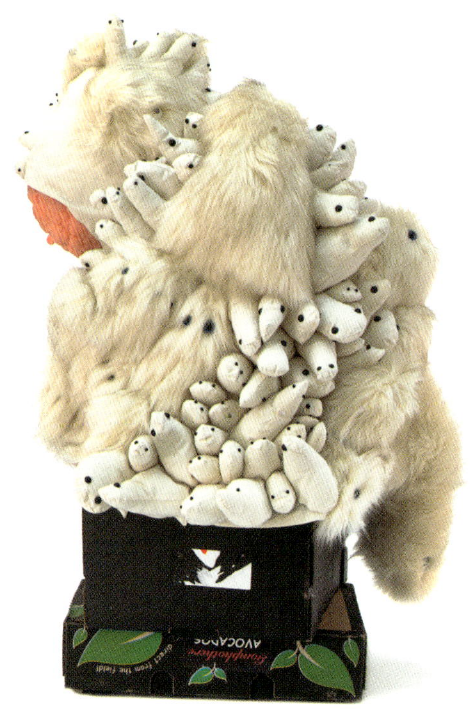

Phyllida Barlow RA
untitled: noplace; 2016
Mixed media
H 175 cm

Neil Jeffries RA
Orange Thought
Oil on metal
H 34 cm

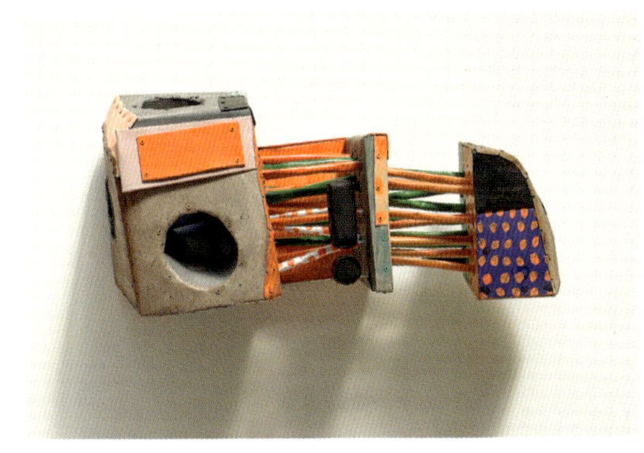

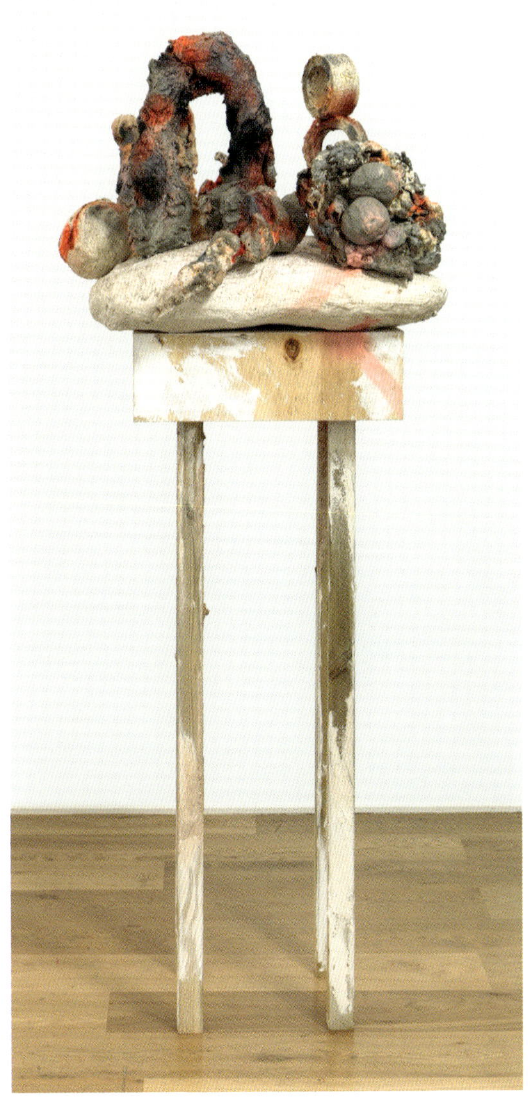

Prof David Mach RA
Silver Hart
Coat hangers and steel
160 × 143 cm

Laura Ford
Silent Howler (1)
Bronze
H 107 cm

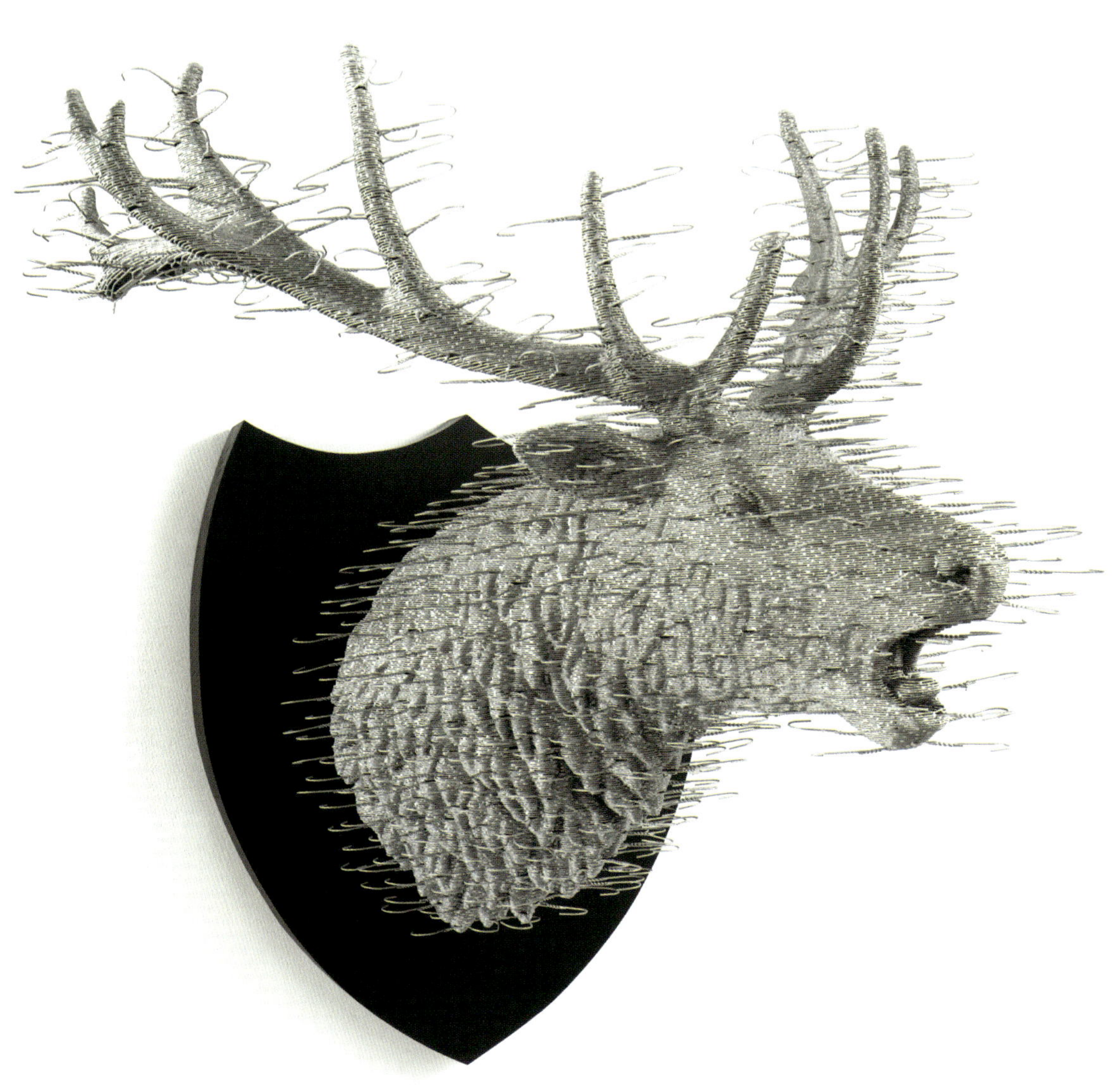

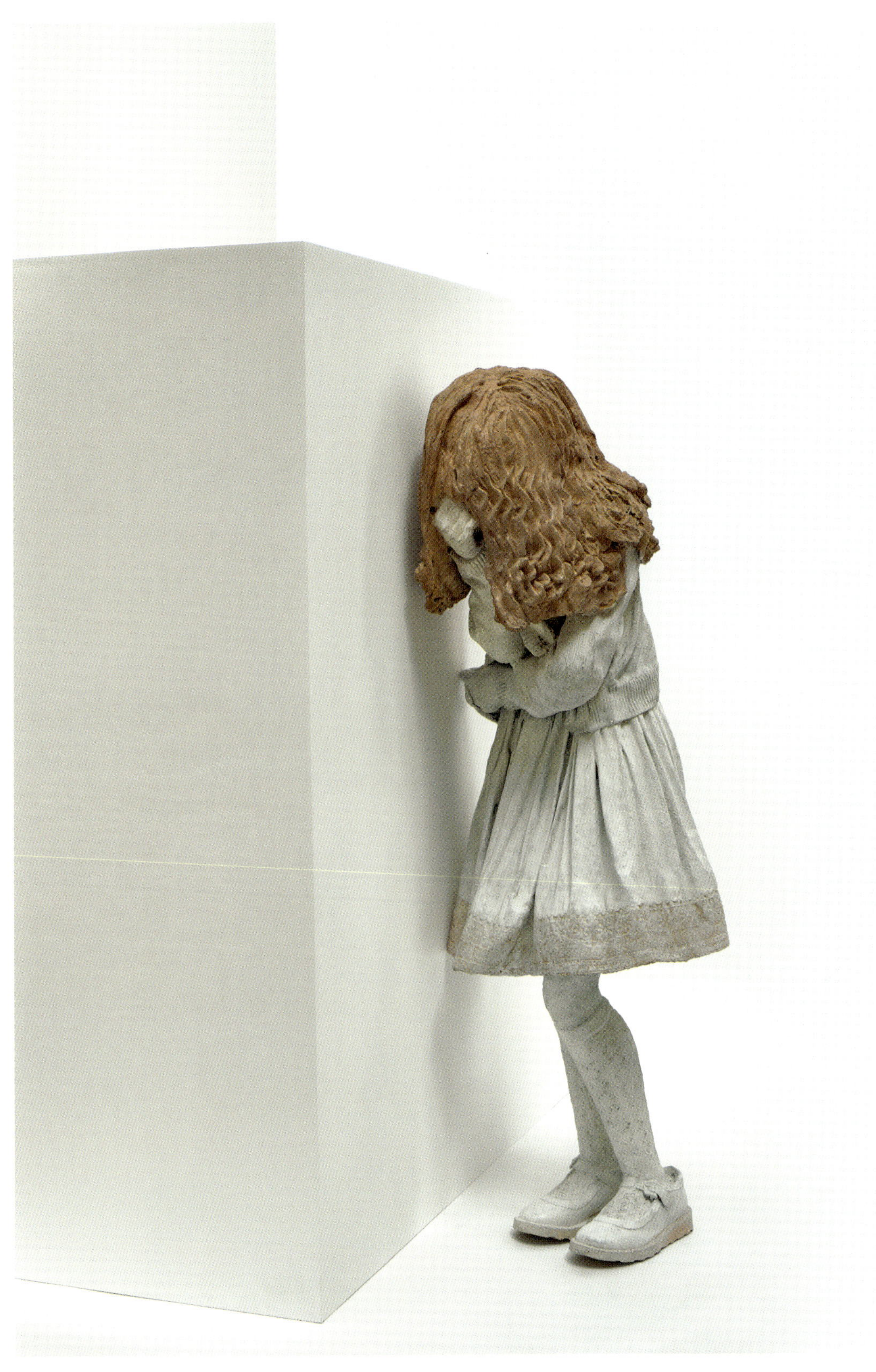

Bob and Roberta Smith RA
What Unites Human Beings is Huge and Wonderful
Signwriters' paint on found doors
197 × 154 cm

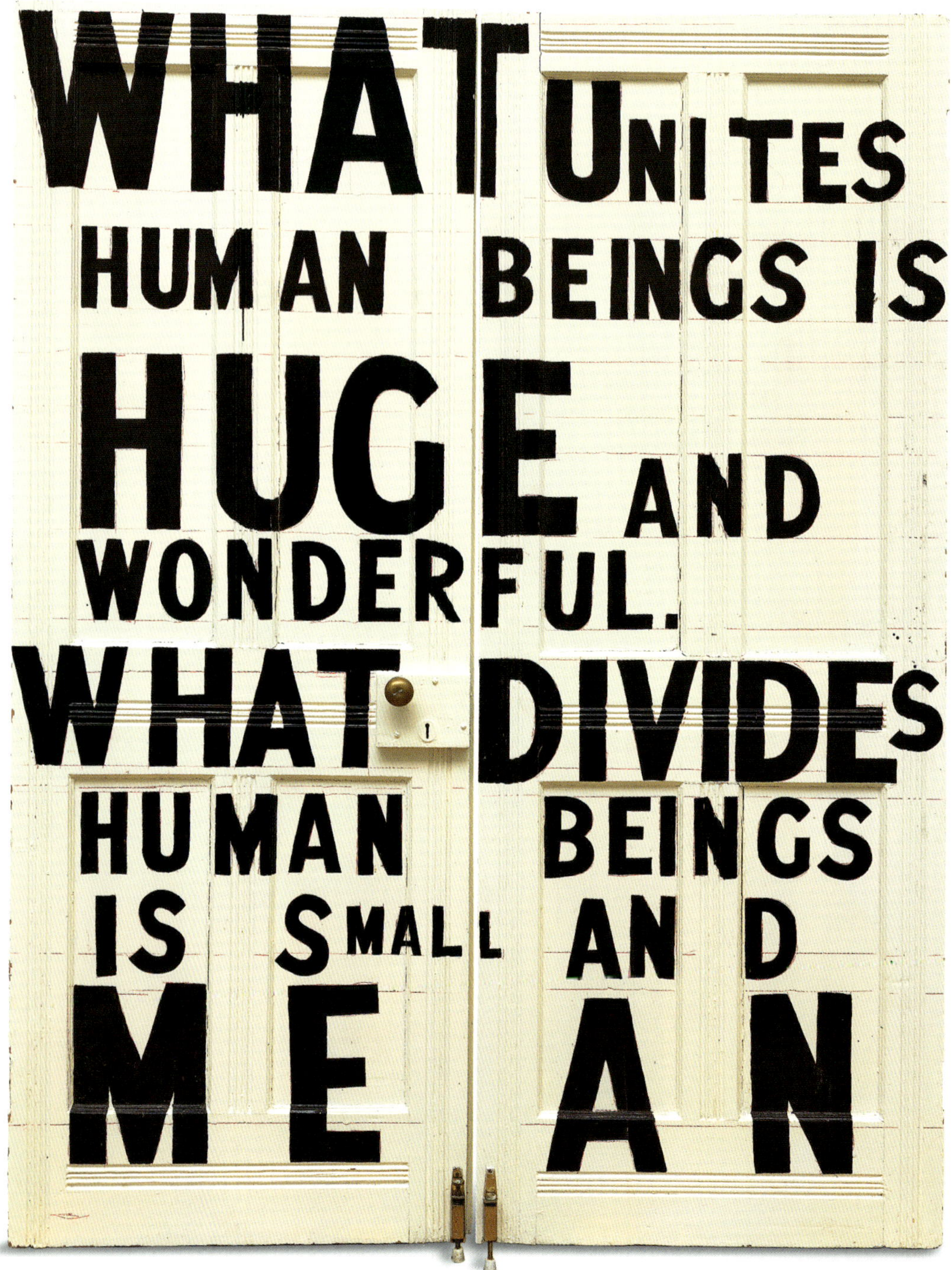

Richard Wilson RA
Wheelhouse
Mixed media
H 47 cm

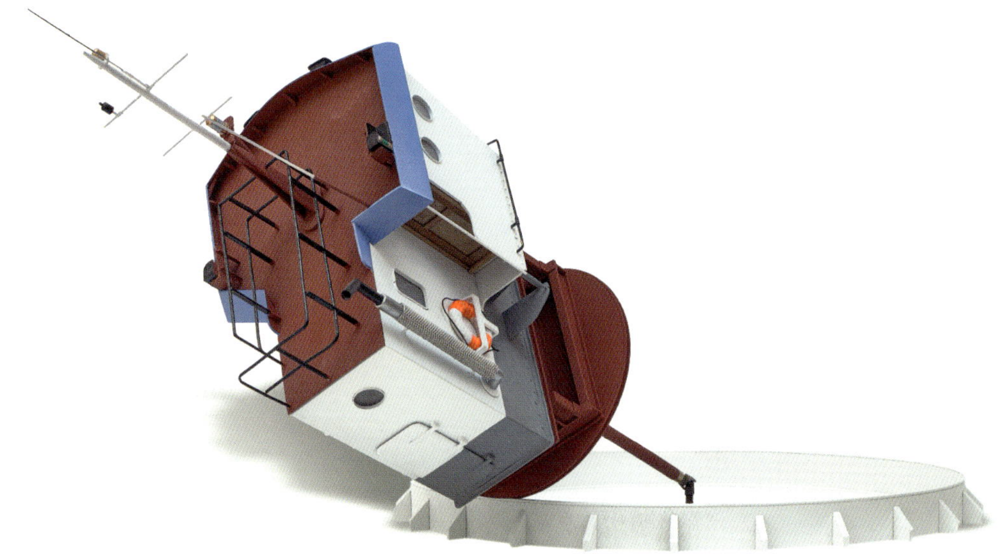

Eric Parry RA
Design for a Large Rug
Pencil and watercolour
60 × 60 cm

Tal R
Satie Moon Walking
Mixed media
H 102 cm

Sir Anish Kapoor CBE RA
Untitled
Alabaster
90 × 60 cm

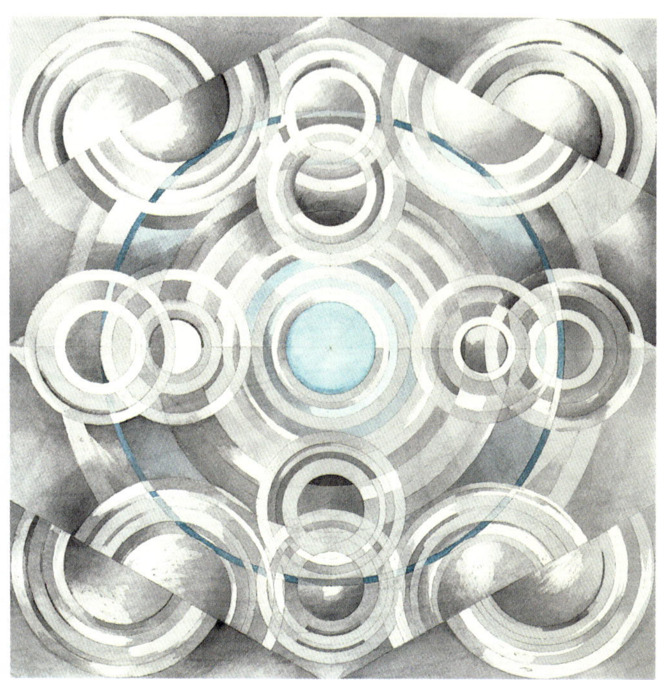

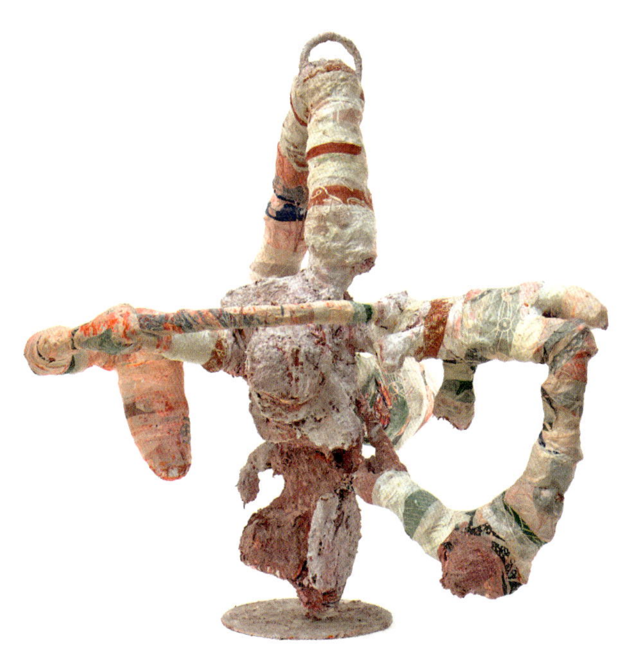

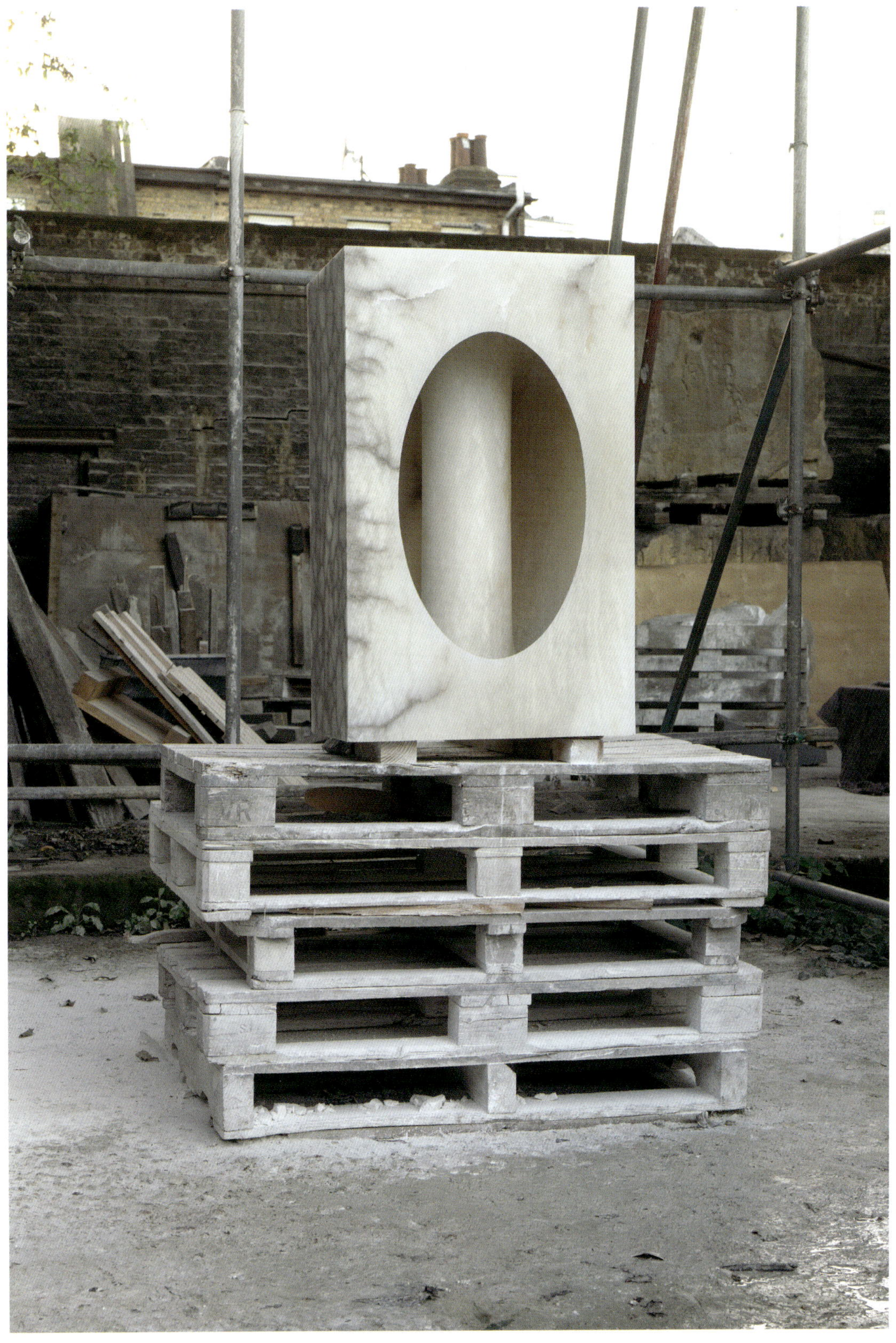

Manijeh Yadegar Hall
C22-02 and C1-03 (Diptych)
Oil
37 × 83 cm

Jeff Lowe
Solitude
Welded aluminium
H 47 cm

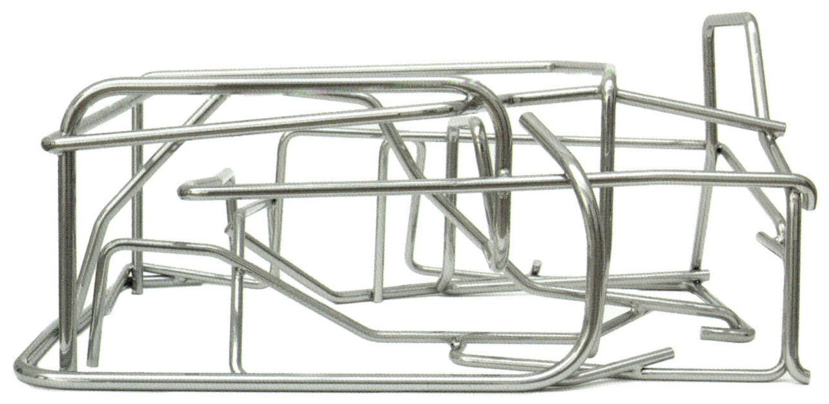

Nigel Hall RA
Around Tiger Island
Painted wood
H 43 cm

Vanessa Jackson RA
Riff II
Oil
30 × 26 cm

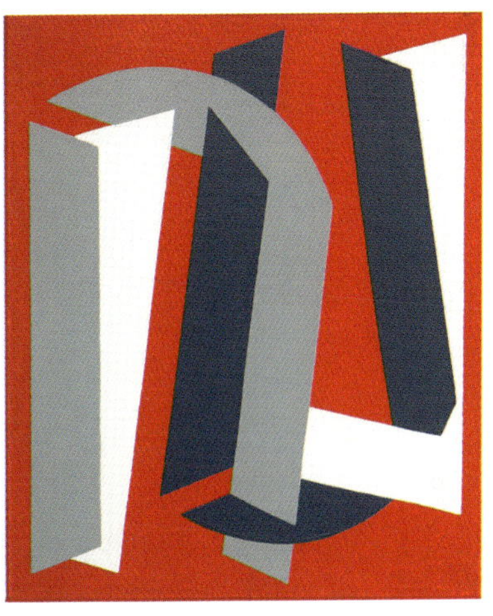

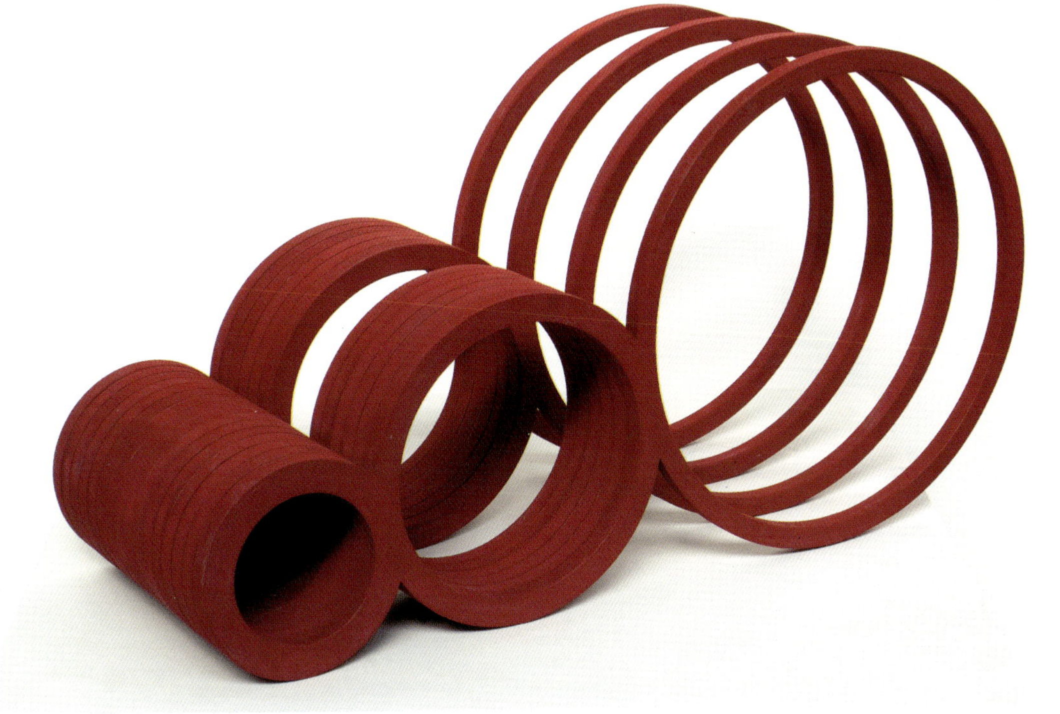

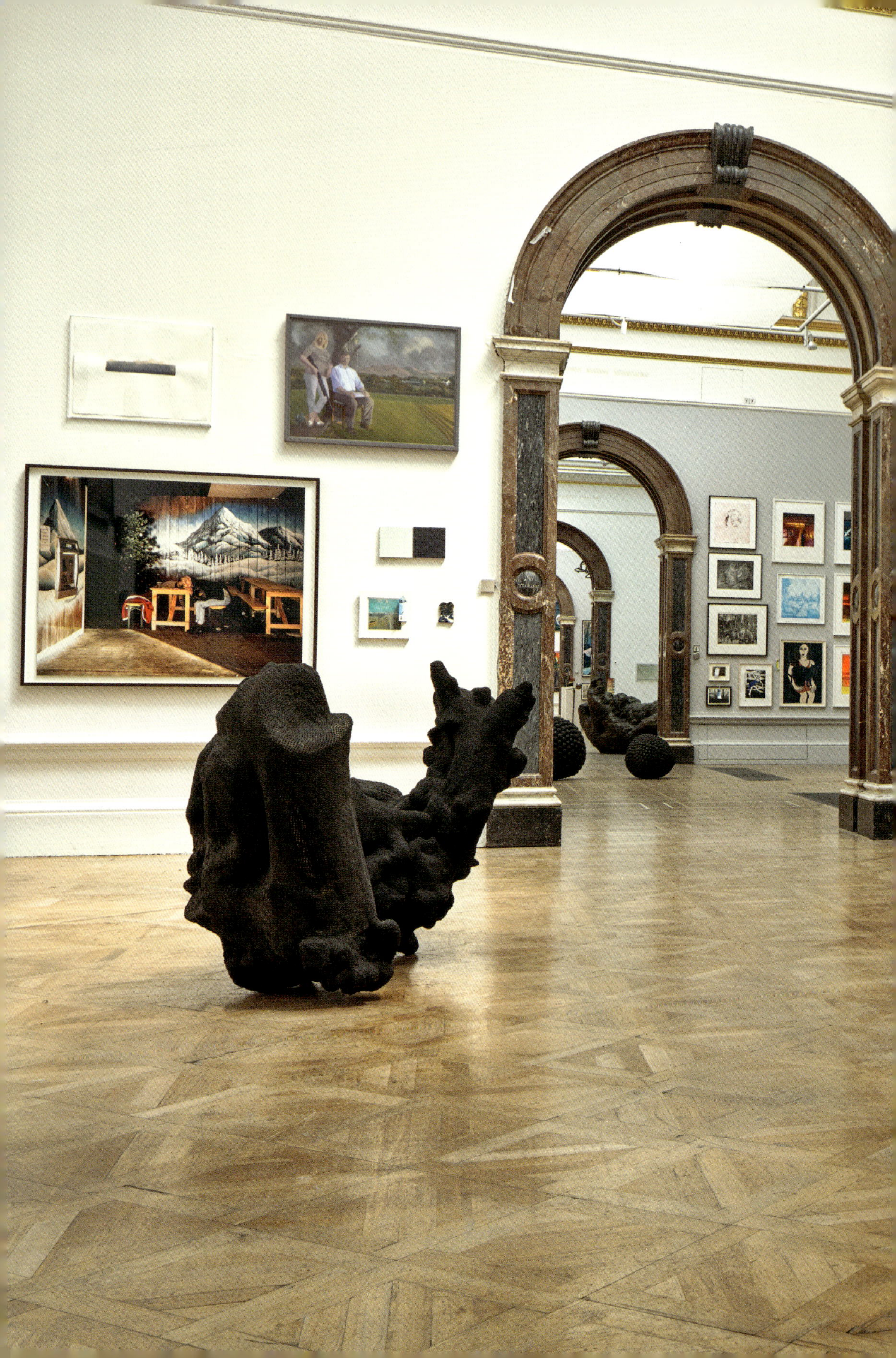

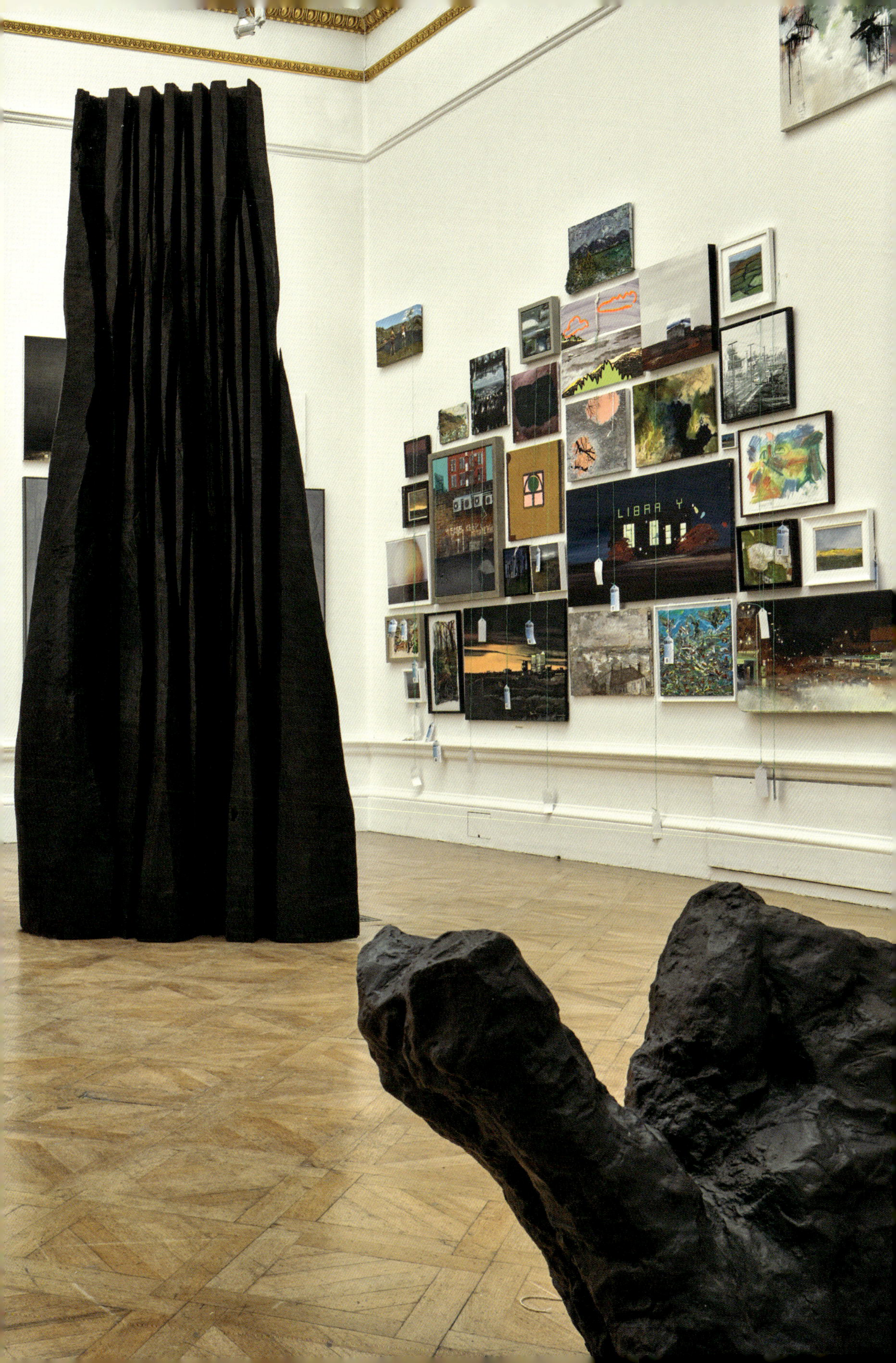
LIBRA Y

Timothy Hyman RA
My London Cosmos
Oil on wood
39 × 30 cm

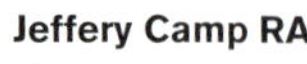

Jeffery Camp RA
Azure
Oil on board
57 × 63 cm

Eileen Cooper RA
Ballerina
Oil
152 × 107 cm

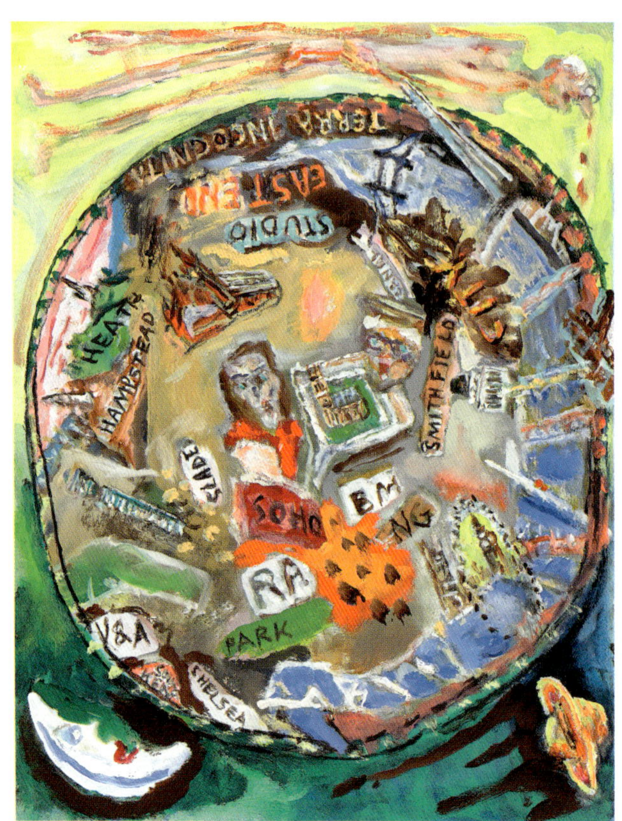

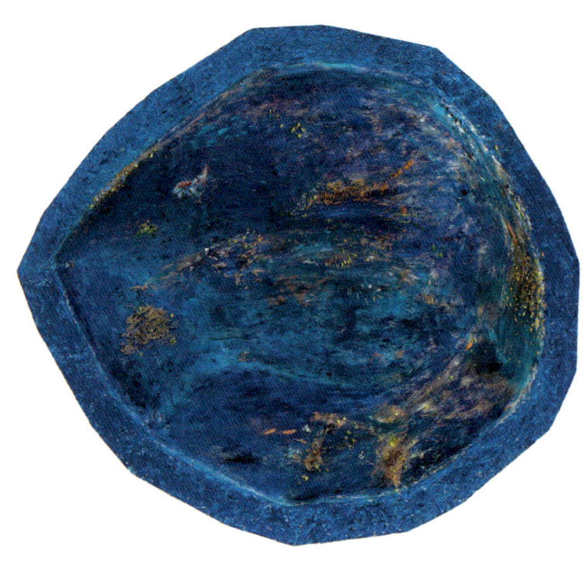

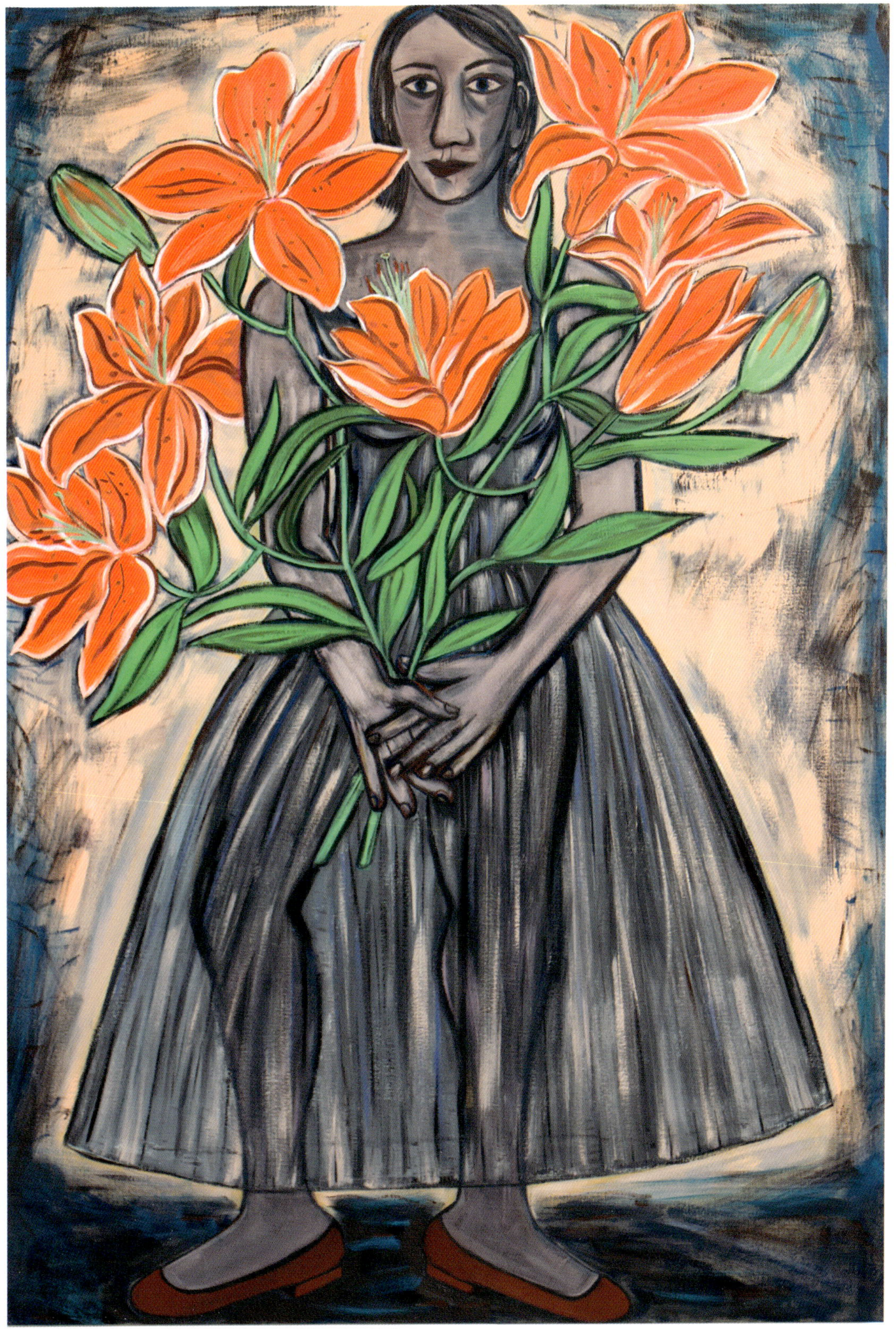

Bernard Dunstan RA
Kitchen Conversation
Oil
29 × 28 cm

Diana Armfield RA
Roses and Sweetpeas on the Kitchen Table
Oil
53 × 43 cm

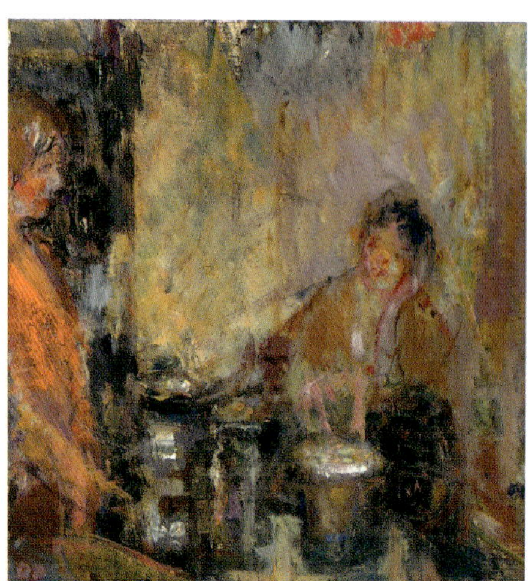

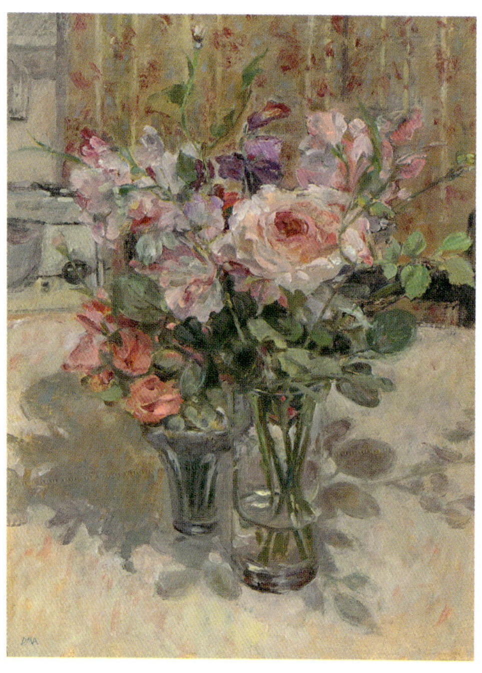

Olwyn Bowey RA
Stag's Head with Stag's Head Fern
Oil
96 × 92 cm

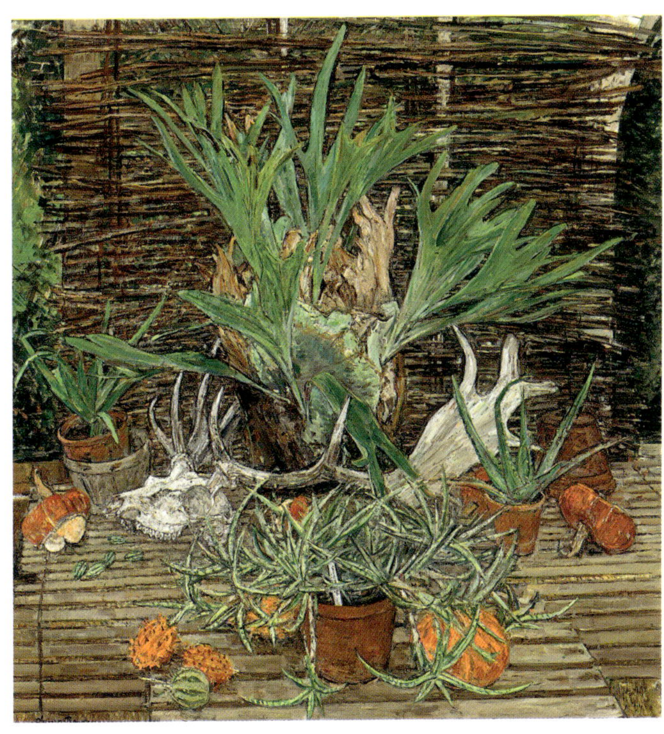

Frederick Cuming RA
Bonfire & Crescent Moon, Hastings Beach
Oil
74 × 74 cm

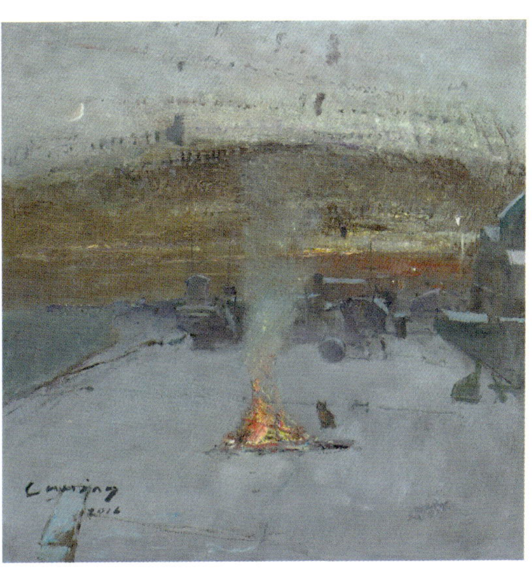

Dr Leonard McComb RA
Pansies
Pastel
50 × 64 cm

Gus Cummins RA
Structural Reform
Acrylic
58 × 78 cm

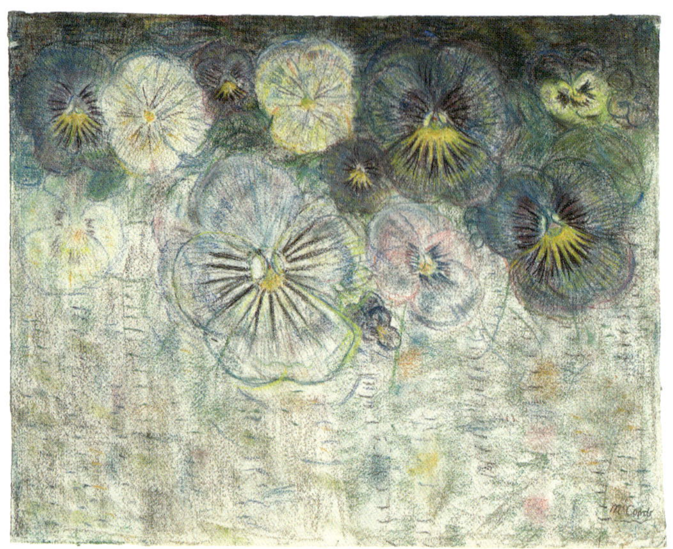

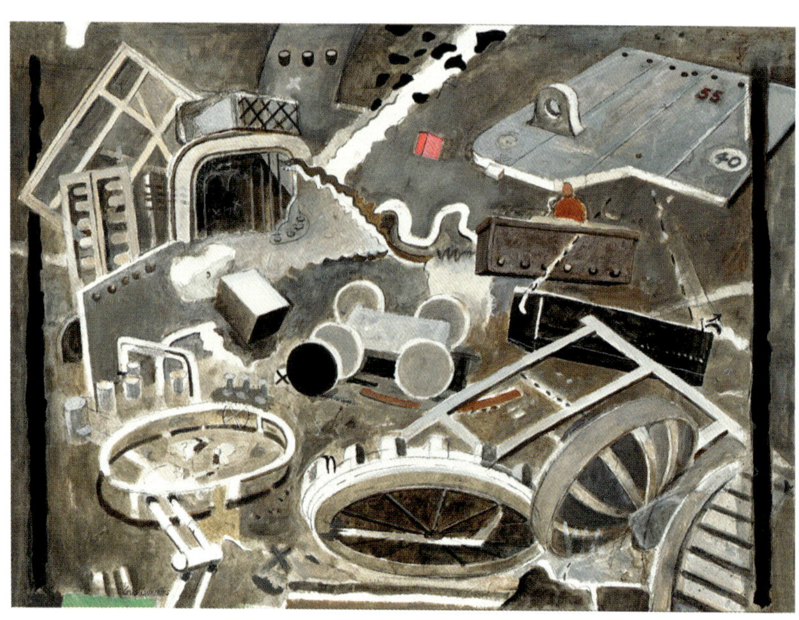

Anthony Eyton RA
Studio in the Morning
Oil
166 × 139 cm

June Berry
Morning Rendez-vous
Oil
51 × 59 cm

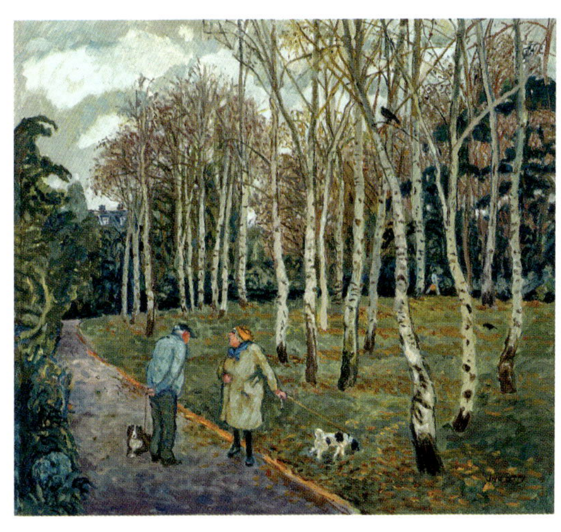

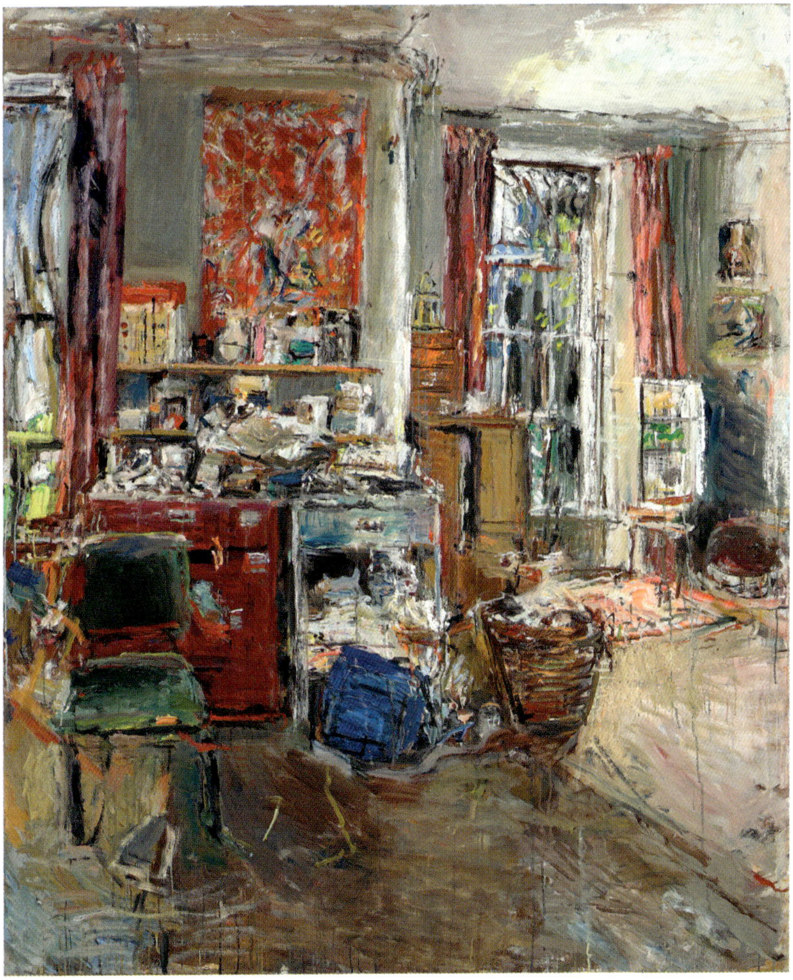

John Wragg RA
I Saw Him Dance
Acrylic
59 × 58 cm

Anthony Green RA
A Modern Olympia III
Oil on board
136 × 124 cm

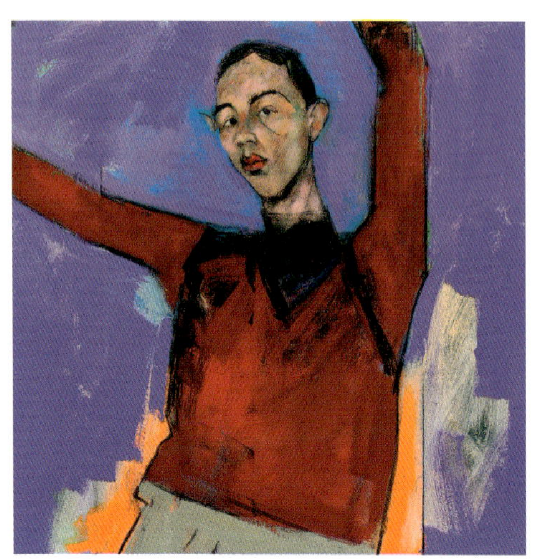

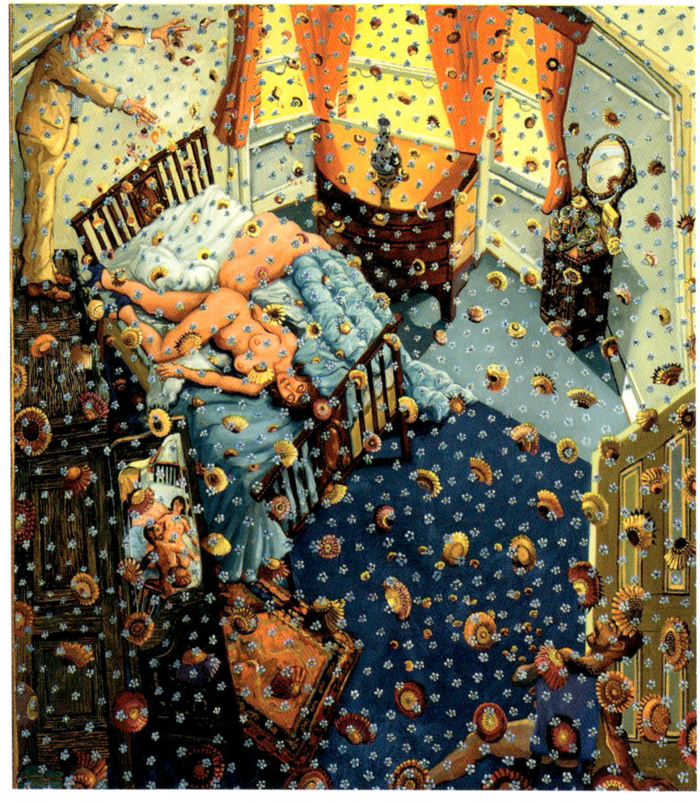

Sonia Lawson RA
Woman and Children
Chalk, pencil and charcoal
88 × 88 cm

Philip Sutton RA
My Granddaughter 'Rivka'
Oil
93 × 93 cm

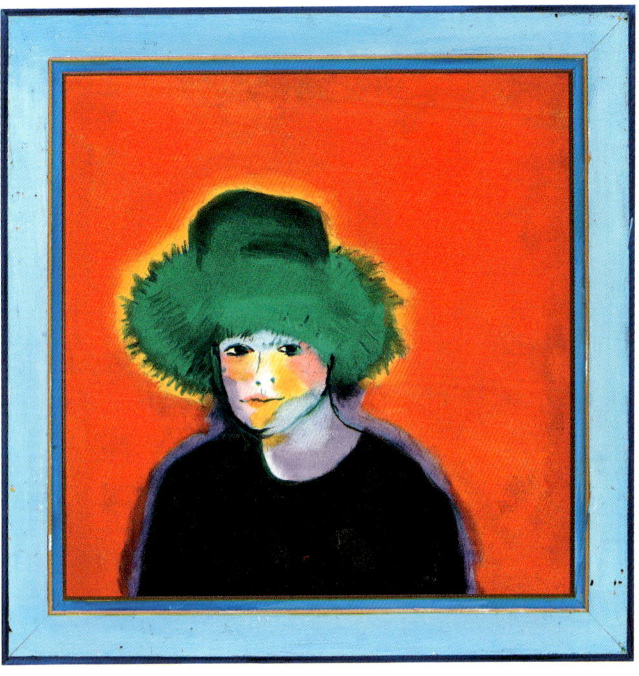

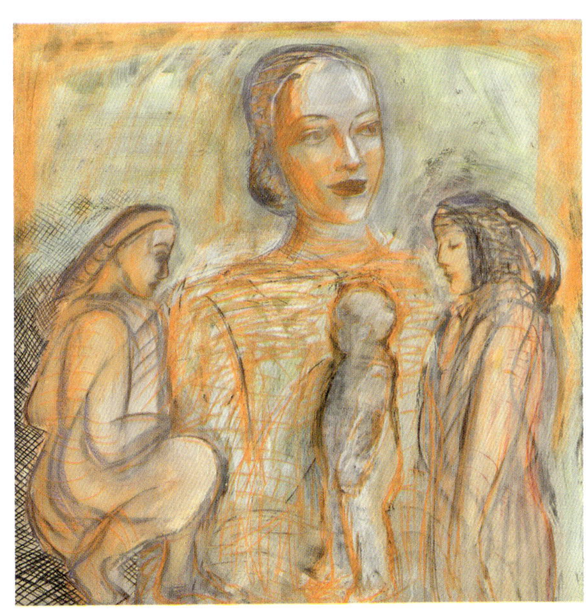

Ken Howard OBE RA
Venice Triptych
Oil
77 × 88 cm

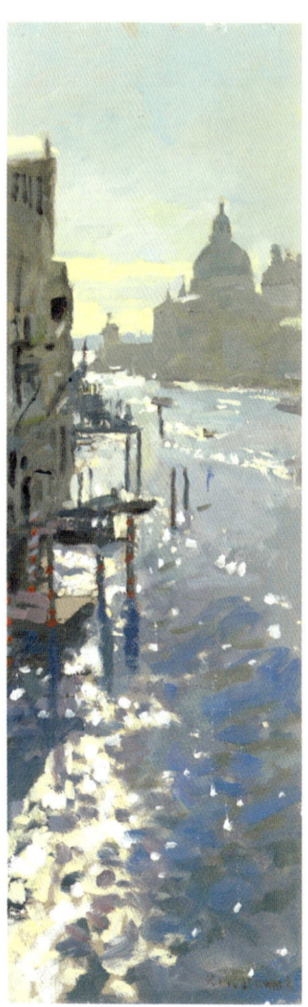
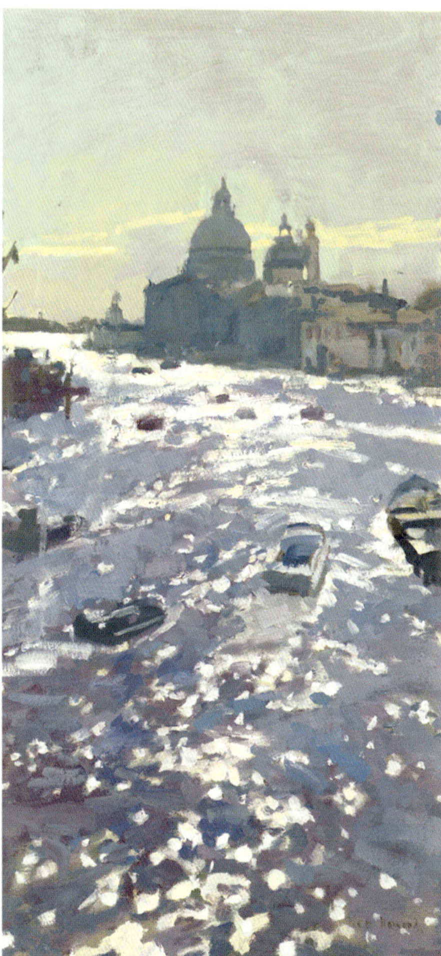
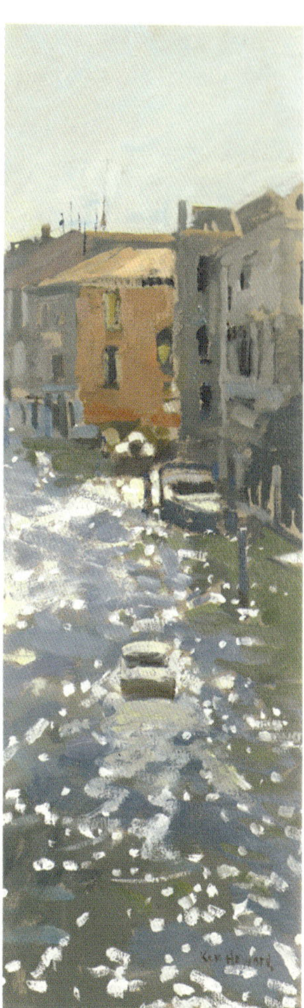

Bill Jacklin RA
Storm Over the City II
Oil
106 × 122 cm

Dr David Tindle RA
Windows and Walls
Egg tempera on board
72 × 53 cm

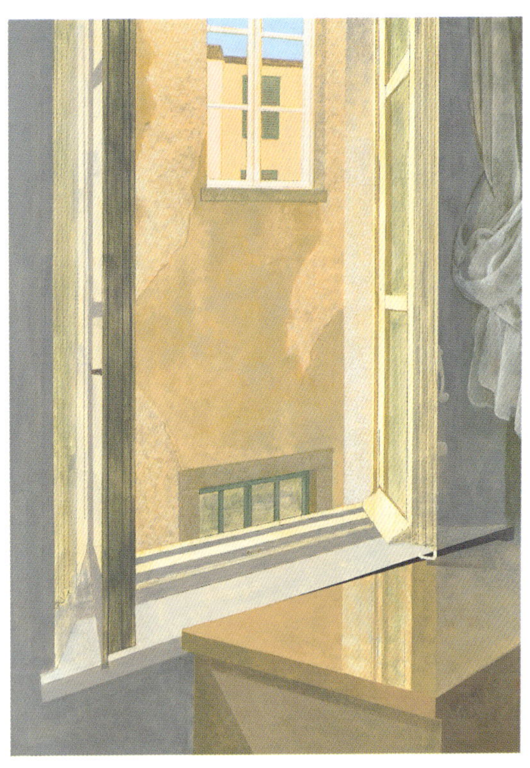

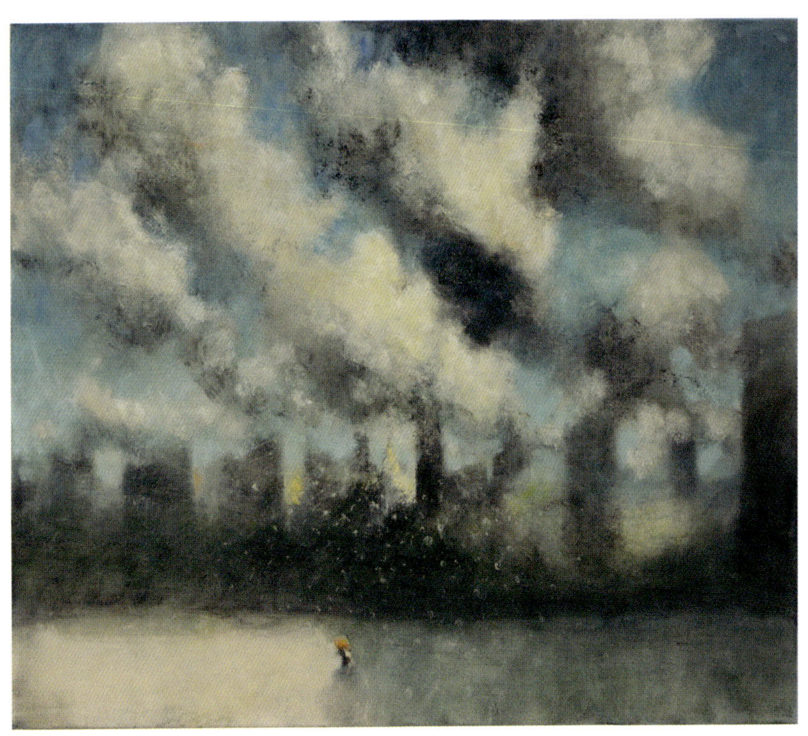

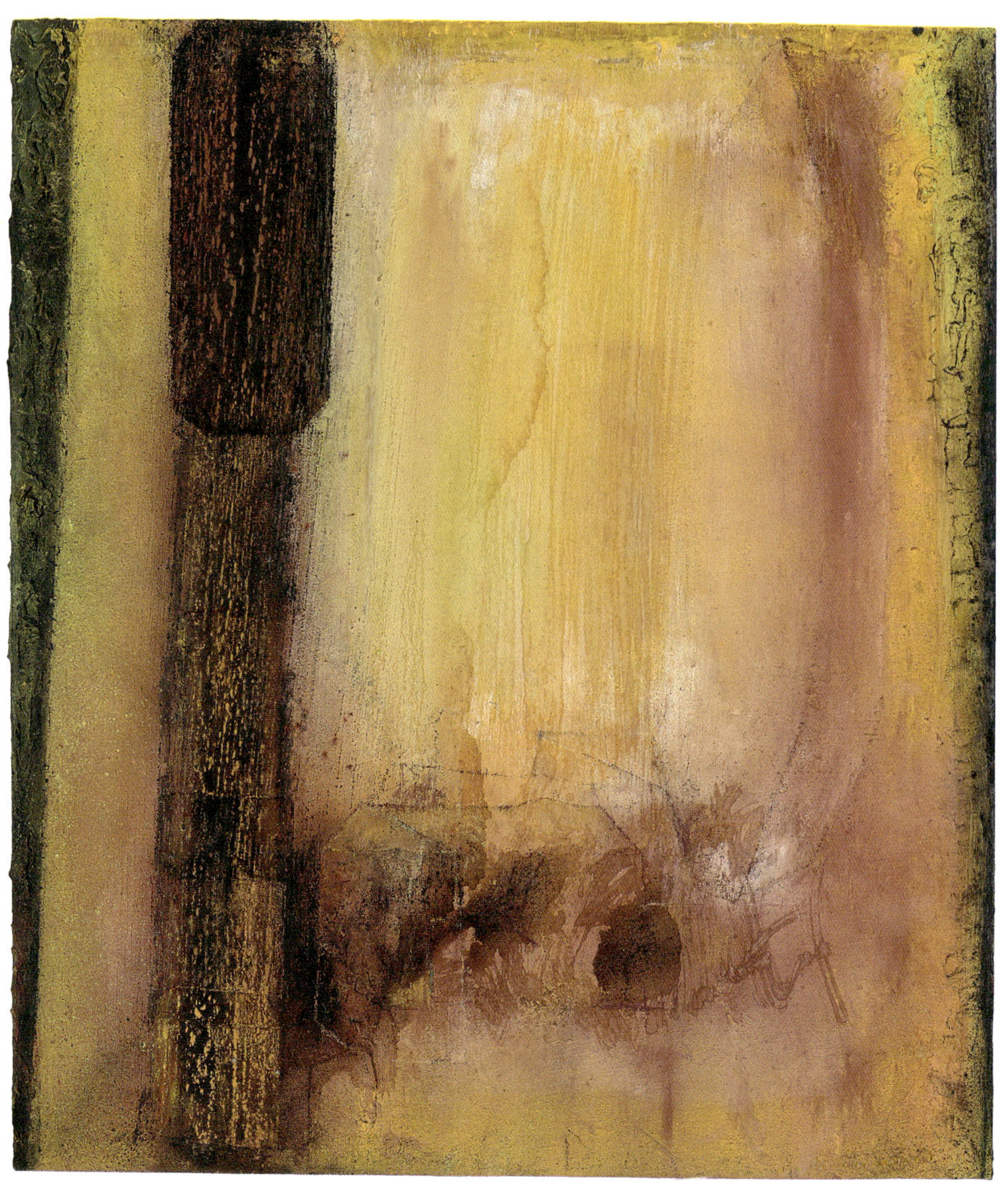

Kenneth Draper RA
Reflections on a Quiet Place
Mixed media
153 × 138 cm

Donna McLean
Thomsen
Oil on board
27 × 26 cm

Mick Rooney RA
Autumn
Aquatint
60 × 50 cm

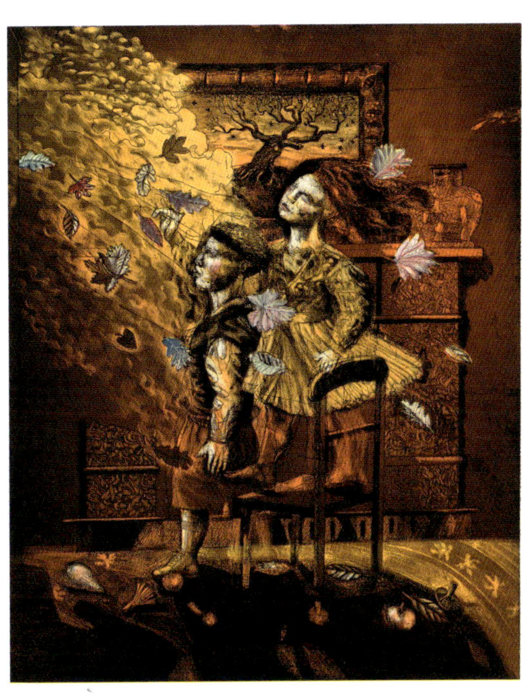

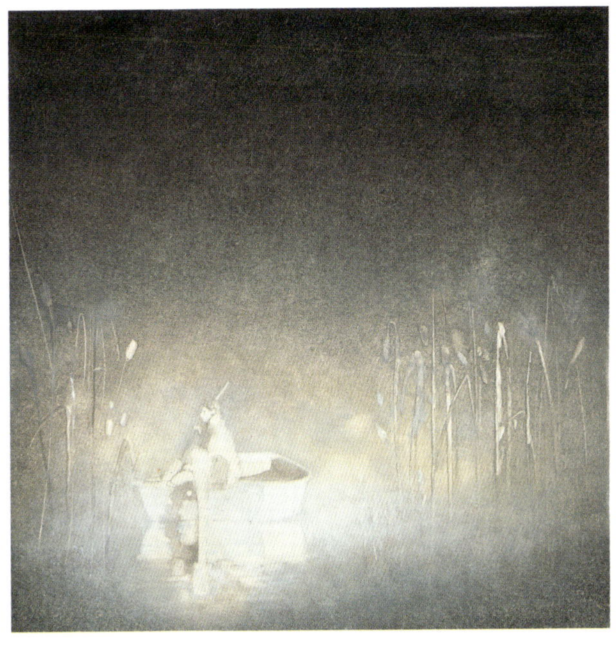

David Pearce
Green Stickback
Acrylic on linen
50 × 60 cm

Gabriella Boyd
Such Soft Hair
Oil
70 × 60 cm

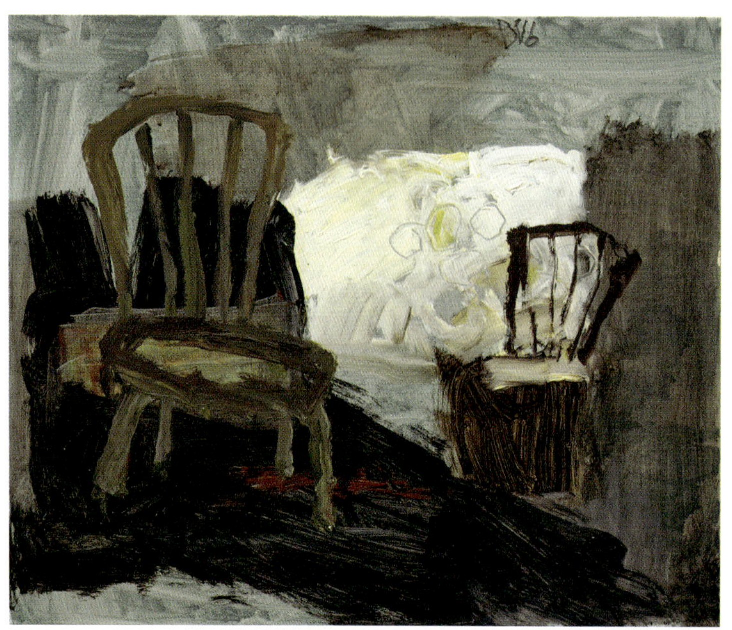

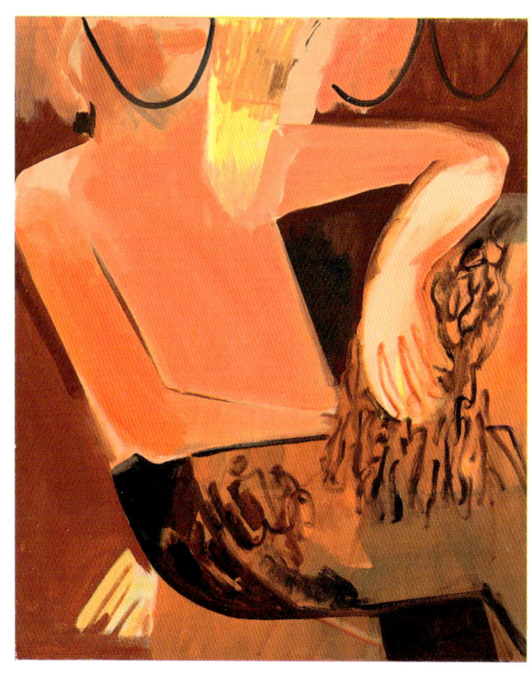

Dan Perfect
Puppetmaster
Ink, watercolour, gouache and soft pastel
64 × 78 cm

Lindsey McLean
Two Figures in their Landscape
Oil on board
14 × 22 cm

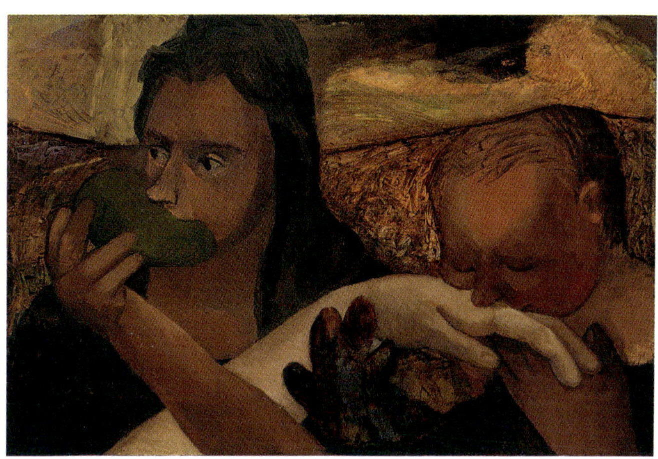

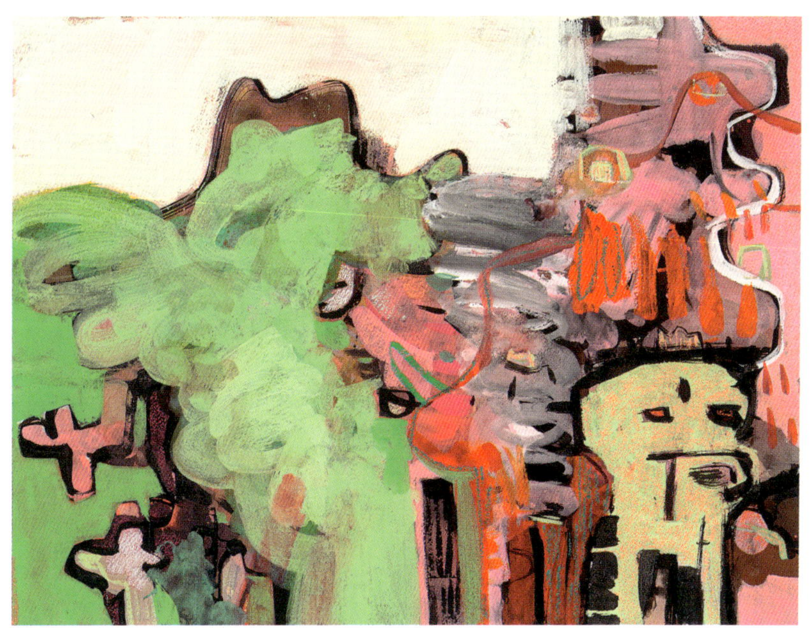

Kiki Smith
In a Bower
Hand-coloured etching and aquatint
61 × 90 cm

Melinda Gibson
Untitled III (Lunar Caustic)
Pigment print
21 × 15 cm

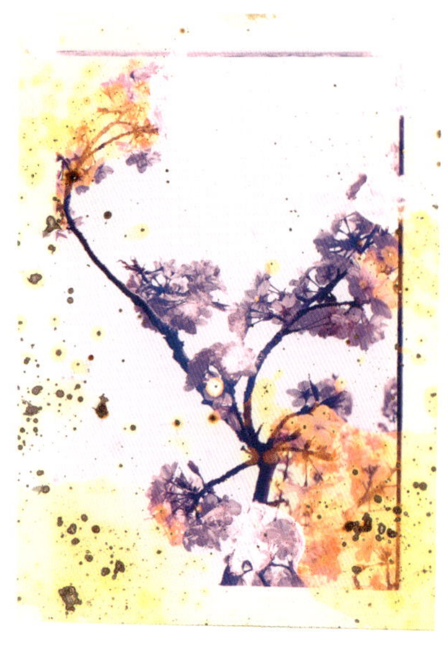

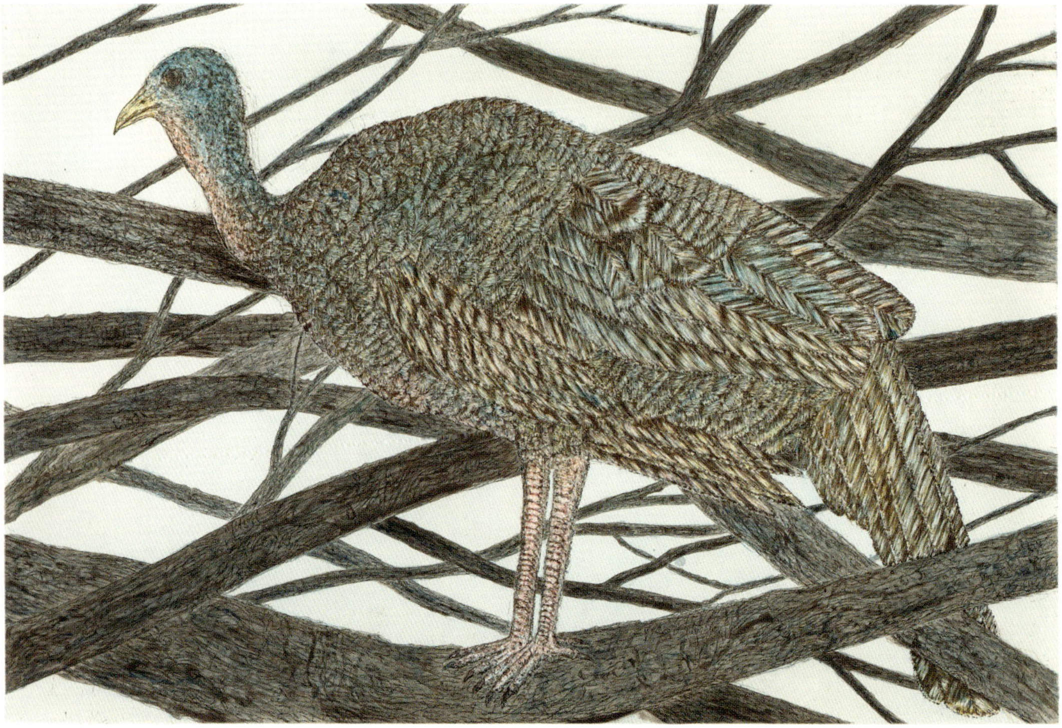

Victoria Ahrens
River Dialogue
Photo-etching
20 × 29 cm

Katja Angeli
Lovers (Diptych)
Digital print and collage on Japanese paper
59 × 46 cm each

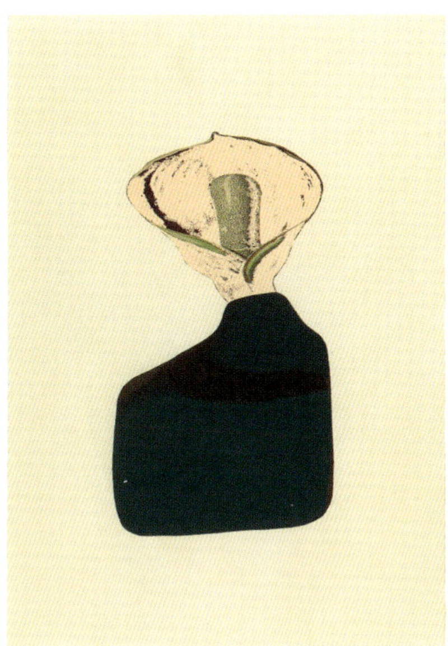

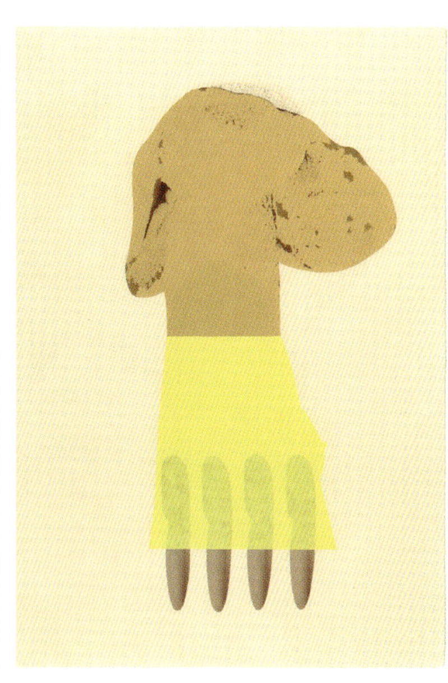

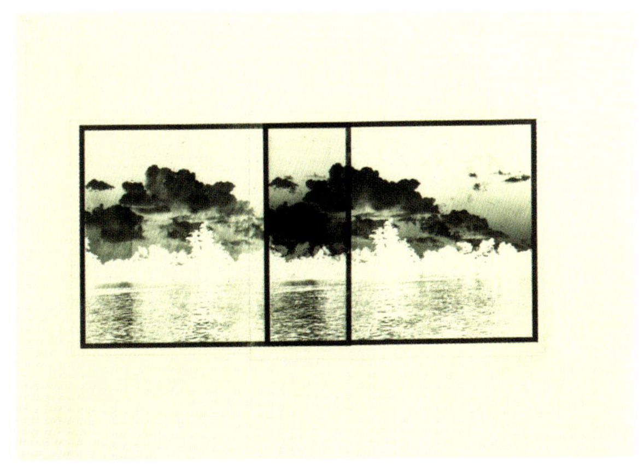

Julia Farrer
Snare I
Etching and aquatint
37 × 50 cm

Claire Willberg
Wiggle Grid
Etching and chine-collé
20 × 15 cm

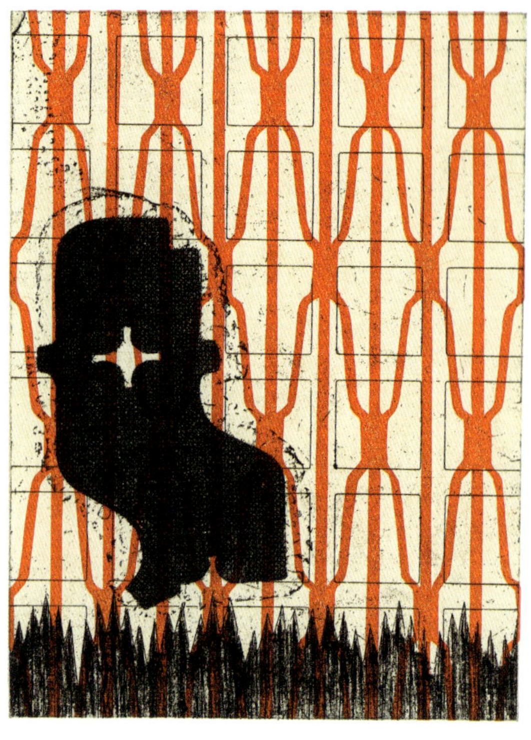

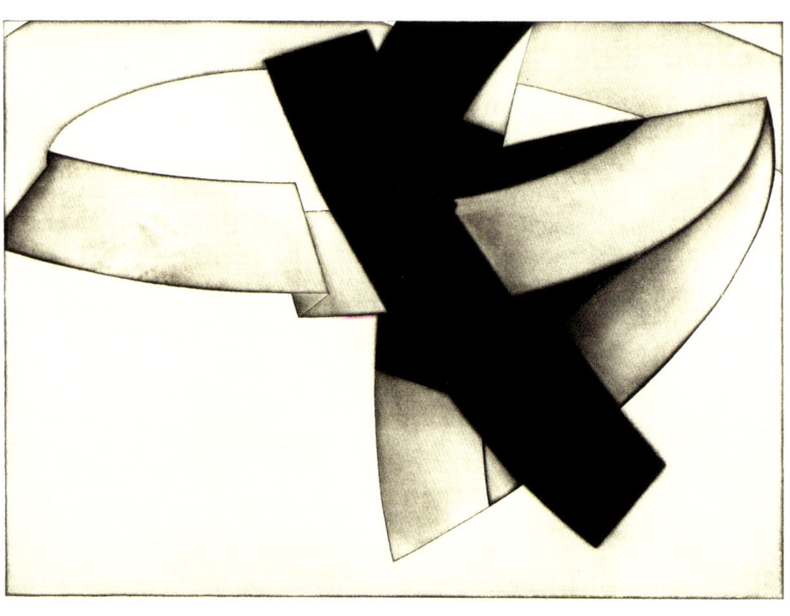

James Fisher
Margaret Morse
Woodcut
50 × 47 cm

Tim Long
Goodbye Mr Pixels (detail)
Woodcut
55 × 48 cm

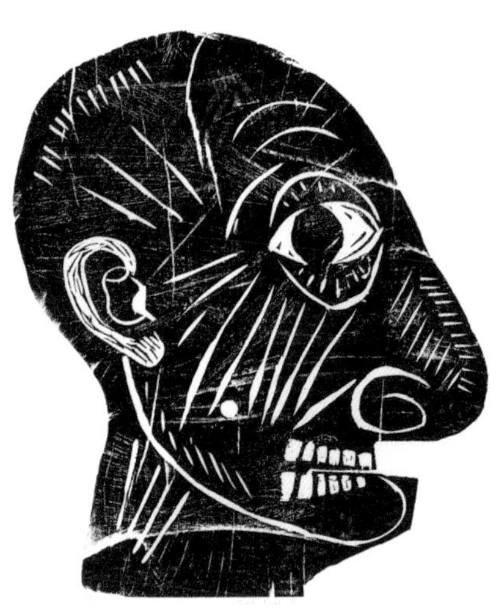

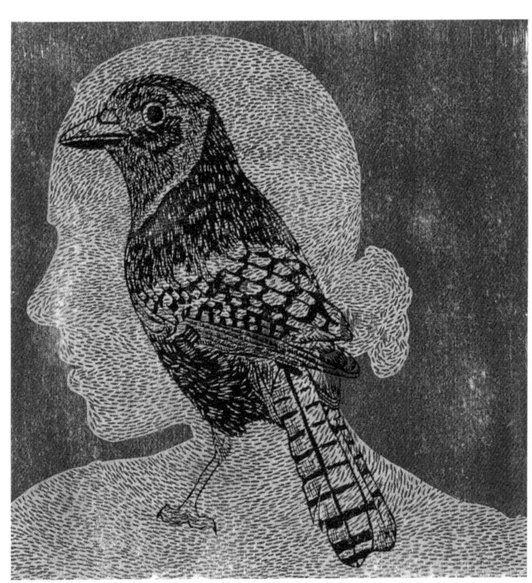

Jock McFadyen RA
Pink Flats 2
Oil
96 × 189 cm

Tony Noble
Two for Joy
Oil on panel
111 × 86 cm

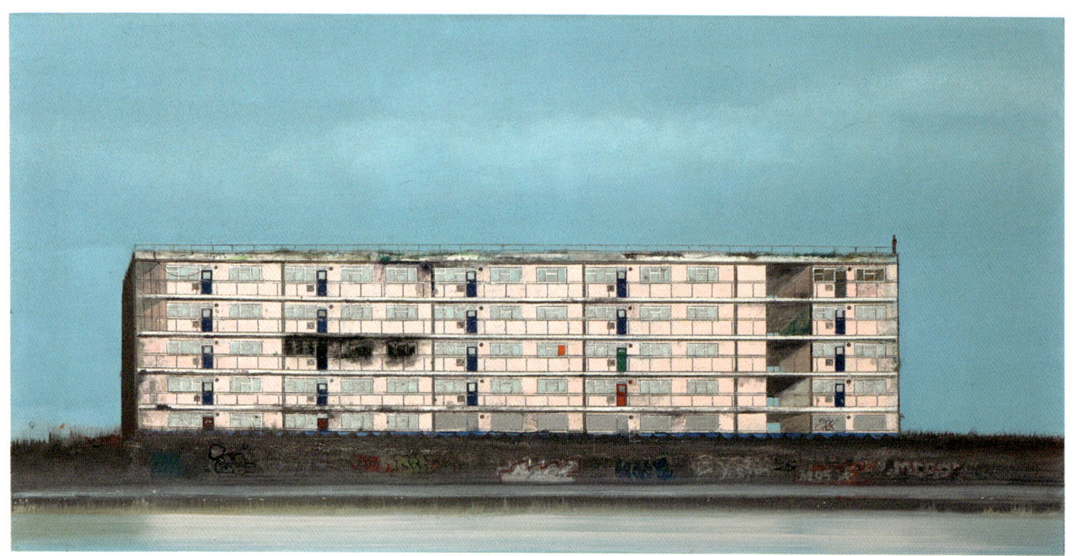

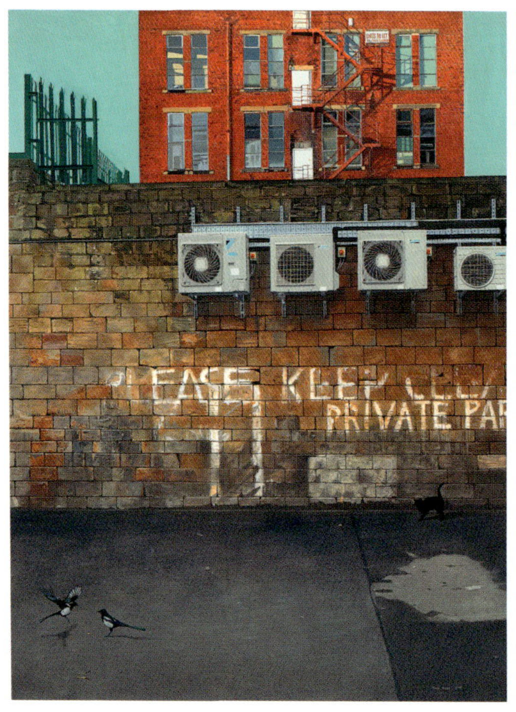

Comhghall Casey
Toy Caravan (CKO 443)
Oil
37 × 42 cm

India Dewar
Slice of the Multibrane Loaf
Oil on prepared bread
15 × 10 cm

Bridget Bernadette Karn
Frosted Woodland
Wool
60 × 30 cm

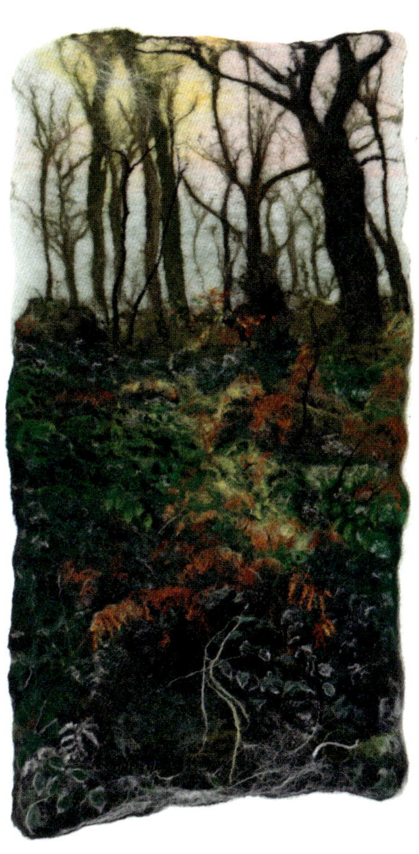

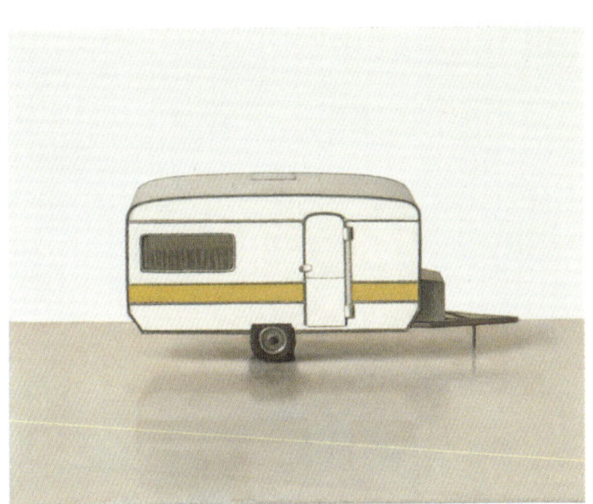

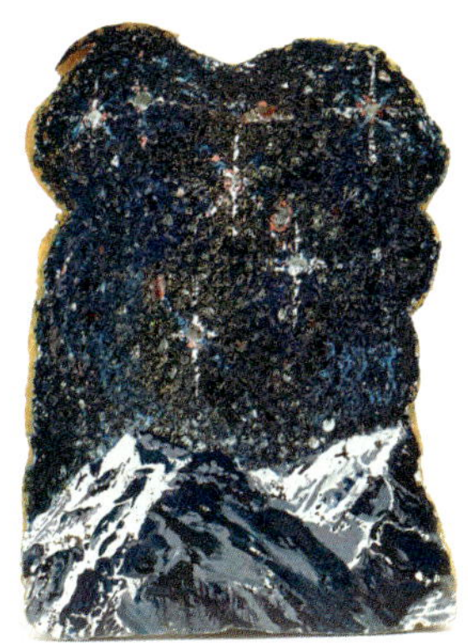

Keith Milow
The Old & New Law VII
Acrylic
100 × 200 cm

Hugh O'Donnell
Sentinel
Acrylic on wood relief
46 × 27 cm

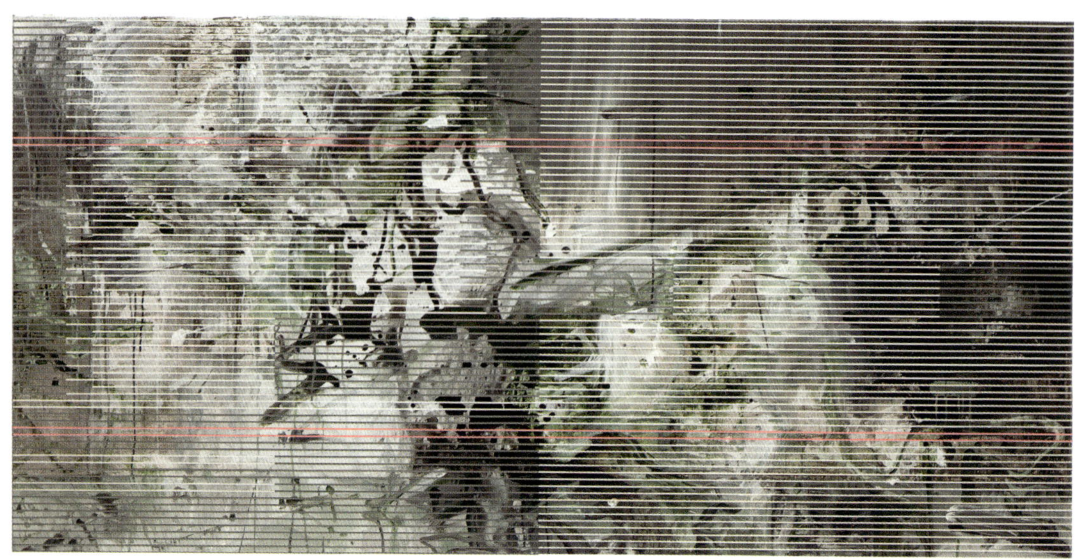

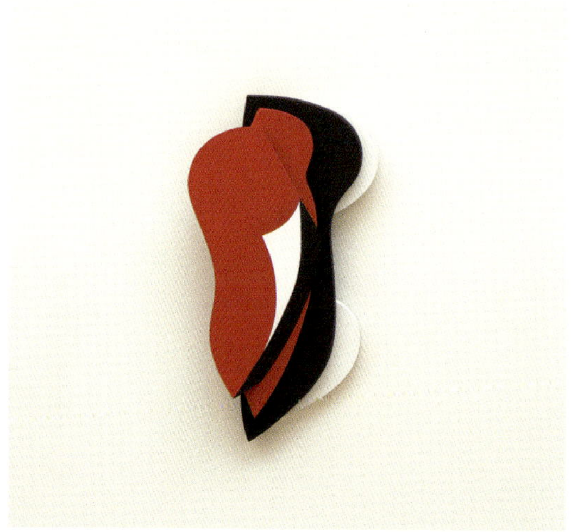

Alex Hanna
Pill Packs (Adjacent Dark)
Oil on board
20 × 25 cm

Jane Cordery
Dover, In Blue
Acrylic
64 × 64 cm

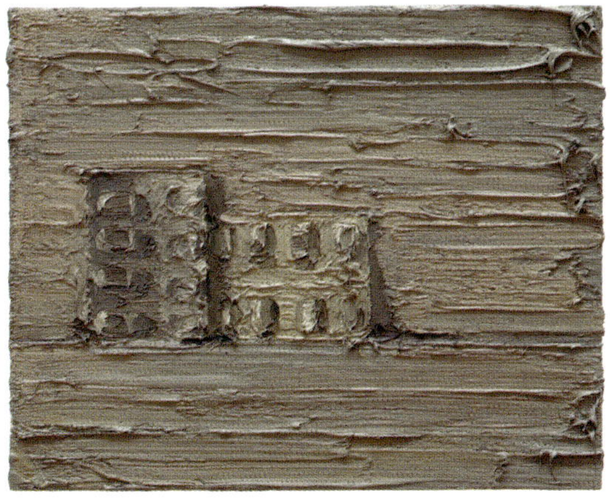

Estela Alba
Noli me Tangere
Oil and car spray paint on aluminium
175 × 119 cm

Derek Boshier
Black Dog
Acrylic
151 × 90 cm

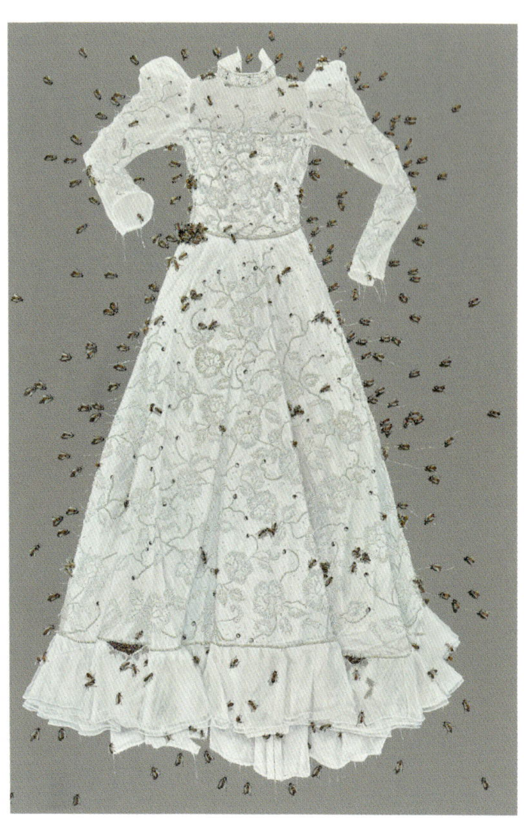

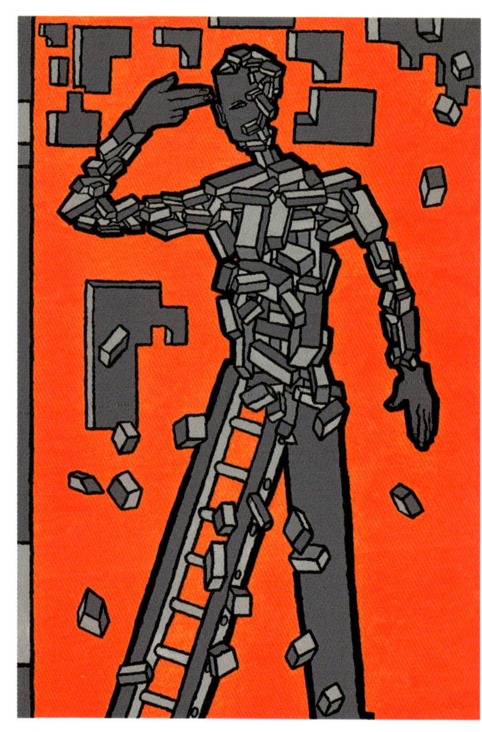

Prof Sir Quentin Blake CBE RDI
Companions
Chinagraph pencil
57 × 77 cm

Andrzej Jackowski
At the Lining – Flowers
Lithograph and chine-collé
67 × 91 cm

John Hewitt
Ancestral Figures: Mid-Victorian Couple
Pencil
43 × 42 cm

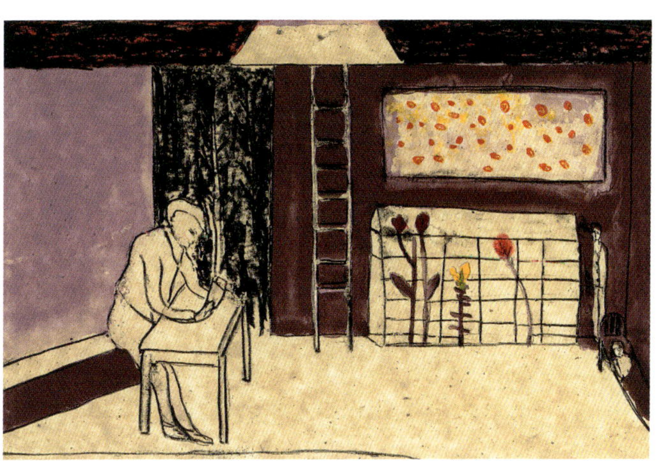

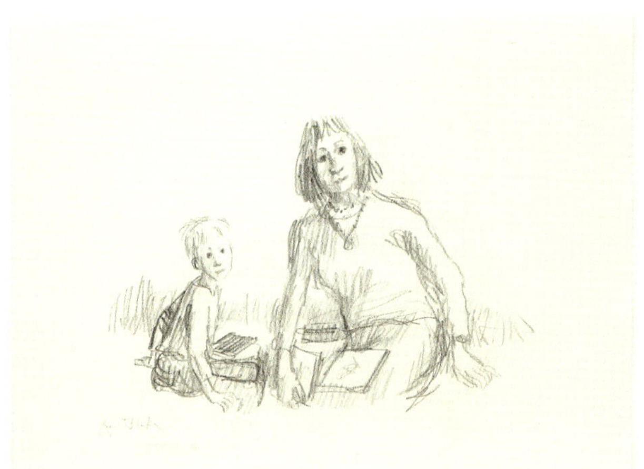

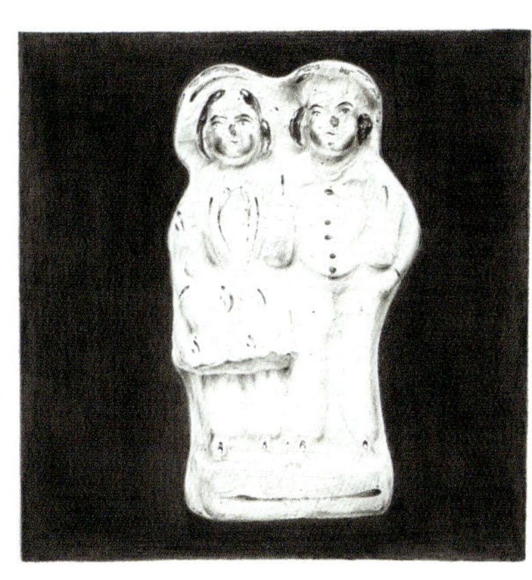

El Anatsui Hon RA
Avocado Coconut Egg (ACE)
Aluminium and copper wire
260 × 270 cm

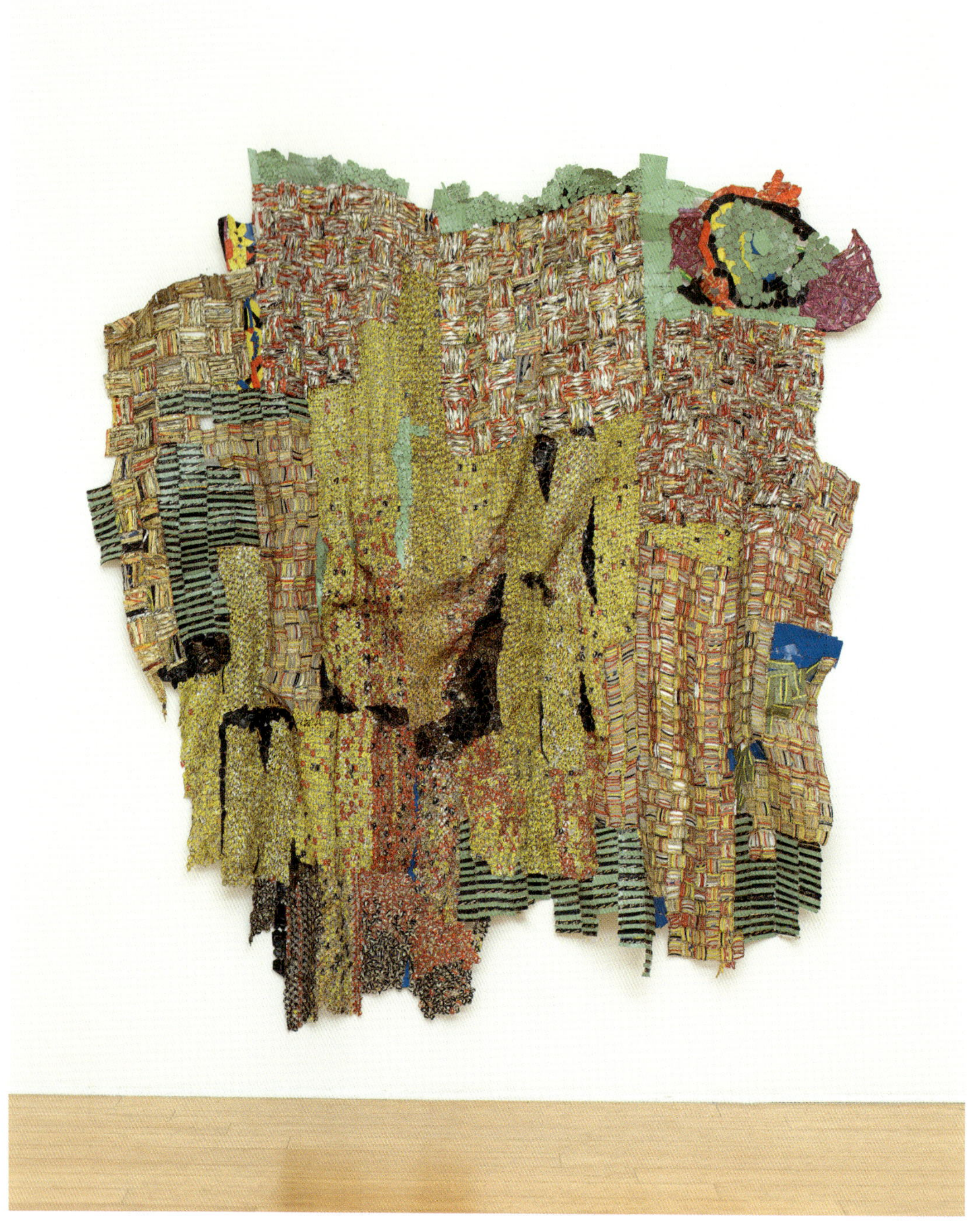

Marina Abramović Hon RA
Carrying the Skeleton (I)
Colour chromogenic print
203 × 180 cm

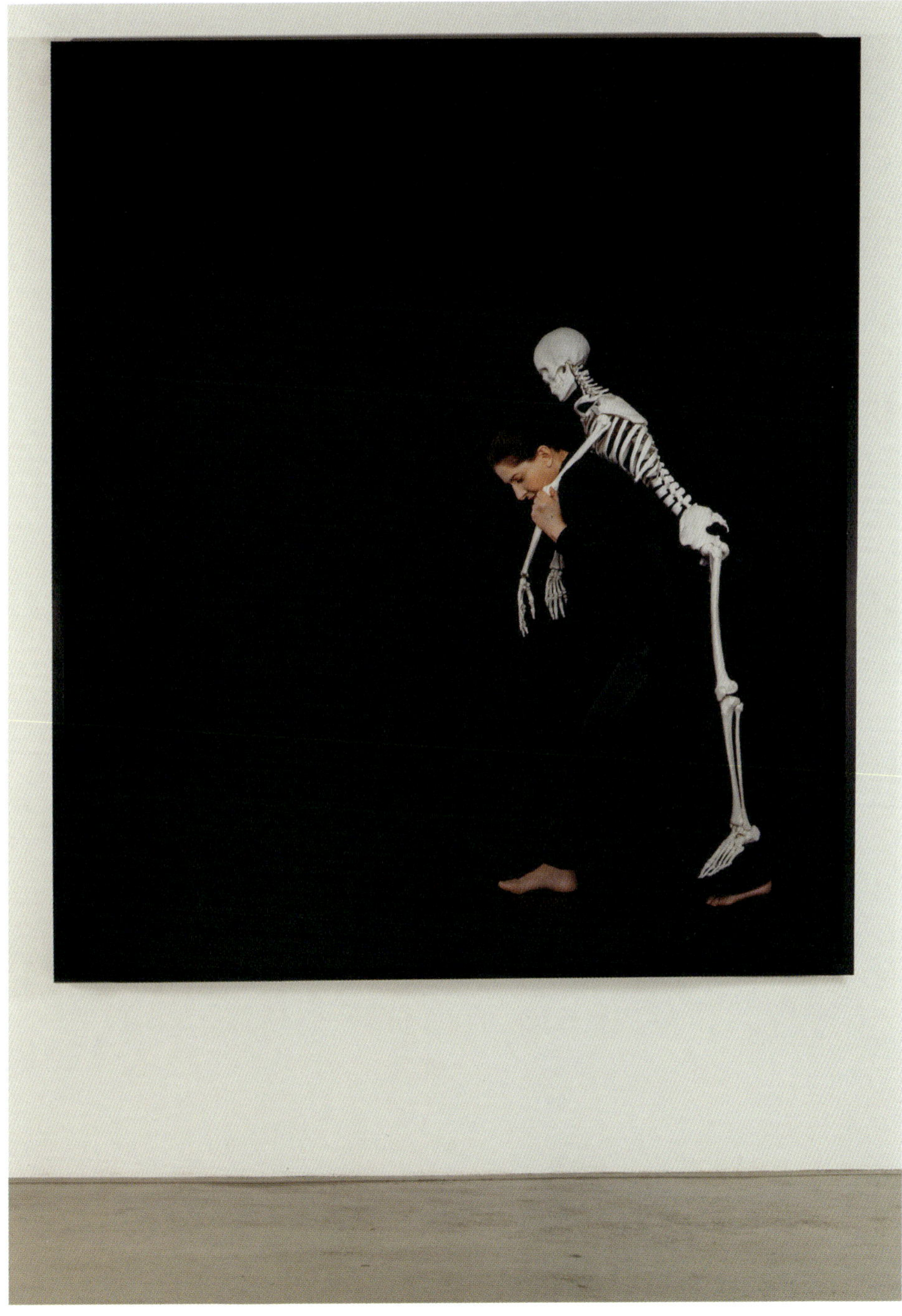

Prof Bryan Kneale RA
Untitled (Green)
Mixed media
29 × 29 cm

Alison Wilding RA
Traacks
Brass and pear wood
H 25 cm

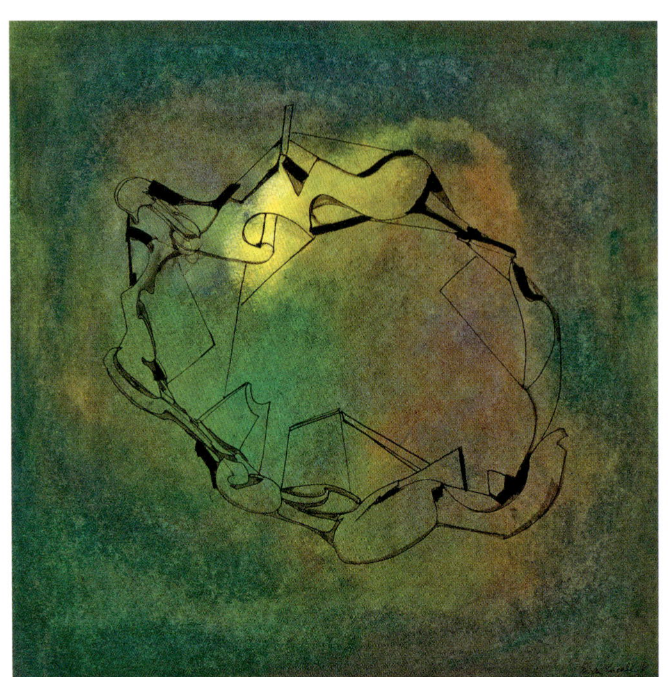

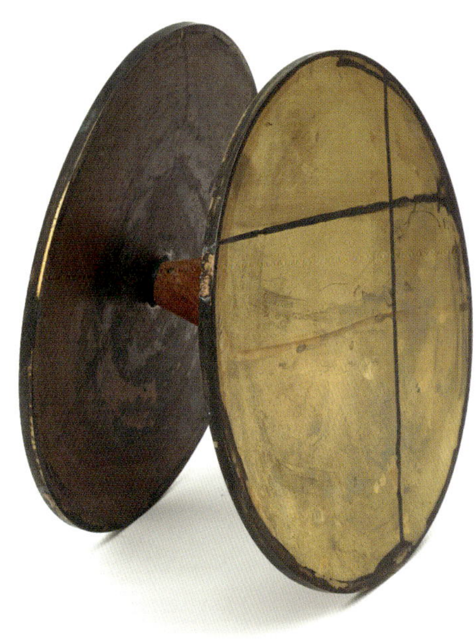

Ann Christopher RA
Held Memory
Stainless steel
H 7.5 cm

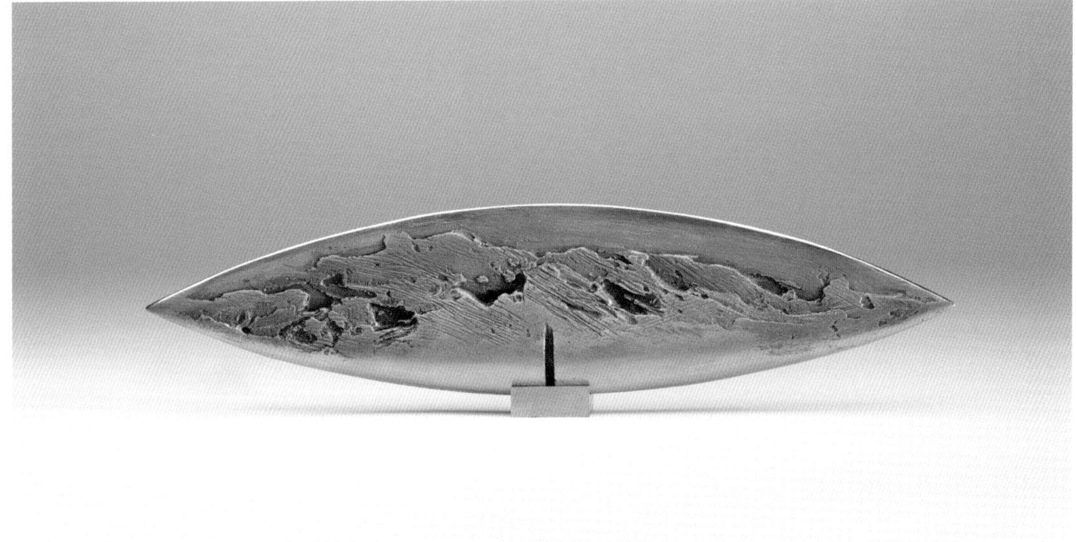

Mitch Epstein
Weeping Beech, Brooklyn Botanic Garden
Gelatin silver print
101 × 76 cm

Thomas Ruff
neg◊stil_13
C-type print
29 × 22 cm

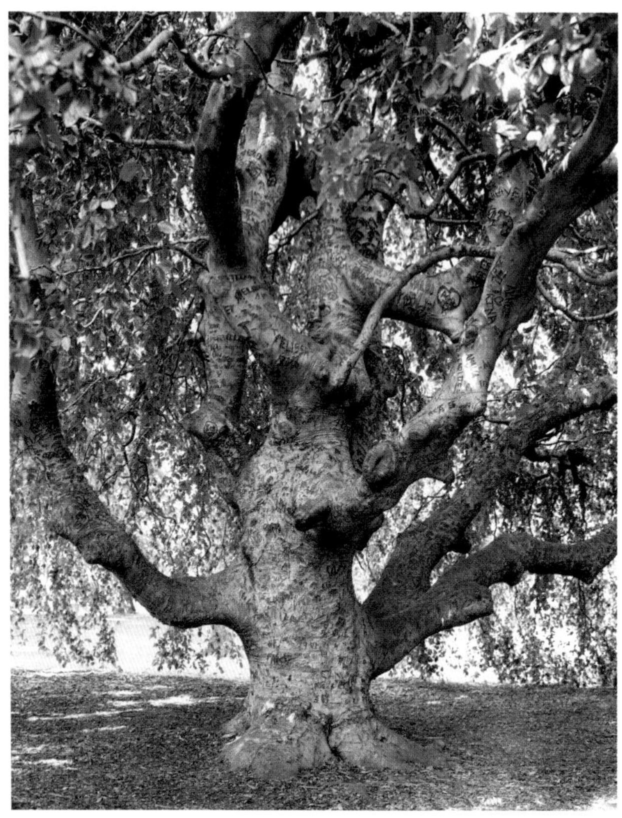

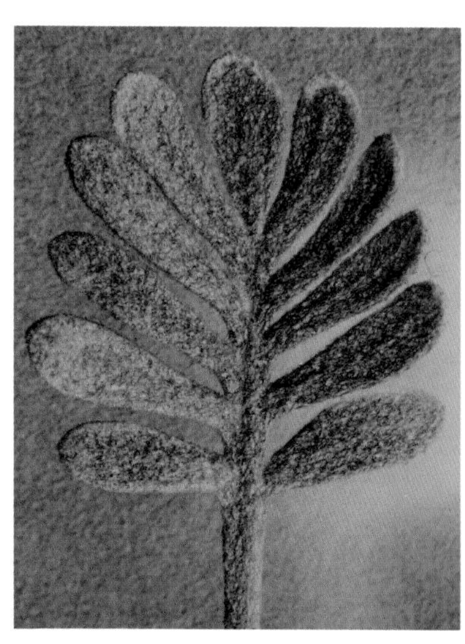

Lidia Patelli
Pelican
Photographic print
112 × 75 cm

Helen Sear
Caetera Fumus
C-type print on Perspex
105 × 86 cm

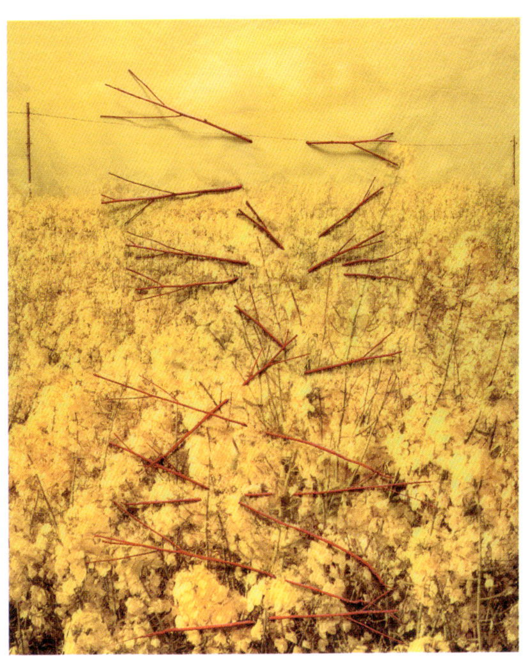

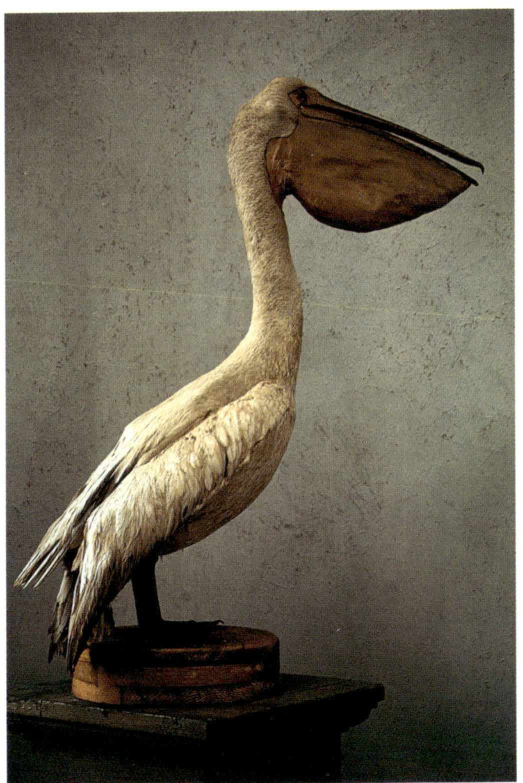

Tugce Karapinar
Opaque and Transparent
Photographic print
42 × 52 cm

Julie Cockburn
Stargazer
Hand embroidery and graphite on found photograph
42 × 35 cm

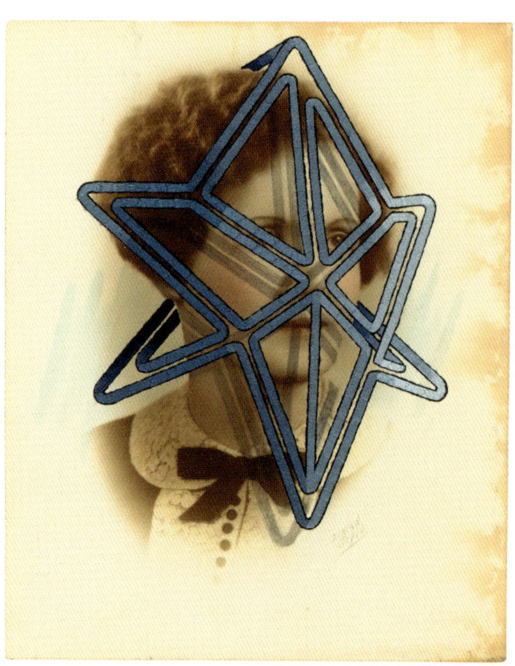

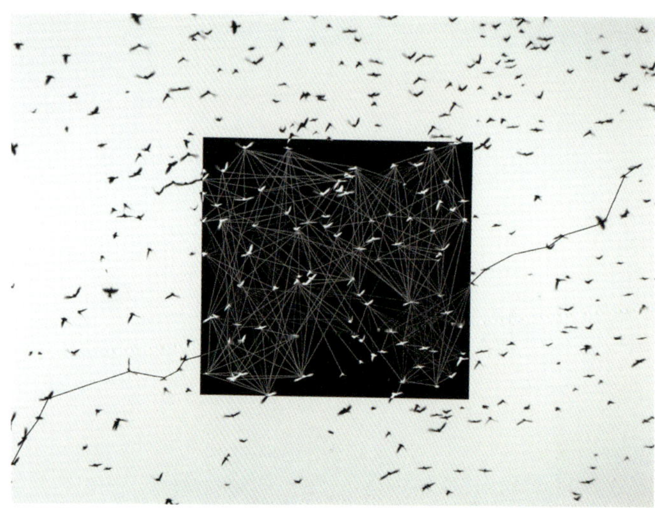

Mark Neville
Rave in the Basement of the Elks Lodge, Braddock
Silver gelatin print
127 × 154 cm

Sanna Charles
Dancing with the Dead in my Dreams
Giclée and inkjet print
40 × 27 cm

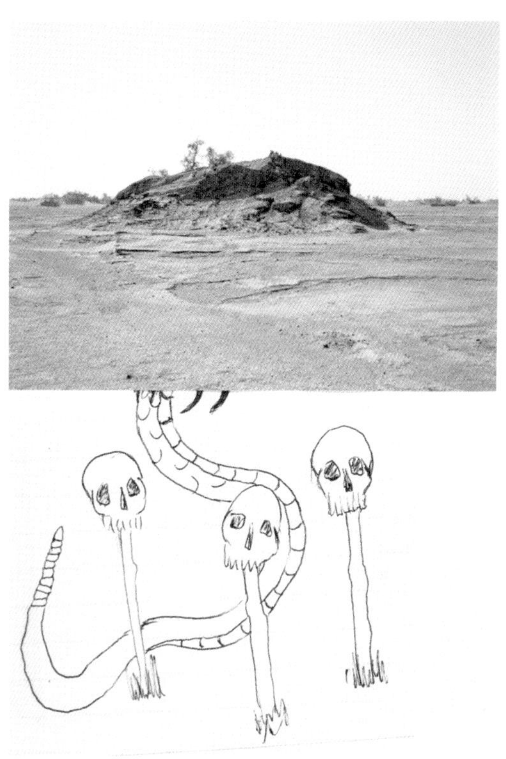

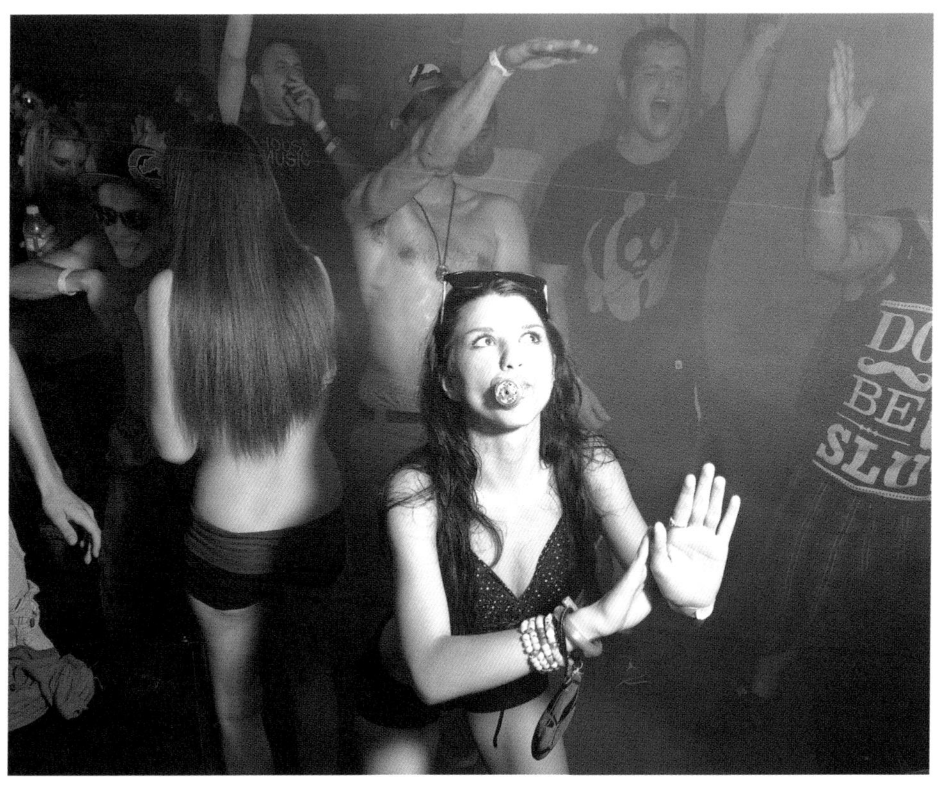

Jimmy Cauty
The Aftermath Dislocation Principle Part 3: The Bridge
Styrofoam, plastic and shipping container
H 183 cm

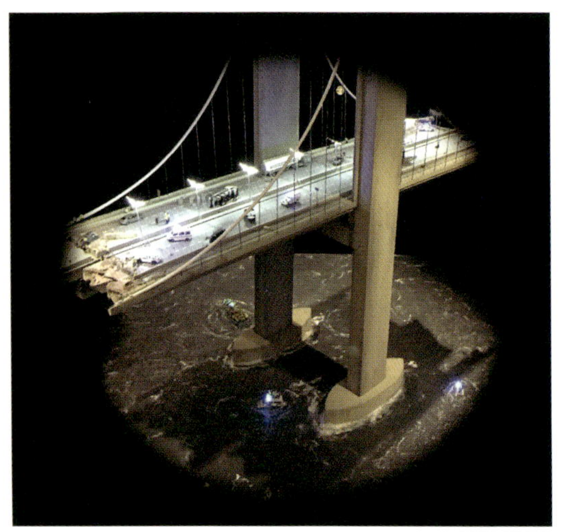

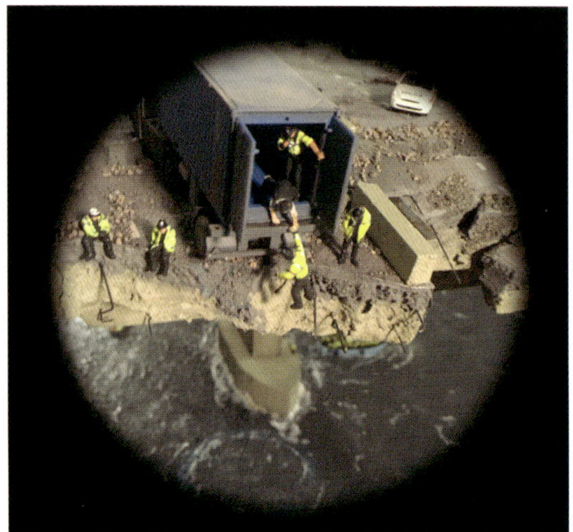

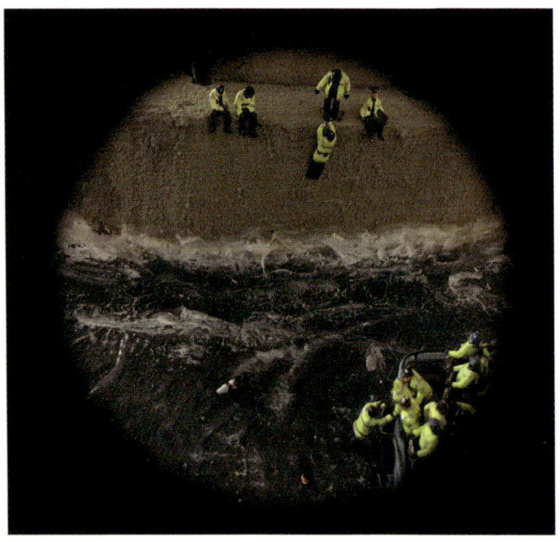

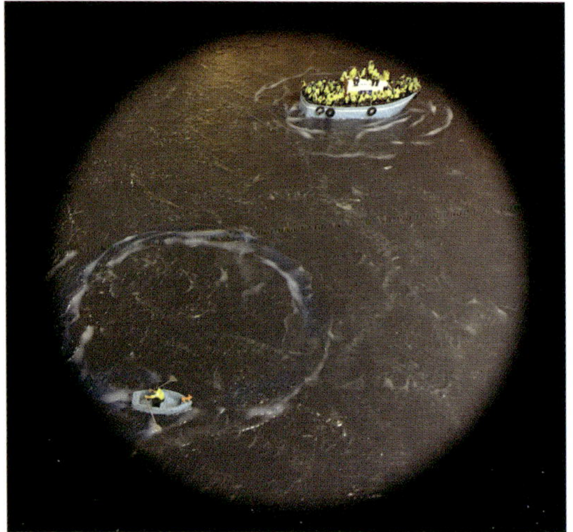

Julie Massie
Fragile Edges
Porcelain
D 53 cm

Joseph Walsh
Magnus Modus
Ash
H 56 cm

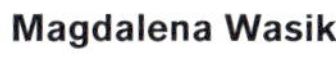

Magdalena Wasik
Series I: Elevation Study
Black clay
H 29 cm

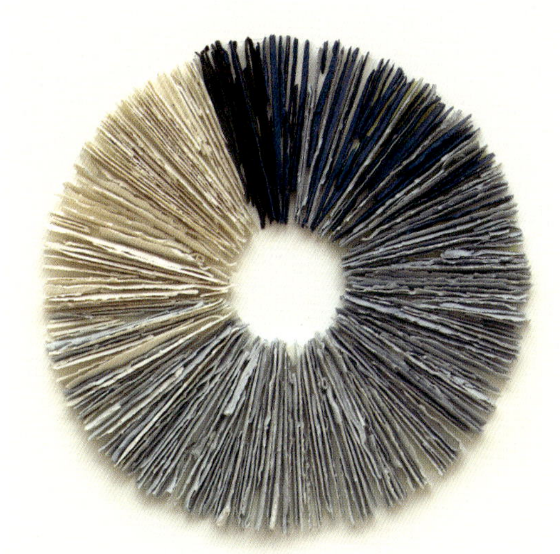

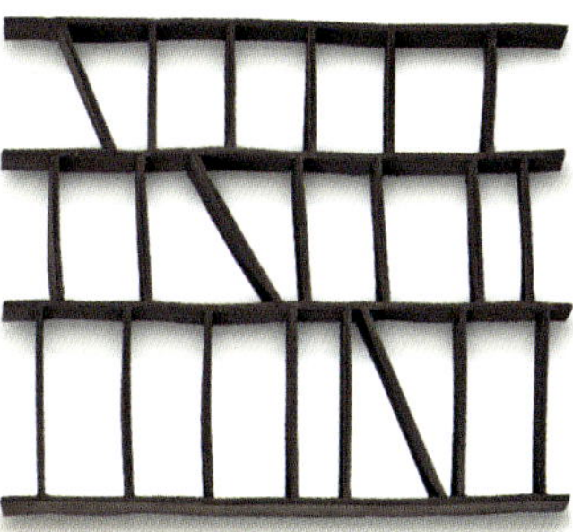

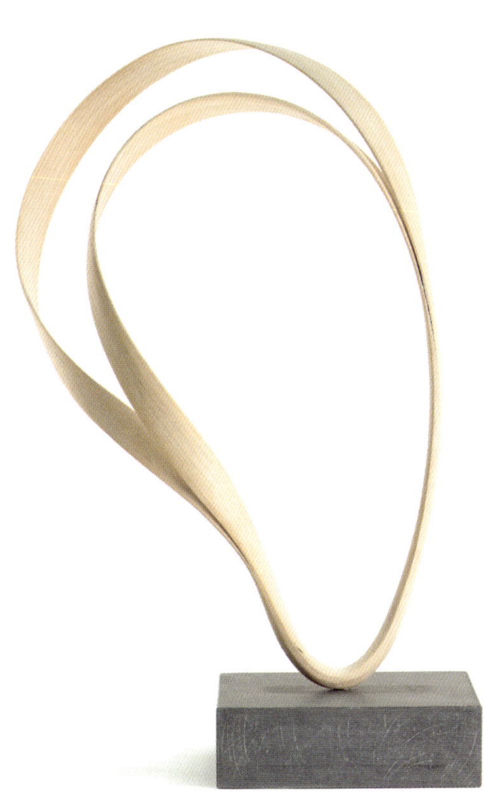

Christopher Le Brun PRA
Goldengrove
Oil
240 × 340 cm

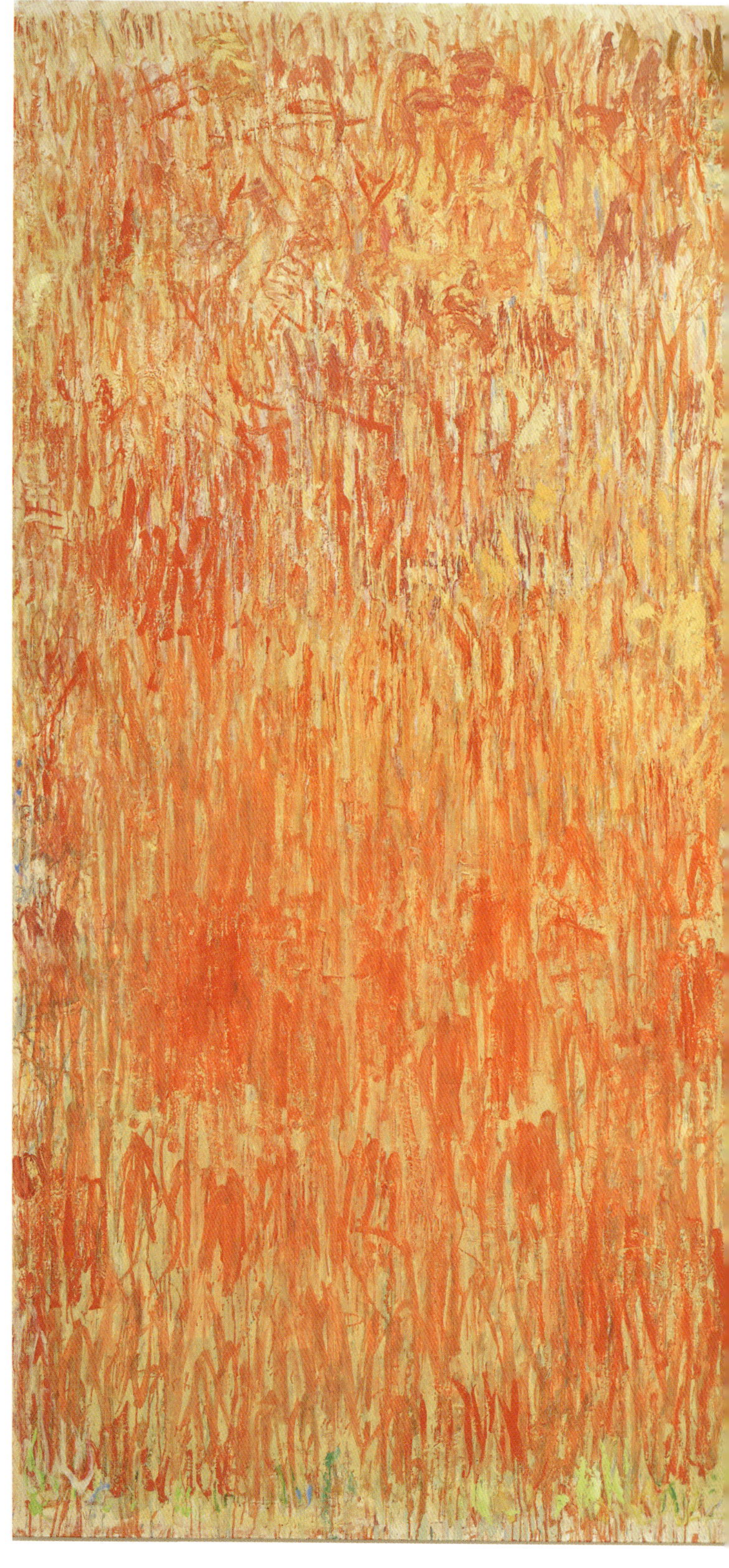

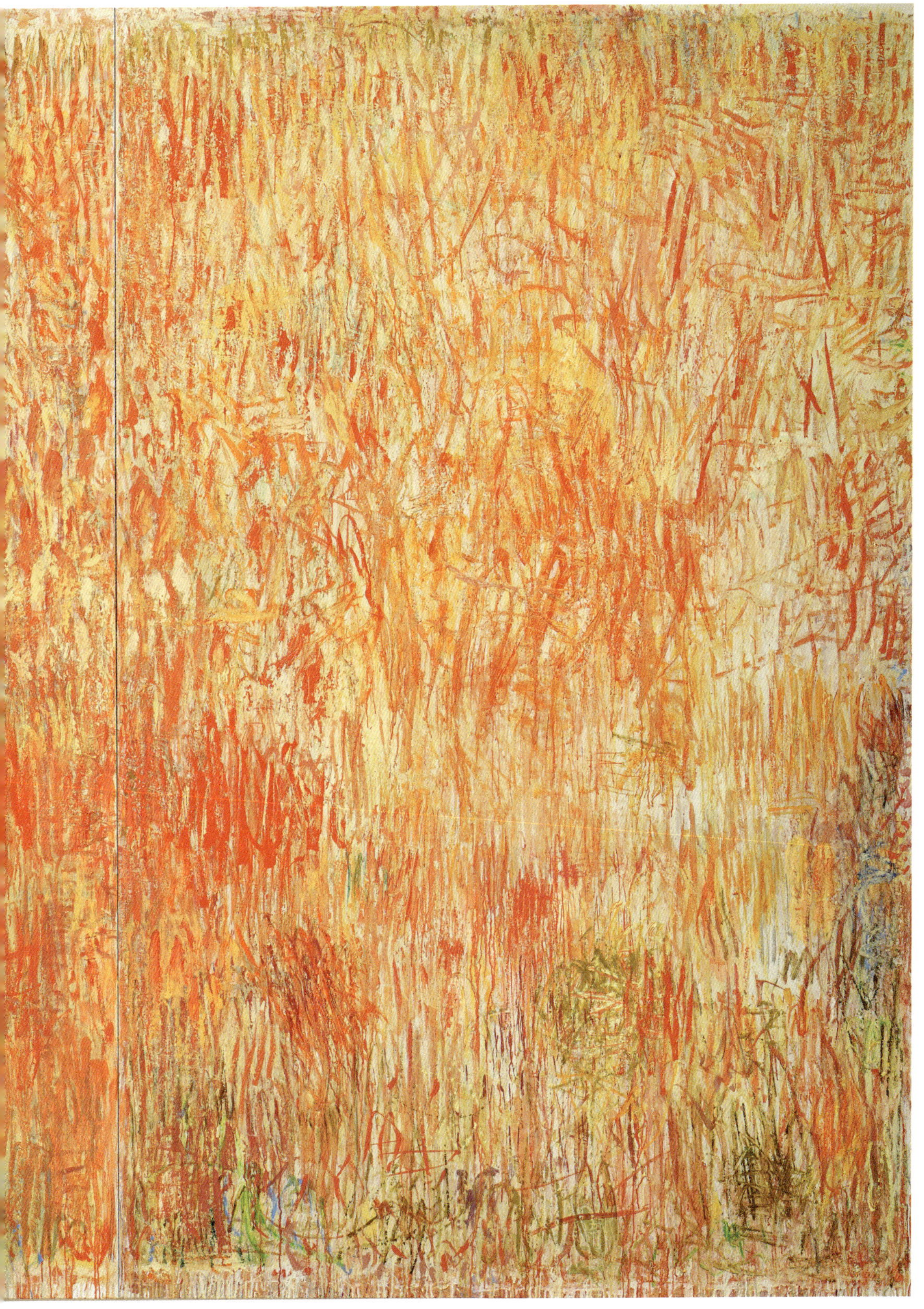

Bill Woodrow RA
Green Circle
Oil on paper
88 × 134 cm

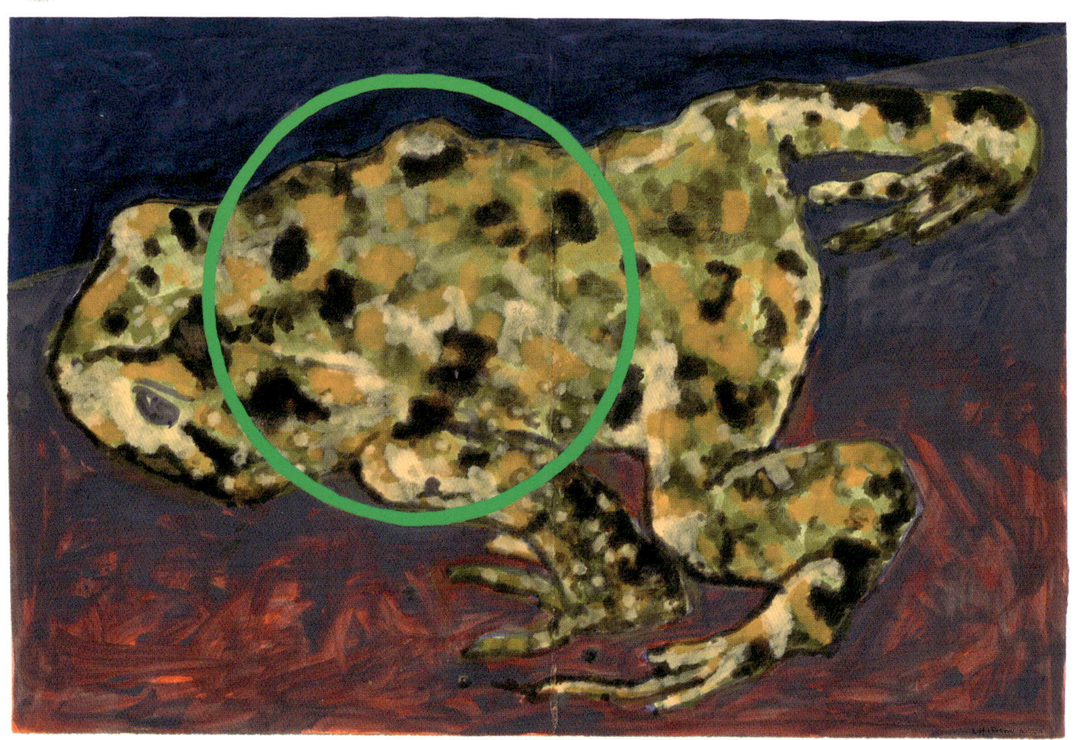

Stephen Chambers RA
Stupid Stupid: Cow & Brother
Etching
22 × 18 cm

Prof Cathie Pilkington RA
Primal Scene
Lithograph
30 × 38 cm

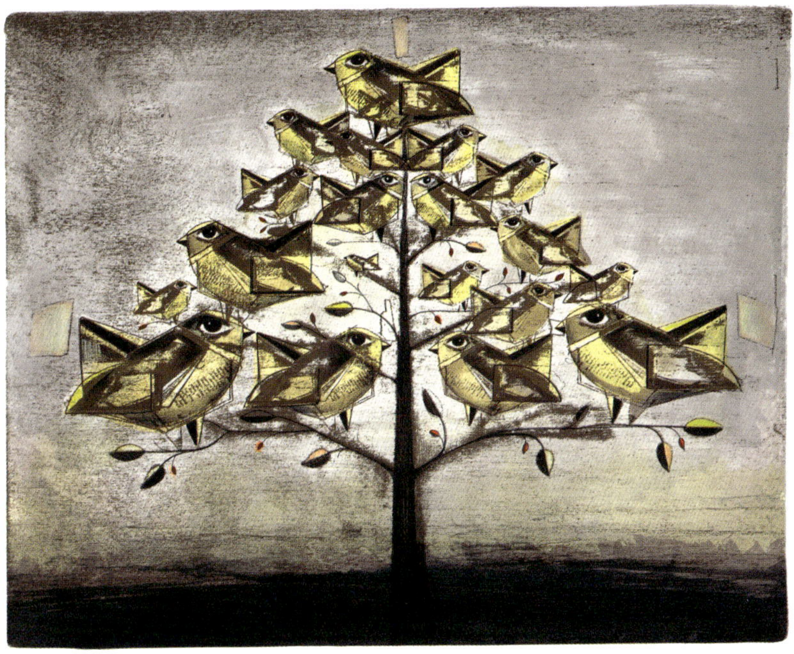

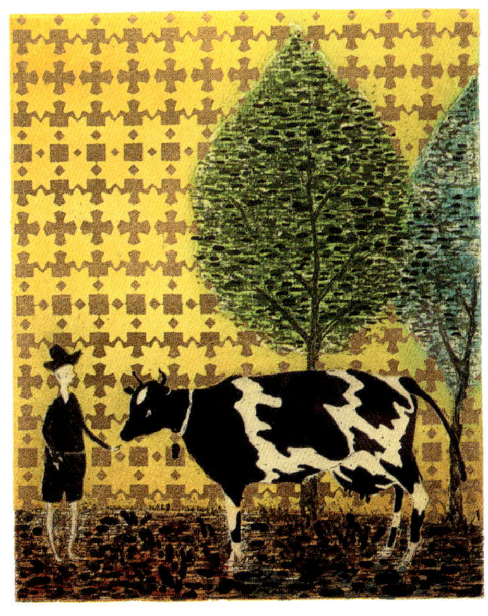

Richard Long CBE RA
Honky Tonk Women
Carborundum and acrylic on paper
124 × 249 cm

Index

Royal Academy of Arts in London, 2016

Registered charity number 1125383

Officers

President: Christopher Le Brun PRA
Keeper: Eileen Cooper RA
Treasurer: Prof Chris Orr MBE RA
Secretary and Chief Executive: Dr Charles Saumarez Smith CBE

Past Presidents

Sir Nicholas Grimshaw CBE PPRA
Phillip King CBE PPRA

Senior Royal Academicians

Prof Norman Ackroyd CBE
Diana Armfield
Gillian Ayres CBE
Basil Beattie
Dame Elizabeth Blackadder DBE
Olwyn Bowey
Frank Bowling OBE
James Butler MBE
Jeffery Camp
Prof Sir Peter Cook
Edward Cullinan CBE
Frederick Cuming HON D LITT
Prof Trevor Dannatt
Dr Jennifer Dickson
Bernard Dunstan
Anthony Eyton
Lord Foster of Thames Bank OM
Peter Freeth
Anthony Green
Sir Nicholas Grimshaw CBE PPRA
David Hockney OM CH
Sir Michael Hopkins CBE
Ken Howard OBE
Prof Paul Huxley
Tess Jaray
Eva Jiricna CBE
Allen Jones
Prof Phillip King CBE PPRA
Prof Bryan Kneale
Paul Koralek CBE
Sonia Lawson
Dr Leonard McComb
Leonard Manasseh OBE
Michael Manser CBE
Mick Moon
John Partridge CBE
Tom Phillips CBE
Lord Rogers of Riverside CH
Prof Michael Sandle
Terry Setch
Philip Sutton
Joe Tilson
Dr David Tindle
William Tucker
Anthony Whishaw
John Wragg
Rose Wylie

Academicians

Prof William Alsop OBE
Ron Arad
Phyllida Barlow
Prof Gordon Benson OBE
Tony Bevan
Sonia Boyce MBE
John Carter
Prof Brian Catling
* Stephen Chambers
Sir David Chipperfield CBE
Ann Christopher
Eileen Cooper
Stephen Cox
Prof Tony Cragg CBE
Michael Craig-Martin CBE
Gus Cummins
Richard Deacon CBE
Tacita Dean OBE
Spencer de Grey CBE
Anne Desmet
Kenneth Draper
Jennifer Durrant
Tracey Emin CBE
Prof Stephen Farthing
Sir Antony Gormley OBE
Prof Piers Gough CBE
Nigel Hall
Thomas Heatherwick CBE
Gary Hume
* Louisa Hutton
Timothy Hyman
* Bill Jacklin
Vanessa Jackson
Neil Jeffries
Prof Chantal Joffe
Sir Anish Kapoor CBE
Prof Michael Landy
* Christopher Le Brun PRA
Richard Long CBE
* Jock McFadyen
* Prof David Mach
Prof Ian McKeever
John Maine
Lisa Milroy
Prof Dhruva Mistry CBE
Mali Morris
Farshid Moussavi
David Nash OBE
Mike Nelson
Prof Humphrey Ocean
Hughie O'Donoghue
Prof Chris Orr MBE
Cornelia Parker OBE
Eric Parry
Grayson Perry CBE
* Prof Cathie Pilkington
Dr Barbara Rae CBE
Fiona Rae
Peter Randall-Page
* David Remfry MBE
* Prof Ian Ritchie CBE
Mick Rooney
Eva Rothschild
Rebecca Salter
Jenny Saville
Sean Scully
Tim Shaw
Conrad Shawcross
Yinka Shonibare MBE
Bob and Roberta Smith
Alan Stanton OBE
Emma Stibbon
Wolfgang Tillmans
Rebecca Warren
Gillian Wearing OBE
Alison Wilding
Chris Wilkinson OBE
* Richard Wilson
* Bill Woodrow

* *Hanging Committee 2016*

Honorary Royal Academicians

Marina Abramovic
Prof El Anatsui
Prof Tadao Ando
Georg Baselitz
Jim Dine
Marlene Dumas
Olafur Eliasson
Frank O Gehry
Prof Rebecca Horn
Prof Arata Isozaki
Jasper Johns
William Kentridge
Anselm Kiefer
Per Kirkeby
Jeff Koons
Daniel Libeskind
Bruce Nauman
Mimmo Paladino
Ieoh Ming Pei
Senator Renzo Piano
Ed Ruscha
Julian Schnabel
Richard Serra
Cindy Sherman
Frank Stella
Rosemarie Trockel
James Turrell
Ai Weiwei
Peter Zumthor

Royal Academy of Arts

The Royal Academy of Arts has a unique position as an independent institution led by eminent artists and architects whose purpose is to promote the creation, enjoyment and appreciation of the visual arts through exhibitions, education and debate. The Royal Academy receives no annual funding via government, and is entirely reliant on self-generated income and charitable support.

You and/or your company can support the Royal Academy of Arts in a number of different ways:

- Almost £60 million has been raised for capital projects, including the Jill and Arthur M Sackler Wing, the restoration of the Main Galleries, the restoration of the John Madejski Fine Rooms, and the provision of better facilities for the display and enjoyment of the Academy's own collections of important works of art and documents charting the history of British art.
- Donations from individuals, trusts, companies and foundations also help support the Academy's internationally renowned exhibition programme, the conservation of the Collections and education projects for schools, families and people with special needs; as well as providing scholarships and bursaries for postgraduate art students in the Royal Academy Schools.
- As a company, you can invest in the Royal Academy through arts sponsorship, corporate membership and corporate entertaining, with specific opportunities that relate to your budgets and marketing or entertaining objectives.
- By including a gift to the Royal Academy in your will, you could help to protect all that we stand for, and ensure we are there as a voice for art and for artists, whatever the future may hold. Your gift can be a sum of money, a specific item or a share of what is left after you have provided for your family and friends. Any gift, regardless of the size, can have an impact, and will allow art lovers to enjoy the Royal Academy in the years to come.

To find out ways in which individuals can support this work, or a specific aspect of it, please contact Karin Grundy, Head of Patrons, on 020 7300 5671.

To explore ways in which companies, trusts and foundations can become involved in the work of the Academy, please contact the Sponsorship and Partnership Team on 020 7300 5706/5813

For more information on remembering the Academy in your will, please contact Matthew Watters on 020 7300 5677 or legacies@royalacademy.org.uk

Membership of the Friends

The Friends of the Royal Academy was founded in 1977 to support and promote the work of the Royal Academy. It is now one of the largest such organisations in the world, with around 90,000 members.

As a Friend you enjoy free entry to every RA exhibition and much more...

- Priority booking to all events the public
- Exclusive Previews and Private Views
- Access to the Keeper's House
- *RA Magazine* quarterly
- A dedicated programme of events
- Free entry to all exhibitions with a family guest

Why not join today?

- At the Friends desk in the Front Hall
- Online at www.royalacademy.org.uk/friends
- Ring 020 7300 8090 any day of the week
- E-mail friends@royalacademy.org.uk

About the author

Richard Davey is a visiting fellow at the School of Art and Design, Nottingham Trent University, and the university's coordinating chaplain. He is the author of *Anthony Whishaw* (RA Publications; 2016), and has contributed to many other books, including *Anselm Kiefer* (RA Publications; 2014).

Head of Summer Exhibition and Curator (Contemporary Projects)
Edith Devaney

Summer Exhibition Organisers
Nancy Cooper
Christopher Eperjesi
Katherine Oliver
Alexandra Searle
Paul Sirr
Cleo Stringer
Elana Woodgate

Royal Academy Publications
Beatrice Gullström
Alison Hissey
Carola Krueger
Natalie Kulenicz
Peter Sawbridge
Nick Tite

Book design: Adam Brown_01.02
Photography: John Bodkin, DawkinsColour (unless otherwise stated)
Colour reproduction: DawkinsColour
Printed in Wales by Gomer Press

British Library Cataloguing-in-publication Data
A catalogue record for this book is available in the British Library

ISBN 978-1-910350-52-2

Illustrations

Page 2: Detail of *Untitled* by Gert & Uwe Tobias
Pages 4-5: Installation of Kutluğ Ataman *The Portrait of Sakıp Sabancı*
Page 6: Installation view of Gallery IV with Carol Robertson's *Dark Star 2* being hung
Pages 8-9: Installation shots and animation still of *Spyre* by Ron Arad RA
Page 11: Cathie Pilkington RA photographing the installation of the Lecture Room
Page 12: The installation of Gallery V in progress
Page 14: Richard Wilson RA in front of Jane Harris' *Familiar – Devil's Advocate*
Page 17: Richard Wilson RA photographing during installation
Pages 18-19: Richard Wilson RA, Jock McFadyen RA, Cathie Pilkington RA, David Remfry MBE RA and David Mach RA during the installation of Gallery III
Page 20: Bill Jacklin RA overseeing the installation of Gallery I
Pages 22-23: Installation view of Gallery I
Page 24: Ian Ritchie CBE RA during installation
Pages 26-27: Installation view of the Large Weston Room
Page 29: Jock McFadyen RA overseeing the installation of Gallery IV
Pages 30-31: Jock McFadyen RA and Richard Wilson RA during the installation of Gallery IV
Page 32: Stephen Chambers RA surveying the installation of Gallery V
Pages 34-35: Stephen Chambers RA installing Gallery VII
Page 36: Christopher Le Brun PRA with Richard Wilson RA during installation
Pages 38-39: Installation shot of Gallery III with detail of Heather and Ivan Morison, *Will You Please Be Quiet, Please* in the foreground
Page 40: David Remfry MBE RA directing the installation of Gallery III
Pages 42-43: Installation view of Gallery VIII
Page 44: David Mach RA installing the Lecture Room
Page 46: Cathie Pilkington RA installing the Lecture Room, with detail of *Eric* by Tim Shaw RA in the foreground
Pages 48-49: Installation view of the Lecture Room with *Marsland* by Gillian Ayres CBE RA, William Alexander's *Reinventing the Wheel* and Yinka Shonibare MBE RA's *Balloon Man* in the foreground
Page 50: David Mach RA and Bill Woodrow RA
Pages 52-53: Installation view of Gallery X
Pages 54-55: Richard Wilson RA directing the installation of Gallery VI
Pages 64-65: Installation view of the Wohl Central Hall with *2 hose petrified Petrol Pump* by Allora & Calzadilla in the foreground
Pages 76-77: Installation view of Gallery VI with Aono Fumiaki's *Mending, Substitution, Consolidation, Coupling – Restoration of a Sake Bottle Collected in Watari-Cho Arahama, Miyagi, Japan, After the Great East Japan Earthquake and Tsunami (Memorial Configuration)* in the foreground
Pages 132-133: Installation view of Gallery IX with *Plosion 1 (Yellow)* by Conrad Shawcross RA in the foreground
Page 146-147: Installation view of Gallery IV with *Dark Matter* by David Mach RA (left), *Big Black* by David Nash OBE RA and *Study for Odalisque* by William Tucker in the foreground

Photographic Acknowledgements

Pages 4-5, 6, 11, 12, 14, 17, 18-19, 20, 22-23, 24, 28, 30-31, 32, 34-35, 36, 40, 42-43, 44, 46, 50, 54-55, 63: Photography: Phil Sayer
Page 2: Courtesy of the artists and Maureen Paley, London
Page 16: © Jane & Louise Wilson. All Rights Reserved, DACS 2016
Page 21: Courtesy of the artist and Marlborough Fine Art
Page 22: Ian Ritchie Architects Ltd.
Page 57: © Boyd & Evans, courtesy of Flowers Gallery London and New York
Pages 58-59: © Gilbert & George. Courtesy White Cube
Page 60: (top image) Peter Fischli David Weiss, Zürich 2016 Courtesy Sprüth Magers, Matthew Marks Gallery, Galerie Eva Presenhuber; (bottom image) Courtesy the artists and Buchmann Galerie Berlin
Page 61: © Allora & Calzadilla, courtesy of Lisson Gallery. Photography: Ken Adlard
Page 62: (top image) Artwork © The Singh Twins: www.singhtwins.co.uk; (bottom image) Courtesy of Nicole Gnesa Gallery
Page 66: © Jake & Dinos Chapman
Pages 68-69: Private Collection. Courtesy of Sonnabend Gallery, New York. © Estate of Bernd and Hilla Becher
Page 70: © Jane & Louise Wilson. All Rights Reserved, DACS 2016
Page 72: (top image) Courtesy of the artists and Galerie Daniel Templon, Paris – Brussels; (bottom image) Courtesy of the artists and BlainSouthern. Photography: Peter Mallet
Page 73: (top image) Courtesy of the artists and Maureen Paley, London; (bottom image) Courtesy the artists and Sprovieri
Page 74: Courtesy of Dalziel + Scullion
Page 75: Courtesy of Langlands & Bell and Alan Cristea Gallery
Page 78: Courtesy of David Krut Workshop (DKW)
Page 79: Photography: Paladino Studio
Page 81: Courtesy of the artist and Marlborough Fine Art
Page 82: Courtesy of Mick Moon and Alan Cristea Gallery
Pages 84-85: © Anselm Kiefer. Photo © White Cube (Charles Duprat)
Page 86: Courtesy of the Artist and UNION Gallery, London
Page 87: Copyright The Artist, courtesy Sadie Coles HQ, London
Page 88: Courtesy of the artist and Maureen Paley, London
Page 89: Courtesy of Gordon Cheung and Alan Cristea Gallery
Page 92: Photography: Rose Jones
Page 93: Courtesy of Gillian Ayres and Alan Cristea Gallery
Page 95: Photography: Antony Makinson at Prudence Cuming Associates Ltd., London
Page 97: Printed and published by Advanced Graphics London
Page 99: Photography: Jian Wei Lim
Page 100: © Ellsworth Kelly
Page 101: © Georg Baselitz 2016. Photo © Jochen Littkemann, Berlin. Courtesy of White Cube
Page 102: Courtesy of Miriam De Burca and Alan Cristea Gallery
Page 103: Courtesy of Glasgow Print Studio
Page 104: (top image) Courtesy of Yinka Shonibare Studio; (bottom image)Courtesy of Michael Craig-Martin and Alan Cristea Gallery
Page 105: Courtesy of Cornelia Parker and Alan Cristea Gallery
Page 106: Courtesy of the artist and Marlborough Fine Art
Page 108: (top image) Courtesy of Ian Davenport and Alan Cristea Gallery; (bottom image) Courtesy of Christiane Baumgartner and Alan Cristea Gallery
Page 109: (top image) Courtesy of Julian Opie and Alan Cristea Gallery; (bottom image) Courtesy of Jim Dine and Alan Cristea Gallery
Page 110: Courtesy of Ian McKeever and Alan Cristea Gallery
Page 113: Courtesy of the Artist. Photography: Robert Glowaki
Page 114: (top image) Photography: Iain Gildea; (bottom image) Courtesy of the artist and Marlborough Fine Art
Page 115: Courtesy of Idris Khan and Alan Cristea Gallery
Page 117: Photo: Ben Bisek
Page 119: David Chipperfield Architects, Arup, Harry Gugger Studio, Robrecht en Daem Architecten, Vogt Landscape, Publica and Alinea Consulting
Page 123: (bottom image) Photo Credit: Julian Calder
Page 124: (top image) © Farshid Moussavi Architecture; (bottom image) Photo credit: Jack Hobhouse
Page 129: (top image) Courtesy of Richard Woods and Alan Cristea Gallery
Page 131: Photography: Leon Chew
Page 137: (bottom image) Courtesy of the artist and Hauser & Wirth. Photography: Alex Delfanne
Page 143: Courtesy of the artist. Photography: Dave Morgan
Page 145: (bottom image) Photography: Colin Mills
Page 149: Photography: Maciej Urbanek
Page 156: © Courtesy of the artist and Richard Green Gallery
Page 157: (bottom image) Courtesy of the artist and Marlborough Fine Art
Page 171: (bottom left image) Courtesy of the artist and Marlborough Fine Art
Page 172: Image courtesy October Gallery, London. Photography: Jonathan Greet
Page 173: © Marina Abramović; Courtesy of Lisson Gallery. Photography: Adam Reich
Page 175: Photography: Steve Russell
Page 176: (bottom image) Courtesy of Gagosian Gallery © Thomas Ruff / DACS, 2016
Page 179: (bottom image) Courtesy of Mark Neville and Alan Cristea Gallery
Pages 182-183: Photography: Stephen White
Pages 186-187: Courtesy of Richard Long and Alan Cristea Gallery